GREAT CAMPAIGNS

The Fredericksburg Campaign

GREAT CAMPAIGN SERIES

GREAT CAMPAIGNS

THE FREDERICKSBURG CAMPAIGN

October 1862 - January 1863

Victor Brooks

COMBINED PUBLISHING
Pennsylvania

PUBLISHER'S NOTE

The headquarters of Combined Publishing are located midway between Valley Forge and the Germantown battlefield, on the outskirts of Philadelphia. From its beginnings, our company has been steeped in the oldest traditions of American history and publishing. Our historic surroundings help maintain our focus on history and our books strive to uphold the standards of style, quality and durability first established by the earliest bookmakers of Germantown and Philadelphia so many years ago. Our famous monk-and-console logo reflects our commitment to the modern and yet historic enterprise of publishing.

We call ourselves Combined Publishing because we have always felt that our goals could only be achieved through a "combined" effort by authors, publishers and readers. We have always tried to maintain maximum communication between these three key players in the reading experience.

We are always interested in hearing from prospective authors about new books in our field. We also like to hear from our readers and invite you to contact us at our offices in Pennsylvania with any questions, comments or suggestions, or if you have difficulty finding our books at a local bookseller.

For information, address:
Combined Publishing
P.O. Box 307
Conshohocken, PA 19428
E-mail: combined@combinedpublishing.com
Web: www.combinedpublishing.com
Orders: 1-800-418-6065

Library of Congress Cataloging-in-Publication Data.
Brooks, Victor.
   The Fredericksburg Campaign : October 1862-January 1863 / Victor Brooks.
      p. cm.-- (Great Campaigns)
   Includes index.
   ISBN 1-58097-033-8
   1. Fredericksburg (Va.), Battle of, 1862. I. Title. II. Series.

E474.85 .B84 2000
973.7'33--dc21   00-022685

Maps by Paul Dangel
Printed in the United States of America.

A note on usage: To simplify matters, the identities of Union units are in *italics*; times have been rendered on a 24-hour basis.

Contents

Maps

Sidebars

Introduction

In the late summer of 1862, only months after it appeared that the cause of Southern independence was doomed, the Confederacy attempted its most ambitious combined offensive of the war, invading the border states of Kentucky and Maryland. President Jefferson Davis and his advisors hoped to add these two prosperous states to their new nation and perhaps gain foreign recognition in the bargain. This situation was an incredible turnaround from the gloomy days only a few months earlier when the South had suffered a series of disasters including the loss of the huge garrison of Fort Donelson, Tennessee, a bloody repulse at the battle of Shiloh, Union capture of New Orleans, the largest city in the Confederacy, and the approach of General George McClellan's enormous *Army of the Potomac* to the suburbs of the capital city of Richmond. Then, as suddenly as the blue-coated tide surged forward, it quickly receded. Union offensives from Mississippi to Virginia ground to a halt and hard hitting Rebel counterattacks pushed the Yankees northward. By early September, General Braxton Bragg's Army of Tennessee and General Robert E. Lee's Army of Northern Virginia were marching into Kentucky and Maryland and the governors and citizens of almost every adjacent Northern state were in a panic. While Bragg prepared to install a new Confederate governor of Kentucky in the Bluegrass State, Lee's lean, confident graycoats sparred with advance elements of McClellan's army as it tried to cover Washington and push the Rebels back across the Potomac River.

The Yankee and Confederate armies were pulled inexorably toward the picturesque town of Sharpsburg, Maryland as the campaign hurtled towards its climax. McClellan held an enormous advantage over his Southern opponent as he outnumbered the rebels nearly two to one and, through an incredible stroke of luck, had obtained a copy of Lee's entire operational orders lost by a careless Confederate officer. As scattered Union divisions began concentrating to smash the Rebels, Lee threw up hastily prepared defenses along Antietam Creek with his back to an unfordable Potomac River only a short distance away. Then, on Wednesday, September 17, 1862, the *Army of the Potomac* lunged again and again at the badly outnumbered Rebels in a desperate attempt to annihilate a dangerously exposed enemy. In the bloodiest single day of the Civil War, Yankees and Rebels charged through cornfields, wheatfields, orchards, and sunken roads, until by nightfall two exhausted armies reluctantly pulled apart after almost 25,000 men had been killed or wounded.

While Robert E. Lee had orchestrated a series of tactical moves that had at least temporarily saved his army, the Rebels were battered, outnumbered and cut off from any source of reinforcements. The *Army of the Potomac* had suffered heavily as well, but thousands of blue-coated soldiers had never seen action that day and thousands of other Yankees were even now marching through the darkness to provide McClellan with an even larger numerical advantage the next day. If the general who was called the Young Napoleon simply concentrated all of his fresh units and launched a determined attack all along the Confederate line, there was a very real chance that the main Rebel army would be captured or annihilated by nightfall Thursday and the Southern Confederacy's existence would be measured in weeks or even days. However, if McClellan's famous caution rose once again to the surface, the war would continue and, most likely, the scene of the fighting would shift back down to Virginia. Thus, as darkness enveloped the bloody battlefields near Sharpsburg, Maryland, the citizens of another quaint town a little more than 100 miles to the south were about to have their community's name added to the awful place-names of the Civil War. No one, in the picturesque colonial town of Fredericksburg, Virginia knew it on this warm late summer night, but a chain of events was about to be set in motion that would place almost 200,000 soldiers literally on their doorsteps.

CHAPTER I

Aftermath of Antietam

Thursday, September 18, 1862, dawned sunny and hot over a Maryland countryside that had just been the scene of the single bloodiest day of the American Civil War. George Brinton McClellan's hard fighting *Army of the Potomac* had very nearly shattered Robert E. Lee's equally tenacious Army of Northern Virginia along the Antietam Creek which flowed through the small town of Sharpsburg. Now such mundane local landmarks as the West Woods, the Cornfield, and the Dunker Church entered the realm of American legend as 2,100 dead bluecoats and 1,600 corpses in gray and butternut lay sprawled around fields, roads, and fences that one eyewitness called a "landscape turned red." An additional 10,000 Yankees and 9,000 Rebels groaned and writhed in pain from a variety of severe injuries incurred in the bloody stalemate. At 0800 on this bright Thursday morning, General McClellan wired a situation report to Abraham Lincoln's latest choice for the position of commander in chief of the Federal armies, Henry Wager Halleck. The paunchy, balding, scholarly commander, who was nicknamed "Odd Brains" in the pre-war army, carefully read the dispatch from the handsome 36-year-old field general who was now frequently called "the Young Napoleon." McClellan insisted excitedly, "The battle of yesterday continued for fourteen hours and until after dark. We held all we gained, except a portion of the extreme left.

Our losses were very heavy, especially in general officers. The battle will probably be renewed today." A short time later, McClellan wrote to his wife, "The spectacle yesterday was the grandest I could conceive of; nothing could be more sublime. Those in whose judgement I rely tell me that I fought the battle splendidly and that it was a masterpiece of art."

While McClellan's direction of the battle was far less of a masterpiece than he explained to Halleck or his wife, he was in an excellent position to score a decisive victory over his Southern opponents. Twelve thousand Federal reinforcements were marching into Union camps as McClellan wrote his dispatches, including eight regiments of Pennsylvanians under Brigadier General Andrew Humphreys, who had just conducted an all night march of 23 miles in order to participate in an anticipated second day of battle that seemed very likely to culminate in a Yankee victory. The arrival of fresh units gave McClellan over 62,000 uninjured men, over half of whom had not even participated in Wednesday's ferocious encounter—more than twice the strength of his adversary. However as blue-coated units were deployed for a possible advance on the Confederate lines, the Young Napoleon's famous caution began to replace the exuberance of earlier Thursday morning. McClellan began mentally formulating a lengthening list of reasons why a renewed offensive could threaten the very existence of the *Army of the Potomac*, and with it, the American Union.

On the other side of the extended battle line, fewer than 25,000 Confederate soldiers cleaned their weapons, ate their meager rations, and patiently waited for their commanding general to decide whether to hold the army's position or attempt a withdrawal across the nearby Potomac River back into Virginia. A combination of high levels of straggling between Virginia and Maryland and the horrendous casualties of the previous day's battle had reduced the already legendary Army of Northern Virginia to its smallest size until the final surrender at Appomattox Court House, 31 bloody months in the future. However, a combination of dogged determination, awareness of the character flaws of his opponent, and the

Wounded Confederate prisoners being tended by their Union captors after the battle of Antietam. Shelter halves have been stretched between rifles to shield the wounded from the late September sun.

instincts of a riverboat gambler had prompted Robert E. Lee to decide to hold the field against an adversary that was almost three times as numerous and receiving additional reinforcements almost hourly. The charismatic Virginian fully intended to fight a second day at Sharpsburg with an army that quite literally deployed no reserves; every man capable of firing a musket was at the front line. There were no reserve units to plug breaches in the lines and no real fallback positions on this side of the Potomac. Lee simply assumed that a body of men that had rolled up an astounding series of victories during the past several months could more than hold its own against an opponent commanded by an overly cautious general, who never seemed capable of using his vast numbers to any decisive advantage on the battlefield.

Lee was determined and confident, but in reality the Maryland campaign would be judged as one of the general's least spectacular moments of the entire war. The Virginian had crossed the Potomac while thousands of his men straggled on the south side of the river and then exposed himself to destruction when he divided his already outnumbered army into as many as six detachments. The opportunity for annihilation was then enhanced even further when a copy of the general's Special Orders for the campaign was carelessly lost by a subordinate and quickly found by one of McClellan's men. Even the cautious Young Napoleon exclaimed, "With this paper, if I cannot whip Bobby Lee, I shall be willing to go home."

The Confederate commander was able to hold the Yankees at bay just long enough to concentrate most of his army along the Antietam Creek at Sharpsburg. However, while McClellan's traditional caution allowed Lee enough time to cross the Potomac back into Virginia and collect his thousands of stragglers for a new campaign, Lee deliberately sought a confrontation with the oncoming Federal army, an act of defiance that might have virtually ended the war in a single afternoon. As one of Lee's artillery commanders, General E. Porter Alexander, insisted, "The more that one studies the situation, the more amazed he must be at the audacity which deliberately sought a pitched battle in the open field, without a yard of earthworks, against a better equipped army of double his force, and with a river close behind him, to be crossed by a

General George McClellan won the battle of Antietam, but his excessive caution allowed the Confederate army to slip away under cover of darkness.

single ford, peculiarly bad and exposed in case he had to retreat. A defeat would certainly have involved the utter destruction of his army." Only the superb fighting ability and tenacity of the men in gray and butternut prevented annihilation from occurring on September 17, yet on Thursday morning Lee belligerently held his battered men in their positions and dared George McClellan to attack him, probably knowing full well that a persistent and fully coordinated Yankee assault could very well destroy the Army of Northern Virginia. However, Lee had read his adversary correctly and the momentarily expected assault never developed.

Two hours after McClellan dispatched his account of the battle to General Halleck, General William B. Franklin, commander of the *Army of the Potomac VI Corps*, entered the Young Napoleon's headquarters and proposed an assault on the high ground around Nicodemus Hill behind and on the flank of the Confederate position in the West Woods. Franklin's suggestion for a specific attack on a specific location must have jolted McClellan back into his customary caution. He quickly retreated from the confident attitude that permeated his dispatch to Washington and began conjuring up visions of Rebel divisions circling around the assault force and thrusting directly at the national capital while Union troops were tied down along Antietam Creek. The Federal field commander insisted, "One battle lost and almost all would have been lost, Lee's army might then have marched as it pleased on Washington, Baltimore, Philadelphia, or New York." Franklin's proposed assault was never officially canceled as much as it was progressively postponed throughout that sunny Thursday morning and afternoon.

While McClellan rapidly lost confidence in the ability of his army to fight a second day at Sharpsburg, Robert E. Lee continued to gain confidence in the fighting abilities of his outnumbered men. He noted that "though still too weak to assume the offensive, we awaited without apprehension the renewal of the attack." However, as the afternoon moved toward dusk with no sign of a Union assault, Lee began to suspect that the battle of Antietam had largely run its course. The aggressive Virginian still wanted another crack at McClellan, but he now admitted that he needed to gather up his stragglers before considering a new offensive into Maryland at some other point along the Potomac. Thus after assuring himself and his men that holding the field all day on September 18 constituted a technical victory against the Yankees, Lee ordered the able-bodied men to continue to hold the lines while a steady stream of Confederate ambulances, supply wagons, and artillery caissons began lurching toward Boteler's Ford.

As the darkness deepened on this cloudless, late summer night, the Army of Northern Virginia began a staged withdrawal of units back to the Potomac River. Earlier that month, the invasion of Maryland had been inaugurated with regimental bands playing "Maryland, My Maryland," a popular pro-Southern tune of the time. However, after Lee's invitation to Marylanders to "throw off the shackles" of Northern tyranny had been largely ignored by the prosperous inhabitants of that state, and the "liberating" army had been mauled at Sharpsburg, the song was far less pleasant to Rebel ears. When the band of the 18th Mississippi Regiment began playing the tune during the crossing back into Virginia, a barrage of curses and catcalls greeted the musicians. Despite the capture of Harpers Ferry and its garrison, and the bravery demonstrated by the Rebel soldiers at Antietam, the campaign was seen as best left in the past with new challenges in Virginia clearly on the horizon.

At dawn on Friday, September 19, a Federal signalman reported, "I have scanned the whole ground from right to left and at this moment there is not a rebel in sight." This Union soldier had witnessed the result of an all-night Confederate retrograde in which thousands of men and horses and hundreds of wagons and cannons had crossed the Potomac at Boteler's Ford. By morning, Confederate rear-guard commander General John G. Walker could inform his superior that, except for a single damaged cannon and a few broken-down wagons, the entire Army of Northern Virginia was now on the Virginia side of the river. A substantially relieved General Lee uttered a single "Thank God!" in response and immediately

William N. Pendleton mishandled the Confederate artillery at both Fredericksburg and Gettysburg, but he and Robert E. Lee maintained a close personal friendship.

began pondering opportunities to snare McClellan in a trap when the *Army of the Potomac* made its own crossing into the Old Dominion. However, until McClellan could be enticed into a battle on Confederate terms, the first order of business was to pull the graycoats out of range of the powerful Federal artillery. As General William N. Pendleton noted, "Our troops that had been briefly resting in the valleys were now ordered further inland, to be out of the reach of the shells so numerously hurled by the enemy, yet near enough to turn readily upon and perhaps destroy the adverse army should it force the passage of the river and take position between our forces."

Pendleton, who was in command of the reserve artillery of the Confederate army, was given responsibility for delaying a Federal crossing until the rest of the army had been reformed a few miles below the river. The Episcopalian priest-turned general deployed 33 guns along the Potomac with 11 more cannons in reserve, while also assuming command of Lawton's and Armistead's brigades to provide infantry support in case the Yankees decided to cross immediately. At this point, Union corps commander Fitz John Porter ordered a massive Federal artillery bombardment to cover a probing operation conducted by the elite *1st United States Sharpshooters* and the *4th Michigan Regiment* who were ordered to cross the Potomac and test the Rebel defenses.

The Federal advance could not have come at a worse time for the defenders, as General Lawton had been wounded at Antietam and General Armistead was temporarily assigned as provost marshal, leaving both brigades under the command of colonels and making Pendleton the ranking officer at the Potomac lines. Pendleton placed sharpshooters along the riverbank to warn of an enemy landing and ordered his men "not to fire merely in reply to shots from the other side but only to reply to any attempt at crossing." Unfortunately, the former minister had no idea how many men he actually commanded. Since a typical Confederate brigade fielded about 1,500 men, Pendleton probably assumed that he had about 3,000 infantrymen to support his gunners. Without confirming these assumed figures, Pendleton deployed 200 men well upstream to guard his left flank and then rushed another 100 men two miles downstream to cover a suspected landing point, holding the remainder of the two brigades at Boteler's Ford to repel an enemy crossing. However, the 2,700 men Pendleton assumed to have deployed were in reality barely a tenth that number as both of these brigades had been virtually annihilated at Antietam and now fielded fewer than 300 men each. Thus, after Pendleton's detachment of 300 troops out of support range, fewer than 300 riflemen remained to challenge two much larger Federal regiments. Soon, after the defenders had been dangerously thinned down by Pendleton's detachments, the bluecoats came splashing across the Potomac and a battery of Confederate field pieces was almost immediately overrun.

When Pendleton saw four of his precious guns being captured and 40 other pieces in danger of meeting a similar fate, he left the battlefield and hurried inland to the headquarters of Brigadier General Roger A. Pryor to request additional infantry. Pryor, a former Virginia congressman who had been instrumental in the surrender negotiations at Fort Sumter the previous year, replied that he had no troops to spare and directed him to his division commander. At this point, the fate of 25 percent of the artillery of the Army of Northern Virginia hung in the balance. The general responsible for these almost irreplaceable weapons was essentially doing the work of an enlisted courier as he spent most of this Friday afternoon and evening drifting further up the chain of command towards Lee's headquarters. Pendleton finally arrived at his commander's headquarters after midnight and found Lee sleeping under an apple tree. He woke his fellow Virginian with the startling news that the advancing Yankees had most likely captured the entire reserve artillery of the Army of Northern Virginia. One of Lee's aides noted that the startling news "lifted me right off my blanket and I moved away fearful I might betray my feelings," but "General Lee exhibited no temper and made no reproach."

While Lee was being extremely charitable to a general who had terribly bungled his assignment, the situation on the Potomac was actually far less critical than Pendleton feared. During the artillerist's absence, a small column of Confederate cavalry had arrived to temporarily blunt the Yankee drive and Pendleton's subordinates had implemented a skillful retrograde which had saved 40 of the 44 cannons. By the morning of September 20, the situation at the river had stabilized, and when Porter pushed three additional Union brigades across in a leisurely fashion, Lee decided to give them a bloody nose. General Ambrose Powell Hill was ordered to deploy his division around the growing Federal bridgehead and, with Jubal A. Early's men in support, push the Yankees back across the river. Hill's astoundingly rapid march from Harpers Ferry to Sharpsburg had saved the Confederate right flank at Antietam on Wednesday and on this Saturday morning he was eager for a resumption of the fighting. After pushing his men through "the most tremendous artillery fire I ever heard" the Light Division swept towards Porter's bridgehead "as if each man felt that the fate of the army was centered in himself." The bluecoats, after meeting only scattered resistance on their cautious probes inland, had not expected the tidal wave of fury unleashed by A. P. Hill's Rebels and entire regiments hastily withdrew toward the Potomac near the village of Shepherdstown. When graycoat brigades under Generals William D. Pender and James J. Archer began threatening to cut off access to the ford, Porter unleashed a massive artillery barrage from the north bank of the Potomac and sent orders to his advance units to use the covering fire to pull back to Maryland. The most exposed Federal unit was the *178th Pennsylvania Regiment* which had been cut off from its supporting units by the Rebel attacks and was now essentially on its own. The regiment was one of the most poorly armed in McClellan's army as the men had been equipped with Belgian rifles of dubious reliability. When the retreating Yankees began blazing away at the advancing graycoats, over half of the guns misfired and the Federals became almost helpless. Within minutes, 269 men, most of the regiment, were killed, wounded, or captured, while an additional 100 Unionists from other units were cut down or captured in the fallback. At a cost of 30 killed and 231 wounded, A. P. Hill's division had crushed the first Union offensive after Antietam and driven another nail into the coffin of George Brinton McClellan's command of the *Army of the Potomac*.

George McClellan had been badly singed by Lee's sharp response to his cautious advance into Virginia. Now the Young Napoleon became convinced that it was folly to leave Maryland until his army was properly reorganized and refitted; a process that could easily consume several months. While Abraham Lincoln was able to use the modest Union success at Antietam as a springboard to issue a preliminary Emancipation Proclamation, the president realized that continued popular support of the war effort was predicated on much more than simply repelling Rebel invasions of the North. A major offensive which would annihilate Lee's army and capture the Confederate capital of Richmond was crucial to maintaining the delicate coalition of Republicans and War Democrats that was always on the verge of unraveling, particularly since the war now seemed to have entered an effective stalemate. Lincoln was now convinced that McClellan had allowed a virtually annihilated Rebel army to slip through his fingers back

Fitz John Porter was a corps commander loyal to McClellan, and was court-martialed after McClellan's dismissal.

into Virginia and he personally traveled to the *Army of the Potomac* headquarters to urge McClellan to take the offensive "before the government loses patience in its general." However, not only did McClellan fail to heed this ominous "advice" and set the *Army of the Potomac* into motion, the Union field commander was about to be subjected to another humiliating operation launched by his outnumbered adversary.

General James Ewell Brown Stuart had already completed a spectacular ride around the *Army of the Potomac* during the Peninsula campaign earlier in the year, and McClellan had received scathing attention from the Northern press for his failure to counter this embarrassing escapade. Now Robert E. Lee concluded that a similar raid into Maryland and Pennsylvania could provide substantial strategic and psychological dividends for the Confederate cause. In early October, two weeks after Antietam, Lee was becoming increasingly concerned about his opponent's intentions and capabilities. He decided to use his superb cavalry arm to secure vital intelligence about the Federals, and hopefully disrupt the Yankee supply lines enough to discourage McClellan from launching a fall offensive. Lee decided to send several regiments of cavalry under J. E. B. Stuart on a wide-ranging operation that would slip past the flank of the Federal army and allow the gray-coated troops to descend on Chambersburg, Pennsylvania. Just north of the town was an important railroad bridge which crossed a branch of the Concocheague Creek. If that span was destroyed, the trains of the Cumberland Valley Railroad would be unable to deliver supplies to McClellan's army at the Union rail center of Hagerstown, Maryland. The interruption of this rail service would force the Federals to rely exclusively on the Baltimore and Ohio Railroad for food and ammunition, a situation that would provide McClellan with no fallback facilities and probably reduce the Pennsylvanian's already faltering enthusiasm for launching an autumn campaign into Virginia.

On the morning of Wednesday, October 8, 1862, J. E. B. Stuart received Lee's orders at his headquarters on the Dandridge plantation and the delighted cavalry commander set in motion the raid into the North. Lee had authorized Stuart to take 1,200 to 1,500 men on the expedition, and directed the mounted column to capture horses, gather intelligence, and seize hostages to be exchanged for pro-Confederate Marylanders, who had been arrested by Federal authorities. The commanding general left the details to Stuart as he noted "reliance is placed upon your skill and judgement in the successful execution of this plan." Stuart had enough confidence in his superior's trust in his judgment that he increased the size of the expedition to 1,800 men in five detachments under William H. "Rooney" Lee, Wade Hampton, William E. "Grumble" Jones, William Micham, and Matthew Calbraith Butler, while 21-year-old Major John Pelham was assigned to provide artillery support with a four-gun battery of field pieces. By Wednesday evening cavalry officers in dress uniforms were dancing at a huge farewell ball at the Dandridge mansion while Stuart himself provided the music for several dances. The next afternoon the units selected for the raid were formed in the nearby town of Darkesville, which would serve as the jump-off point for the operation.

At daybreak on Friday, October 10, almost 2,000 jaunty, confident, gray-coated horsemen crossed the Potomac River, overwhelmed a small Federal patrol posted at McCoy's Ford, and started trotting along the old National Road. The Rebel troops had just missed colliding with six regiments of Yankees that had passed over the same spot less than an hour earlier, and the proximity of significant Federal forces almost immediately impacted on Stuart's strategy. The Rebel cavalry leader was strongly tempted to capture the bulging supply warehouses at the Federal depot in Hagerstown, but noted afterward, "I was satisfied from reliable information that the notice the enemy had of my approach would enable him to prevent my capturing it." Thus Stuart bypassed the Yankee cornucopia and, arranging his command into an advance force, a main force, and a rear guard of 600 men each, spurred northward toward Chambersburg and its vital bridge.

Wade Hampton rode into the Pennsylvania community at the head of his advance force and demanded the town's surrender. After the mayor and councilmen capitulated, the South Carolina planter became temporary "military governor of Chambersburg" and directed his eager troops to spread out and confiscate anything that might be of value to the Confederate cause. The town's leading bankers had already moved most of the money to hiding places outside of the community, but the Rebels quickly discovered a Federal supply depot bulging with 5,000 new rifles, hundreds of picks and shovels, and a huge cache of new blue overcoats. While Hampton's men appropriated the new clothing, weapons, and equipment, a column under General "Grumble" Jones swooped down on the Concocheague bridge. However, the span was a mammoth iron structure that proved impervious to the axes and torches wielded by the Rebels and Jones was forced to inform his commander that his men simply did not have the equipment to seriously disrupt rail service over the structure. Stuart was still satisfied that he had scored a significant psychological triumph during this raid and his main concern now became the safe arrival of the troops back in Virginia.

The graycoats were now heading south through a thoroughly alarmed countryside and the Virginia cavalier needed to exercise all of his talents to avoid a closing pincers of Yankee horsemen and infantry. The nearest Potomac fords were west of the Rebel column but Stuart surprised his men by ordering a gallop to the east. Stuart rode ahead of the column accompanied by his aide, Captain William Blackford, and, af-

General Alfred Pleasonton played an important role in organizing the Union cavalry, but he was eclipsed as the cavalry later developed into a major combat arm under Philip Sheridan.

ter a short silence, pulled out a map and began to explain the reasoning behind his seemingly illogical plan. The Confederate cavalry general was convinced that the Federal column they had narrowly missed encountering on the National Road would soon learn of the raid on Chambersburg and begin an immediate westward deployment to prevent the Rebels from crossing the Potomac. Stuart believed that this force of well over 2,000 men was more of a threat than the more scattered Federal detachments to the east who were forced to guard a number of potential crossing sites.

The Confederate column now drove eastward toward the picturesque college town of Gettysburg and then veered toward Emmittsburg, Maryland, just missing a confrontation with one of the more novel forms of Union horsemen, a detachment of Federal lancers. Stuart's scouts captured a Yankee courier who revealed that General Alfred Pleasonton was closing in on the Rebel column with 800 cavalrymen, while General George Stoneman was deploying 5,000 bluecoats along the major fords of the Potomac. The Confederate commander decided that the most favorable crossing location would be White's Ford, three miles below the mouth of the Monocacy River. This ford was a little-used crossing point that seemed less likely to be heavily guarded than a number of more prominent fords. So Stuart decided to gamble that he could get his men back into Virginia before the Yankees concentrated a large enough force to seriously contest the crossing.

The climax of Stuart's raid was a masterpiece of feints, misdirections, and bravado as the Rebel troops, observed clearly by Federal scouts, galloped toward the heavily guarded Edward's Ferry and then, at the last possible moment, veered into a dense forest that led down to White's Ford. Pleasonton had not ignored this location as a possible Rebel crossing point, and Federal sharpshooters deployed along the rim of a nearby quarry and blasted at the gray-coated troops as they emerged from the woods. While dismounted cavalry under Rooney Lee and two of Pelham's cannons dueled with the Yankee riflemen, successive units of troops splashed across the rough waters of the Potomac and galloped into Virginia. In a moment of poor timing that would plague the Federals during the entire Fredicksburg campaign, significant bodies of Union troops arrived at White's Ford just as the Confederate rear guard was climbing onto the Virginia shore and the bluecoats watched in frustration as their quarry escaped virtually unscathed.

Although George Stoneman is primarily known as a cavalry leader, he commanded **III Corps** *of the* **Army of the Potomac** *at Fredericksburg.*

The spectacular Confederate raid into Pennsylvania had cost the Rebels a grand total of two men captured, while producing 280 Federal prisoners, 1,200 commandeered horses, and thousands of new weapons. Perhaps most importantly, Stuart's expedition clearly placed George McClellan on borrowed time as commander of the *Army of the Potomac*. Secretary of War Edwin Stanton, Commanding General Henry Halleck, and, most ominously, Abraham Lincoln were furious at the negative publicity surrounding Stuart's second "ride around McClellan" in less than six months. One Union observer, Colonel R.B. Irwin, summarized Lincoln's scathing reaction to the raid. When the president seemed in unusually high spirits, someone suddenly asked, "What about McClellan?" Without looking at his questioner, the president drew a ring around the floor with a stick or umbrella and said quietly, "When I was a boy we used to play a game called three times round and out. Stuart has been around him twice; if he goes around him once more gentlemen, McClellan will be out!" In reality it would not require another Stuart raid around McClellan to end the Young Napoleon's tenure with the *Army of the Potomac*. As McClellan's highly publicized but glacially paced fall offensive lurched into operation, Abraham Lincoln concluded that the brilliant yet cautious Pennsylvanian was not the man to successfully terminate the War of the Rebellion.

Promotion and Rank in the Confederate Army

By late 1862 the rank structure of the Confederate army was a blend of pre-Civil War traditions of the old United States army and the necessities of fighting a large scale war for almost two years. When the Confederate Congress had met at Montgomery, Alabama, in early 1861, it had authorized a provisional army and created rank and insignia from lieutenant through general. Confederate second lieutenants wore one gold bar, first lieutenants would have two gold bars, captains would wear three gold bars, majors would display one star, lieutenant colonels would receive two stars, full colonels would wear three stars, and generals would be recognized by three stars in a wreath. However, at this point, before hostilities had even started, the largest authorized unit was only a regiment and the highest recognized rank was only a brigadier general. The senior general among the officers of the seven seceded states was Louisiana's Pierre Beauregard who held the rank of brigadier general during the siege and bombardment of Fort Sumter.

After Fort Sumter surrendered and Lincoln called for 75,000 volunteers to suppress the rebellion, four more states joined the Confederacy and the capital was moved to Richmond, Virginia. At this point it was realized that a much larger Confederate army would be needed, and Congress authorized the rank of full general appointing Albert Sidney Johnston, Samuel Cooper, Pierre Beauregard, Joseph Johnston, and Robert E. Lee to that new rank. While these five men were the senior officers of the army, no new insignia was created; they wore the same three stars in a wreath

as the brigadiers, and there was no provision made for intermediate ranks of major general and lieutenant general.

When serious fighting began with the battle of First Manassas, the Confederate army was still basically a collection of state regiments pulled together into provisional brigades to fight the battle. During the winter of 1861-62, with Joseph Johnston commanding the main Southern army then designated the "Army of the Potomac," the brigade structure was formalized by Congress and Johnston began to informally unite several brigades into unofficial divisions. During the spring and early summer of 1862, as the Confederate field army reached almost 90,000 men, Johnston and his successor, Robert E. Lee, began to formalize these new divisions and requested Congress to promote the division commanders to major general. By the end of the Seven Days' battles in early July of 1862 the newly renamed Army of Northern Virginia was formed around a force of about 30 brigades serving in nine divisions. While many of these divisional commanders now held the rank of major general, they were hardly equal in Lee's eyes. The Virginian was convinced that at least two or three of these men were incompetent, and they were quietly transferred to other theaters. Meanwhile, two men, James Longstreet and Stonewall Jackson, had emerged as superior commanders, and Lee decided to make each of these generals informal corps commanders and put them in charge of four or five divisions. After this arrangement worked out well at Second Manassas and Antietam, Lee approached

President Davis with a request for authority to promote two or three men to a new rank of lieutenant general and place them in charge of newly designated corps. Congress authorized this new rank and new organization for all major Confederate armies in the fall of 1862 and this structure would remain intact for the rest of the war.

Promotion through the officer ranks of the Confederate army would remain a controversial issue through the whole war. President Davis, the Confederate Congress, and individual army commanders each retained some level of authority in recommending promotions and the result was hurt feelings, charges of favoritism, and constant behind-the-scenes maneuvering that did little to help the Confederate cause.

Promotion and Rank in the Union Army

The expansion of the United States Army from its pre-war strength of 16,000 troops to a force of nearly one million soldiers provided thousands of men with Unionist sympathies the opportunity to advance in the Federal officer corps. While promotion was glacial in the pre-war army, and 40-year-old first lieutenants were not uncommon, the organization of hundreds of volunteer regiments after Fort Sumter allowed men only a few years out of West Point to become colonels or even generals in an incredibly short time. By the time of the Fredericksburg campaign the expansion of the Union army had impelled Congress to approve about a dozen new generals a month in a process that would ultimately produce 583 generals during the war while colonels were created at an even more rapid rate. However, in late 1862 the organization of the Union army was still severely hampered by the fact that Congress had only approved two grades of general, brigadiers, or one star general, and major general, or two star generals. The result was a chaotic situation. During the Fredericksburg campaign, division commanders, corps commanders, grand division commanders, the *Army of the Potomac* commander, and the commander of all Union armies (Henry Halleck) all wore the two stars of a major general. This problem was actually the result of a decision made by the old Continental Congress almost a century earlier in the early days of the American Revolution. When the Congress authorized a regular Continental army of 88 regiments in 1775 it largely adopted the rank structure of the British army including lieutenants, captains, majors, lieutenant colonels, and colonels. Eight officers were also named to the lowest grade of general that existed in the British army, the rank of brigadier general, and four men were given the next highest rank, major general. The Congress then decided that the next logical rank for the commander of the new army was the next more senior rank of lieutenant general and George Washington was given that title. This essentially gave the Virginian the same rank as the senior British officer in the colonies, Sir Thomas Gage. However, the British army contained two additional grades of general in its organizational structure full general, and a special rank for the King, captain general of the armies. When Washington returned his commission to Congress at the end of the war, he was still a lieutenant general and for over 80 years Congress was reluctant to appoint anyone to a rank equal to the most famous American general in history. Therefore much of the Civil War, including the Fredericksburg campaign, was fought with dozens of major generals but no one of the lieutenant general or full general ranks of their Confederate adversaries. This problem would be partially solved in March of 1864 when Congress resurrected Washington's old rank of lieutenant general and gave the new commanding general of the Union army, Ulysses S. Grant, a third star. Two years later, in July of 1866, Grant was rewarded for his role in defeating the Confederacy by being appointed the first full, or four-star general of the American army.

CHAPTER II

New Strategies in Richmond and Washington

The onset of autumn of 1862 found the leaders of both Confederate and Union governments in the ironic position of sharing a conviction that their side had just missed a golden opportunity to win the war during the past few weeks. Jefferson Davis, sitting in the Confederate White House in late October of the second year of the war, reviewed a series of events of the previous summer that seemed to be a precursor to European recognition of the secessionist cause. Robert E. Lee's hard-fighting Army of Northern Virginia had routed the badly outgeneraled John Pope on the old Manassas battlefield and had sent the larger Yankee army fleeing back into the entrenchments of Washington. General Braxton Bragg's Army of Tennessee had pushed far into Kentucky, inaugurated a Confederate governor for the Bluegrass State, and captured several large detachments of the Yankee army with virtually no losses to themselves. Confederate cavalry wizard Nathan Bedford Forrest had cut to pieces a Union brigade at Murfreesboro, Tennessee, captured almost a million dollars in supplies, and knocked the Federal supply routes into Nashville out of commission. Rebel horseman John Hunt Morgan had captured huge Federal depots at Glasgow and Lebanon, Kentucky, and threatened to push right into Cincinnati. By late summer Confederate commissioners in London and Paris were informing Davis that the British and

French governments were so impressed with Southern military successes that they were considering recognition of the Confederate States of America, forcible disruption of the Union blockade, and even armed intervention if the Northern government spurned suggestions for a cease-fire. At one point both Kentucky and Maryland seemed destined to fully join the Confederacy and there was some expectation that both Bragg and Lee might seize one or more significant Northern cities.

However, just as the Confederacy seemed poised to virtually dictate the terms of peace to a Union government reeling from disasters, the twin Southern offensives began to unravel. First, while McClellan was unable to annihilate Lee's army at Antietam, the Confederates were now once again south of the Potomac River and the *Army of the Potomac* was likely to begin offensive operations in the near future. Then, on the same day that Lee's graycoats were pulling back across the Potomac, Ulysses S. Grant struck a Confederate army under General Sterling Price at the town of Iuka, Mississippi, and inflicted over 1,500 casualties on the Rebels at a loss of only half as many Yankees. Two weeks later, two Confederate columns under General Earl Van Dorn converged on the Union supply depot at Corinth, Mississippi, and were mauled by General William Rosecrans's defenders, who inflicted over 4,000 Rebel casualties at a cost of half as many of their own men. Finally, on October 8, 1862, near the town of Perryville, Kentucky, a parched Union army looking desperately for water collided with a portion of Braxton Bragg's army along the Salt River. An initial contest for water holes escalated into a full-scale battle in which Don Carlos Buell's Yankees lost over 4,000 men while the outnumbered Southerners lost almost as many troops. Bragg declared a Confederate victory and then retreated all the way back into eastern Tennessee, leaving the newly inaugurated Confederate governor of Kentucky with no part of the state to administer. As the Rebel armies withdrew from the border states, the British government reconsidered its stance toward recognition of the Confederacy and the ministry agreed to indefinitely postpone any decision until a more clear-cut pattern emerged in the American war.

Thus, while the Confederate cause seemed to be in better shape than in those spring days when McClellan's men were so close to Richmond that they could hear the town's clocks strike the hour, it was also increasingly obvious that the North, with its superior manpower and resources, had regained the initiative and the next series of battles would be fought on Southern soil. The two men most responsible for Confederate fortunes, Jefferson Davis and Robert E. Lee, each accepted this situation and determined to maximize the opportunities for inflicting a decisive defeat on the Union forces as they pushed further into Confederate territory.

President Davis spent much of late October and November revamping key elements of the Confederate defense establishment in an attempt to parry expected Union blows from the Atlantic Ocean to the Mississippi River. Despite the defeat at Perryville, Davis's confidence in Braxton Bragg remained extremely high while two of the general's staunchest critics in the west, Major General Edmund Kirby Smith and Major General Leonidas Polk, were brought to Richmond for consultations, flattered by the president, and promoted to lieutenant general to salve their ill feelings about serving under Bragg. Defense of the critical Mississippi River strongholds remaining in Confederate hands was entrusted to Lieutenant General John C. Pemberton, a native Pennsylvanian who had sided with the South and had a distinguished record for bravery in the war with Mexico. Davis felt that Pemberton could not only prevent the Yankees from capturing the invaluable fortifications at Vicksburg but would eventually be able to take the offensive against Ulysses S. Grant's growing legions; thus setting up conditions for new operations to permanently add Kentucky and Missouri to the Confederacy.

Two significant senior level positions were also filled in this whirlwind of activity. First, the Confederate president decided to improve communications and command arrangements in the Western theater by naming a full general to lead all forces between the Appalachians and the Mississippi. Davis briefly considered appointing Lee to the post, but feared there would be no one of suitable quality to take over the crucial

Virginia theater. Pierre Beauregard was extremely popular among ordinary Southerners and was commanding a rather secondary theater in South Carolina, but relations between the Creole and his president were so frosty that Beauregard's name was quickly dropped in favor of Joseph E. Johnston. The balding Virginian had just reported himself fully recovered from the serious wounds he had received at Fair Oaks during the previous spring, and while Davis and Johnston now loathed one another, public pressure was mounting to give the popular general an assignment commensurate with his rank and reputation. Therefore, Joseph Johnston would now assume responsibility for a huge theater of operations rivaled in importance only by Lee's Virginia command.

The final reconfiguration of the Confederate military establishment in the autumn of 1862 occurred in the key cabinet position of secretary of war. George Randolph had served in that post for most of the year and had developed a good reputation among senior generals for his modest success in instilling some order and efficiency into the chaotic Rebel war effort, which depended heavily on state contributions of men, money, and supplies. However, by the fall of 1862, Davis perceived Randolph as becoming far too independent minded for his liking, and when the Virginian assumed personal responsibility for several decisions in the Western theater, the president came down hard on his failure to consult the chief executive. Randolph, a wealthy planter with blood ties to most of the leading families in Virginia, was not about to accept such insults from a man of far less distinguished background and pedigree, and the cabinet minister promptly resigned his post. Davis's choice for Randolph's successor was Virginia congressman James A. Seddon, a 47-year-old veteran of Old Dominion politics. Seddon was intelligent and well-organized, but suffered what was, if possible, even worse health than the Confederate president. Observers noted Seddon's "cadaverous" appearance and remarked on his apparent proximity to the afterlife. Now, the Confederate military establishment would have its two senior policy makers seemingly taking turns on being "indisposed" for extended periods of time, an almost intolerable situation for a fledgling nation that was already so heavily outnumbered and outgunned. When this situation was added to the reality that Joseph Johnston was probably not fully recovered from his near fatal wounds at Fair Oaks, Braxton Bragg was plagued with a long list of chronic ailments, and even Robert E. Lee was exhibiting the first signs of a heart condition that would kill him eight years later, the Confederacy was approaching the late autumn campaign season with virtually no significant leaders in anything approaching robust health.

While Jefferson Davis was revamping the Confederate military establishment on a national level, Robert E. Lee was in the process of refitting and reorganizing the army that served as the shield for the secessionist capital. As the Army of Northern Virginia recuperated from the Maryland campaign back in the friendly fields and hills of the Old Dominion, a steady stream of stragglers, recuperated wounded, and new recruits filed into the camps until the rolls of the army had expanded to nearly 78,000 men, nearly twice the force with which Lee had conducted the Antietam campaign and one of the largest concentrations of Confederate fighting men in the entire Civil War. While Lee was pleased at the growing size of his army, he was far less satisfied with the organization of the Rebel force. The Virginian had fought most of his campaigns with a jury-rigged command structure owing to the fact that the Confederate Congress had never authorized any operational unit above a division. Federal army commanders had enjoyed the luxury of assigning many of the command responsibilities to corps commanders who would orchestrate the operation of several divisions; Lee had been forced to respond with an informal ad hoc system in which a particularly talented division commander was given responsibility for his own unit and several other divisions in the vicinity. In practice, this command responsibility had devolved on two generals, James Longstreet and Thomas J. "Stonewall" Jackson, and in the heat of battle the stratagem had worked reasonably well. However, this system worked only because Longstreet and Jackson were the Army of Northern Virginia's two senior division commanders; if a more senior general had been on the field, the result would have been a chaotic command structure.

During the summer and early fall of 1862, Lee had politely pressured Jefferson Davis to reform this inefficient command system, and in early October the president approved a new law that provided for two or more corps in the larger Confederate armies with a commensurate rank of lieutenant general for the commander of this unit. Davis wisely gave Lee free reign to organize as many corps as he wished for the Army of Northern Virginia. Lee responded that, at present, two corps would be sufficient and "I can confidently recommend Generals Longstreet and Jackson in this army," with the added promise that should a third corps become feasible, "next to those officers, I consider A. P. Hill the best commander with me. He fights his troops well and takes good care of them."

When Longstreet and Jackson were confirmed by the Confederate Congress on October 11, their promotion, combined with a long list of generals killed or wounded at Antietam, encouraged a significant restructure of Lee's general officer corps. The Confederate Congress had recently authorized Jefferson Davis to name 20 additional generals to the Confederate army and the president suggested to Lee that he could recommend a large number of these new positions. At this point, of the nine divisions in the Army of Northern Virginia, only four units were being commanded by major generals while only fourteen of the forty brigades were commanded by the brigadier general expected to lead such a unit. Therefore, Lee recommended George E. Pickett, John Bell Hood, Isaac R. Trimble, and Jubal Early for promotion to major general while 15 colonels were recommended for the wreath and three stars of a Confederate brigadier. Davis came under immediate pressure to hold at least some coveted major-generalships for the other Confederate armies, and while Pickett and Hood were promoted, Trimble and Early remained as brigadiers commanding divisions. Four of the new brigadier positions were also held back by the president so that ultimately 11 of Lee's colonels, mostly in Longstreet's corps, received general's commissions, a situation which still left al-

John Bell Hood was one of the most aggressive commanders in the Confederate forces, and was seriously wounded on several occasions.

most half of the Confederate brigades commanded by colonels. A new round of promotions would now have to await the gruesome selection process of death or injury in battle, and, if the commander in chief of the United States army had his way, that battle would not wait until the next spring.

Abraham Lincoln would have been able to find very few areas of agreement with Jefferson Davis in the autumn of 1862, but one point that he did have in common with the president of the Confederacy was the conviction that his armies had enjoyed a golden opportunity to successfully end the war during the past few weeks but had somehow muffed the opportunity. However, while Davis still maintained complete confidence in his principal field commanders, Braxton Bragg and Robert E. Lee, after their invasions of the north were turned back, Lincoln was furious at his two senior field commanders, Don Carlos Buell and George McClellan, for allowing the invaders to escape back into Tennessee and Virginia.

Unlike Davis, who always considered himself more of a military strategist than a politician, Abraham Lincoln was just beginning to realize that generous portions of intelligence, flexibility, and common sense, attributes that he possessed in abundance, might just be more valuable to conducting a successful war than the more formal military education of most of his generals. Not only had all of his field commanders, with the notable exception of Ulysses S. Grant, proved exasperatingly cautious and inflexible in their campaigns, the man he had brought to Washington, to add professional competence to the direction of the war, was proving to be a major disappointment to the president as well. General Henry Halleck was obviously intelligent and was reasonably courteous and cordial to Lincoln. However, he consistently waffled on both sides of every question of military strategy and tactics and absolutely refused to provide specific advice to a president who craved a direct answer to a question. Lincoln noted privately that Halleck was little better than "a first rate clerk" and seemed incapable of providing the leadership and decision-making capabilities that the president was seeking. Henry Halleck's failure to emerge as a prominent senior commander was not necessarily a disaster to the Union cause, as Abraham Lincoln now began to look to his own capabilities and became more confident that he might be capable of directing the Northern war effort from the White House. The president was now rapidly moving away from the popular "On to Richmond" program, which had become the focal point of a majority of civilians and politicians, in favor of a more sophisticated approach to military operations. Lincoln had developed three major tasks for his field armies in the autumn of 1862. First on the agenda was the control of the Mississippi River through Union capture of the remaining Rebel strongholds along its banks, most importantly, Vicksburg, Mississippi. This operation was now primarily the responsibility of Ulysses Grant and Lincoln was already developing a growing instinct that this was the general who would eventually emerge as his most prominent field commander. When critics of Grant's alleged alcohol abuse problems urged his removal, the president's terse reply had been "I can't spare this man, he fights!" At this point Vicksburg was considered the single most invulnerable Confederate bastion by both sides, but Lincoln probably already suspected that "Unconditional Surrender" Grant would produce some solution to that glaring challenge.

Lincoln's second focal point was the eastern section of Tennessee. That region of the Volunteer State was heavily populated with Union loyalists who were being increasingly subjected to confiscation of property, arrests, and even executions by the Confederate government for their disloyalty to the secessionist cause. The compassionate president was deeply concerned with the fate of these citizens who were sacrificing everything for their allegiance to the old flag, and he was determined to do something about their plight. Lincoln also viewed East Tennessee as one of the most strategically vital points of the whole conflict. Union possession of that region would not only serve as a springboard for operations against the vital Rebel rail center of Atlanta in northern Georgia, but also reduce Confederate ability to shuttle supplies and men back and forth between eastern and western field armies. As Lincoln emphasized, "to take and hold the railroad at or east of Cleveland in East Tennessee, I think fully as important as taking and holding Richmond."

Unfortunately, the general responsible for this sphere of operations, Don Carlos Buell, was a cautious and inflexible field commander. The Union victory at Perryville had developed more because of Bragg's failure to unite his scattered forces, and the bravery and energy of emerging stars such as Philip Sheridan, than because of any strategic or tactical genius on the part of the Federal commander. Now, Buell compounded his failure to annihilate the badly scattered Confederate army around Perryville with a positive refusal to push into an eastern Tennessee that he considered too barren and desolate to support a large army on the march. Lincoln delegated Halleck to place a fire under his lethargic Western general and the senior commander urged his friend and colleague to reconsider a move into East Tennessee as "there are many reasons, some of them personal to yourself, why there should be as little delay as possible." Halleck sent a steady stream of telegrams hinting to Buell that he was powerless to prevent the president from removing his friend unless some offensive operation was initiated and responded to Buell's complaints about supply problems with the terse comment "your army can live there if the enemy can." The crisis finally came to a head as the governors of Ohio and Illinois, the states from which most of Buell's *Army of the Ohio* was recruited, demanded that Lincoln remove the field commander in favor of a more energetic commander. When the general blithely announced that rather than invade East Tennessee he was going to make his winter quarters in the comfort of Nashville, Lincoln and Halleck's patience wore out and he was relieved in favor of the intensively energetic William Rosecrans.

The third focal point of Lincoln's developing strategy was no longer the Rebel capital of Richmond but the force that shielded that city, the Army of Northern Virginia. During the "Forward to Richmond" fever which had swept through the national capital during the spring and early summer of 1861, Lincoln had probably been as guilty as any political leader of over-emphasizing the importance of the Confederate capital to the secessionist military capabilities. However, the shock of Bull Run had encouraged the president to reevaluate the importance of Richmond to the Rebel cause and by the fall of 1862 Lincoln was more interested in bagging Lee's army than Jefferson Davis's office. When McClellan allowed this irreplaceable force to escape intact after Antietam, the outraged president disguised his anger, but started thinking seriously of replacing his commander.

By the fall of 1862 McClellan's insistence that his relationship with the president was still entirely cordial was bordering on complete self-delusion. The Young Napoleon's earlier social blunders, including ignoring the president sitting in his parlor while he went upstairs to bed, and calling Lincoln "the original gorilla" in less than discreet conversations and letters, had already challenged the president's legendary patience. Now as McClellan congratulated himself for his "military masterpiece of art" at Antietam, the president was becoming convinced that his general was becoming highly expendable. The aristocratic Pennsylvanian was now committing two cardinal sins: publicly opposing Lincoln's cherished Emancipation Proclamation and taking no action to destroy the main secessionist army. The president resolved to personally visit the *Army of the Potomac* and then decide whether McClellan should be retained or replaced.

The final consultations between McClellan and Lincoln during the first week of October, 1862, were viewed quite differently by the two men. McClellan reported to his wife that the president was "very kind personally" and "very affable" and insisted that "I was the best general in the country." The general reciprocated this perceived positive attention with a general order to his troops instructing the soldiers that whatever their personal views, it was their duty to obey their country's laws and accept the president's Emancipation Proclamation. However, Lincoln's visit was far less congenial than McClellan perceived at the moment.

Lincoln's final visit to the *Army of the Potomac* under McClellan included little of the combination of good humor and sympathy that constituted most of the president's interactions with his soldiers. As this commander in chief reviewed the individual corps, he rode the lines at a quick trot, taking little notice of the men and according to one less than ecstatic

President Lincoln met personally with General McClellan after Antietam in a final effort to avoid dismissing him.

officer "gave not a word of approval, not even a smile of encouragement." When McClellan escorted Lincoln around Antietam battlefield and attempted to explain what had taken place on September 17, the president turned away abruptly and returned to camp. The next day, as Lincoln and his friend Ozias Hatch, a Springfield neighbor who accompanied him, stood on a hilltop and observed the vast encampment below them, Lincoln abruptly asked his companion whether he knew what they were looking at. The somewhat startled Hatch replied, "It is the Army of the Potomac, of course!" The president shook his head gravely and replied, "So it is called, but that is a mistake; it is only McClellan's bodyguard."

Abraham Lincoln returned to Washington convinced that McClellan should be removed, but also optimistic that a change of commanders would not result in some sort of military coup against the government if McClellan was replaced. When the president returned to the capital he confided to a friend that "I am now stronger with the Army of the Potomac than McClellan" and insisted "the supremacy of the civil power has been restored and the Executive is again master of the situation." However, Lincoln decided to give his field commander one more chance to prove himself worthy of command and on October 6, only two days after leaving the camps, he ordered McClellan to "cross the Potomac and give battle to the enemy and drive him south. Your army must move now while the roads are good."

McClellan, not surprisingly, reacted to this terse order by submitting a long list of reasons why it would be almost impossible to initiate a full offensive before spring. Lincoln responded quickly to his general's objections. He dismissed McClellan's reluctance to advance without an operating railroad immediately behind him with the assertion that "the enemy does not subsist his army at Winchester at a distance nearly twice as great from railroad transportation as you would have to cover, he is certainly not more than half as well provided with wagons as you are." The Young Napoleon's insistence that Lee would invade Pennsylvania if the Union army pushed too far into Virginia was equally shrugged off. "You dread his

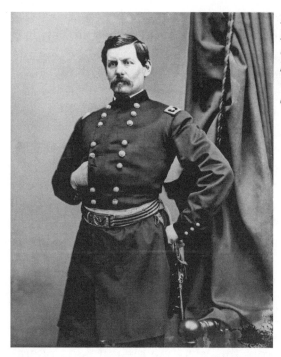

Burnside's advance on Fredericksburg had its origins in orders given to his predecessor McClellan (at left) to undertake more aggressive operations.

going into Pennsylvania. But if he does so in full force, he gives up his communications to you absolutely, and you have nothing to do but to follow and ruin him; if he does so with less than full force, fall upon him and leave what is left behind all the easier." Finally, he reminded McClellan that the Union army was in an excellent position to force Lee into an unwinnable battle if the bluecoat troops could only march at the same speed as their adversaries. "Exclusive of the water line, you are now nearer Richmond than the enemy is by the route that you *can* and he *must* take. His route is the arc of a circle while yours is the chord. The roads are as good on yours as his." Lincoln was convinced that the key to winning the war in the east was to annihilate the Army of Northern Virginia before it retreated back into a series of entrenchments around Richmond that seemed to be nearly impregnable. Thus the president implored his general to press as closely as possible to Lee and try to beat him to Richmond on the inside track with the prospect of fighting a battle in the open where Union numbers and artillery superiority dramatically raised the possibility of victory. As Lincoln noted, "in coming to us he gives us an advantage which we should welcome" while if Lee tried to lunge towards Richmond instead of attacking the Federals "turn and attack him in the rear." He closed by throwing a final challenge to his general. "It is all easy if our troops march as well as the enemy, and it is unmanly to say they cannot do it."

While McClellan made it clear that he believed that Lincoln was minimizing the restrictions under which his army operated, the Pennsylvanian reluctantly ordered the *Army of the Potomac* to move south into Virginia and on October 26, almost six weeks after Antietam, the bluecoats advanced under orders that "this army shall go forward from day to day as rapidly as possible." McClellan's idea of rapid movement was far different than Lincoln's as the 100,000 Yankees covered an agonizingly minuscule distance of only 20 miles in the first eight days of the campaign, a pace that would place the Federals in front of Richmond sometime in the summer of 1863! After resting his army from this less than breathtaking operation, McClellan's forces lurched forward a short distance to Warrenton and then came to another halt as McClellan set up supply lines to Winchester and fortified the gaps in the Blue Ridge Mountains against a possible eastward thrust from Stonewall Jackson's corps deployed in the Shenandoah Valley. As the Yankee army encamped to wait for orders to advance further, McClellan gushed that "we are in the full tide of success, so far as it is or can be successful to advance without a battle." Unfortunately for McClellan, James Longstreet's First Corps of the Army of Northern Virginia was not sitting idly while the Federals penetrated further into Virginia. "Old Pete's" men quickly deployed astride the main railroad to Culpeper Court House after a devastatingly rapid 60-mile march. The Young Napoleon had not been able to take advantage of his position on the chord of the circle that Lincoln had stressed, as the gray-coated infantry had carried out an operation that was the foot soldier's equivalent of J. E. B. Stuart's two "rides around McClellan." As Lincoln had warned a few weeks earlier, "three times and McClellan is out," and the president almost immediately acted to terminate the career of one of the most controversial generals of the Civil War and with this action, promote the genesis of the Fredericksburg campaign.

The Emancipation Proclamation and the Army of the Potomac

During the period between the end of the battle of Antietam and the conclusion of the Fredericksburg campaign the usual military challenges to the *Army of the Potomac* were dramatically complicated by the genesis of Abraham Lincoln's controversial Emancipation Proclamation. The president's intention of freeing all slaves residing in territory still in rebellion as of January 1, 1863, deeply divided the Union army and its commanders. George McClellan, a conservative Democrat who would challenge Lincoln for the presidency two years later, had always made it clear that he only believed in making war on the South for the purpose of bringing the seceded states back into the Union and in no way viewed the war as a crusade against slavery. McClellan also believed, with some justification, that the Emancipation Proclamation would only make the Rebels fight that much harder to preserve their slave property and they would now never be willing to settle for some form of compromise peace. While McClellan issued a perfunctory directive to his soldiers to "accept" the president's proclamation, the wording was so halfhearted and vague that Lincoln felt he had been betrayed by his general.

Burnside's view of Lincoln's edict is more difficult to identify. The Rhode Islander was basically a conservative Democrat in the same mold as his old friend McClellan and he made it clear that he was fighting the war primarily to restore the Union. However, Burnside came from a much more humble background than McClellan and he did not seem to share his predecessor's identification with the aristocratic leaders of the Confederacy. He probably viewed the Emancipation Proclamation strictly in terms of its ability to aid or weaken the Union military effort, and apparently convinced the president that he would dutifully support his commander in chief on any official policy. On the other hand, Burnside's eventual successor, Joseph Hooker, was a newly ardent abolitionist with strong ties to the radical wing of the Republican party. He viewed the proclamation as a key factor in gaining support throughout the North for a fading war effort.

The mixed response of senior generals to Lincoln's edict was probably shared by the men of the *Army of the Potomac*. Since no formal poll of Union soldiers was ever taken on the subject, diaries, letters, and similar documents provide the main indications of Yankee soldiers's opinions of the controversial proclamation. Support for the proclamation tended to run highest in the New England regiments and lowest in the middle Atlantic states, but even in Massachusetts units there were large numbers of soldiers who insisted that they were only fighting to restore the Union. Despite the controversial nature of the Emancipation Proclamation, it seems that very few soldiers actually deserted from the army based on their opposition to Lincoln's edict, and the document itself became more tolerable as the growing number of black soldiers demonstrated their fighting ability in battles against the Confederates.

CHAPTER III

A Change at the Helm

*A*n unusually heavy early season snowstorm blanketed much of northern Virginia on November 7, 1862, and by that Friday evening the snow was falling so rapidly that the headlight of a special military train was barely able to pierce the frozen landscape. This train carried a particularly important passenger, General Catherinus Putnam Buckingham, a white-bearded West Point classmate of Robert E. Lee who had been dispatched directly from Edwin M. Stanton's office with two highly confidential letters. The secretary of war had requested the Ohio general to personally deliver an order of dismissal to George McClellan and an order of promotion to Ambrose E. Burnside to replace the Young Napoleon as commander of the *Army of the Potomac*. Stanton had impressed upon Buckingham the delicacy of his mission, as the secretary of war and President Lincoln each suspected that McClellan might not voluntarily surrender command of the largest army on the North American continent. Therefore, the high-ranking emissary was instructed to initially approach Burnside with the offer of promotion and use every tactic available to convince the bewhiskered Rhode Islander to accept the command. However, if the 38-year-old corps commander absolutely refused promotion, Buckingham was to refrain from delivering the dismissal order to McClellan and return immediately to Washington until Stanton and Lincoln could decide upon an alternate to Burnside.

General Buckingham's train lurched through the deepening snow drifts until it reached the town of Salem, Virginia, but at that point the decidedly middle-aged officer was forced to mount a horse and ride through the icy roads until he came to Burnside's temporary command post almost 15 miles to the south. The Ohioan brushed the accumulated snow from his uniform and entered a small farm building where he discovered the commander of the *IX Corps* perusing a number of sketchy maps. Burnside seemed genuinely surprised to be offered command of the army and protested vehemently that McClellan was performing adequately as commanding general and that he himself was unqualified for such a lofty position. Buckingham finally convinced Burnside that McClellan was about to be dismissed in any case, and added somewhat darkly that if the Rhode Islander did not accept the offer, the mantle of command would most likely fall upon the controversial Joseph Hooker, one of the few men that the mild-mannered corps commander genuinely detested as a backbiting, drunken, scheming malcontent. The mere mention of Hooker swung the issue in Buckingham's favor and Burnside agreed to accompany the general to McClellan's headquarters to inform the Pennsylvanian of the change in command.

Since Burnside himself protested, apparently quite sincerely, that he was not fit for the enormous responsibility being thrust upon him, both contemporary and modern analysts have seriously questioned the wisdom of Lincoln's decision, especially in light of the disaster that was to follow at Fredericksburg. Burnside was just emerging from a very shaky performance at Antietam in which he failed to take advantage of a substantial superiority in numbers to storm over Antietam Creek and roll up Lee's army from its extremely vulnerable right flank. By November of 1862, in strictly military terms, at least four men, Orlando B. Willcox, William B. Franklin, Joseph Hooker, and John F. Reynolds probably offered more skills at commanding the *Army of the Potomac* than Ambrose Burnside. Willcox and Franklin were adequate to slightly above average corps commanders who possessed enough self-confidence to command the army, although nei-

General McClellan surrenders the command of the **Army of the Potomac** *to General Burnside. Before Burnside was appointed to replace McClellan the two had been close friends.*

ther man was particularly imaginative. Joseph Hooker, despite his thinly veiled self-promotion, arrogance, and scheming was still a talented leader who evoked confidence from his men. John Reynolds probably offered the most overall positive attributes as he was highly intelligent, popular with his men, and did not seem incredibly over-awed by the already legendary image of Lee.

While the appointment of Reynolds would seem to have been Lincoln's best move in the fall of 1862, the promotion of Burnside was not as far-fetched as it initially appears. First, the Rhode Islander had the great luck to have commanded one of the few fully successful Union operations in the war up to that point. The expedition against Confederate defenses along the coast of North Carolina had resulted in the capture of nearly 4,000 Rebel soldiers and nearly 80 guns at extremely modest cost to the Union attackers. However, what was not fully evident at the time was that Burnside had enjoyed both substantial numerical superiority and the support of a powerful Federal fleet while confronting largely mediocre Confederate commanders. Second, Burnside also had the good fortune to be viewed as politically acceptable to Lincoln and Stanton. While the newly designated commander was a Democrat who had exhibited few antislavery tendencies, he had acknowledged the need for Union officers to accept the Emancipation Proclamation as a legitimate order from their commander in chief despite personal reservations on their parts. Equally important in a political sense was the fact that Lincoln viewed Burnside as a close personal friend of McClellan and assumed that the men of the *Army of the Potomac* would find this type of transition far less emotional than if a general from the Western armies or one of McClellan's enemies in the *Army of the Potomac* replaced the Young Napoleon. Thus at this particular moment in time, the president viewed Burnside's combination of reasonable military competence and a high degree of political acceptability as an ideal package for an army in transition.

The general who had emerged as the man of the hour spent much of the evening of November 7 accompanying General Buckingham in a ride over snowcovered roads north to Rectortown to McClellan's headquarters. It was well after midnight when the two snowcovered generals arrived in front of McClellan's headquarters tent and they found the commanding general sitting behind a portable desk completing the day's paperwork. The Pennsylvanian received the two near frozen visitors graciously but after a short round of cordial small talk Buckingham rather hesitantly handed McClellan a copy of General Order No. 182 which relieved him from command of the *Army of the Potomac*. The newly dismissed commander maintained his composure and good humor, insisted that Burnside, as a soldier, must obey the offered appointment, and agreed to the new commander's request to remain a few days to ensure an orderly transition. One of the possible reasons for McClellan's graciousness in accepting his dismissal was the fact that rumors had been swirling around Washington that if the president did indeed remove McClellan as commander of the *Army of the Potomac*, he would offer command of all Western armies in compensation. McClellan had no way of knowing that unlike many other army commanders whom Lincoln sacked and then offered positions in another one of the republic's armies, the Pennsylvanian would essentially be retired from active duty at 36 years of age, never to receive another position in the Union forces.

On Monday morning, November 10, 1862, George Brinton McClellan bid farewell to his beloved army during one of the most dramatic military reviews in the entire Civil War. As the Young Napoleon rode through snowcovered fields and received the cheers of thousands of blue-coated soldiers, tears came to his eyes as he admitted that "the scene of today repays me for all that I have endured." As McClellan journeyed to Trenton, New Jersey, to await "further orders" that would never be sent, Ambrose Burnside issued his first orders as commander of the *Army of the Potomac*. The Rhode Islander assured his men that "patriotism and the exertion of every energy is the direction of this army" and that "aided by the full and

McClellan was given a rousing send-off by the **Army of the Potomac** *and continued to be very popular among ordinary soldiers.*

hearty cooperation of its officers and men will, I hope, under the blessings of God, insure its success." He insisted that "with diffidence for myself but with a proud confidence in the unswerving loyalty and determination of the gallant army now entrusted to my care, I accept the command with the steadfast assurance that the just cause must prevail."

Privately, Ambrose Burnside was convinced that he was in over his head as commander of the largest army on either side of the conflict. He wrote to his friend and spiritual adviser the Reverend Augustus Woodbury, "You who know how much I feel any responsibility placed upon me, can readily imagine how much of my time is occupied with this enormous command . . . at times I tremble at the thought of assuming that I am able to exercise so large a command" but insisting "it would have been disloyal and unfriendly to our government not to do it and trusting in God no matter how dark everything now seems to me."

The new commanding general received a somewhat mixed reception from the officers and men of the *Army of the Potomac*. One officer wrote his family that his colleagues accepted the new general "handsomely but not enthusiastically" while another captain noted "we seemed to think there was one they liked much better," the recently departed McClellan. However, an officer in Hooker's command disagreed with this tepid review of events and insisted that "we are well pleased with Burnside, thank God for the prospect ahead now; our soldiers will fight as well for B as McC." Among the majority of enlisted ranks, George McClellan was, and would remain, the most popular commander in the *Army of the Potomac's* history, as he was essentially the father of that army and would always be associated exclusively with that command. However, unlike McClellan's first replacement, John Pope, a blustering stranger from the west who questioned the very manhood of this eastern army, Ambrose Burnside was a known, and generally liked, commodity who, while not seen as an ideal choice, was seen as at least a tolerably acceptable replacement for the beloved "Young Napoleon."

The challenge facing Burnside as he attempted to gain

Ambrose E. Burnside on the day he assumed command of the **Army of the Potomac.** *The unusual cut of his tunic marked him as a Rhode Islander.*

the confidence of a skeptical army was matched by the equally daunting imperative to generate a campaign plan acceptable to Lincoln, Halleck, and Stanton. The president was clearly sending his new commander mixed signals as he assured Burnside that he did not need to move until he was fully prepared but then strongly hinted that failure to fight a major battle with the Rebels before spring would be politically unacceptable. At this moment a number of Lincoln's advisers were insisting that if the Confederacy merely survived until the spring of 1863, Southern independence would simply become a fact, as Northern support for the war seemed to be unraveling alarmingly fast. While the Union army seemed capable of keeping the Rebels from Northern soil, virtually no Confederate territory had been captured in months and the upcoming Emancipation Proclamation threatened to dismantle already shaky border state loyalty. Thus it was imperative that the new commander of the largest army in the republic produce a workable plan for an offensive before the war degenerated into a stalemate that seemed beneficial only to the Rebels.

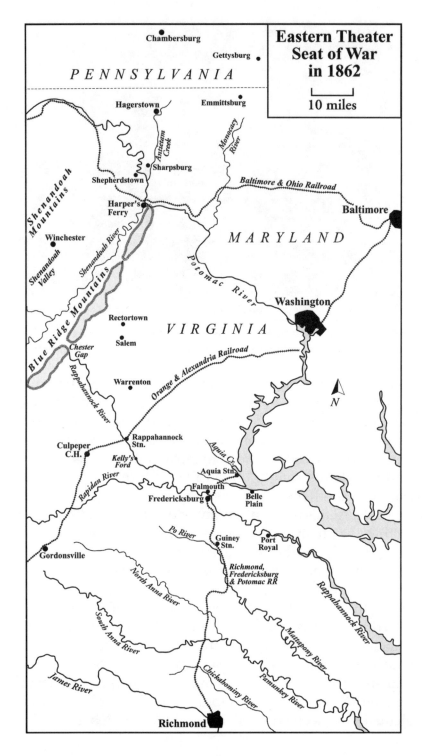

Chambersburg

Gettysburg

**Eastern Theater
Seat of War
in 1862**

10 miles

P E N N S Y L V A N I A

Hagerstown

Emmittsburg

Antietam Creek

Monocacy River

Sharpsburg

Shepherdstown

Baltimore & Ohio Railroad

Harper's
Ferry

Baltimore

Shenandoah Mountains

Winchester

Shenandoah River

M A R Y L A N D

Shenandoah Valley

Potomac River

Blue Ridge Mountains

Rectortown

V I R G I N I A

Washington

Salem

Chester Gap

Rappahannock River

Orange & Alexandria Railroad

Warrenton

N

Rappahannock
Stn.

Aquia Cr.

Culpeper
C.H.

Kelly's Ford

Aquia Stn

Rapidan River

Falmouth

Belle
Plain

Fredericksburg

Po River

Guiney
Stn.

Port
Royal

Gordonsville

*Richmond,
Fredericksburg
& Potomac RR*

Rappahannock River

North Anna River

Mattapony River

South Anna River

James River

Chickahominy River

Pamunkey River

Richmond

Ambrose Burnside was perceptive enough to understand the political crisis facing Lincoln in the autumn of 1862, and he worked quickly to develop the genesis of a plan that he believed could alleviate much of the pressure on the president in the relatively near future. The campaigns of the previous spring and summer had convinced Burnside, along with a large number of other senior officers, that the Army of Northern Virginia was simply too powerful and too well led to be destroyed in a single battle or even a single campaign. Therefore, if Northern support for the war was going to be maintained, at least some significant progress toward ultimate victory was needed in the short run. Burnside believed that the most tangible sign of progress that could be expected in the near future was the capture of the enemy capital at Richmond. However, once Burnside had decided to make a thrust toward the Confederate capital city, he had to determine which of two broad avenues of approach to follow.

One possible scenario was to initiate an essentially accelerated version of his predecessor's current operation which was a fairly concentrated, if glacial, move toward Longstreet's corps deployed around Culpeper Court House, with the hope of engaging and defeating one wing of Lee's army before Stonewall Jackson's force in the Shenandoah Valley could intervene. Ironically this was exactly the operation that a number of senior Confederate generals feared the most as they felt it would enable the Yankees to defeat the two separate halves of the Rebel army in detail before they could be effectively united. General James Longstreet insisted after the war that one of his nightmare scenarios in the fall of 1862 was that Ambrose Burnside would implement McClellan's battle plan without the Young Napoleon's caution. As Longstreet noted, if Burnside had lunged directly for Chester Gap in the Blue Ridge Mountains and held that pass with a screening force, "he might then have held Jackson and fought me or have held me and fought Jackson, thus taking us in detail. This was the only move on the board that could have benefited him at the time he was assigned to the command of the Army of the Potomac. By interposing between the corps of Lee's army he would have secured strong ground and advantage of position. With skill equal to the occasion he should have had success. This was the move about which we felt serious apprehension and we were occupying our minds with plans to meet it when the move toward Fredericksburg was reported."

Lee's willingness to gamble and allow Stonewall Jackson to remain in the Shenandoah Valley to await an opportunity to smash the Yankees from the flank or rear was an audacious decision that might have produced dire consequences for the Confederacy if Burnside had ignored an immediate thrust at Richmond and concentrated on annihilating the Rebel army in the field. However, the Rhode Islander only considered an operation near the Blue Ridge Mountains within the context of an approach to the Rebel capital and he quickly convinced himself that this was the wrong route to Jefferson Davis's presidential mansion.

McClellan had repeatedly badgered Washington with complaints about the inability of the rickety Orange and Alexandria Railroad to supply his enormous army and Burnside had largely agreed with the opinion of his superior. The new commander had visions of Stuart's horsemen slashing his supply line to ribbons as trestles were burned and tracks demolished. In fact even the far more aggressive Ulysses S. Grant rejected this western approach during the decisive 1864 campaign, citing the questionable nature of the supply situation, and approved a more eastern-oriented operation that resulted in the bloody clashes in the Wilderness and Spotsylvania Court House. Thus Burnside jettisoned McClellan's operation and proposed to Halleck "to concentrate the forces near Warrenton and impress upon the enemy the belief that we are to attack Culpeper or Gordonsville, and, at the same time, accumulate a four or five days' supply for the men and animals and then make a rapid move of the whole force to Fredericksburg from that point."

Burnside's proposal received a mixed reception from Abraham Lincoln as it veered dramatically away from the president's developing military strategy to win the war. Lincoln was now fully convinced that Lee's army, not Richmond, was the real prize in the Eastern theater and he was certain that the place to confront the Rebels was as far away from the Confederate capital as possible. Now his new field general suggested a willingness to settle for the consolation prize of the enemy capital as he insisted "the capture of Richmond should be the great object of the campaign as the fall of that place would tend more to cripple the rebel cause than almost any other military event, except the absolute breaking up of their army." Clearly, Burnside was offering Lincoln a half a loaf, a reasonably high prospect of capturing Richmond with an implied promise of more decisive operations against the Army of Northern Virginia sometime during the following year. This was not the operation that the president expected and he promptly sent Henry Halleck and two of his department heads down to Burnside's headquarters to discuss the new commander's rationale for his proposal.

On the frigid night of Wednesday, November 12, Halleck arrived at Burnside's Warrenton headquarters accompanied by General Montgomery C. Meigs, quartermaster general, and General Henry Haupt, superintendent of military railroads. Burnside and the trio from Washington spent most of the night and much of the following day reviewing the new commanding general's proposed operation. Burnside admitted that "General Halleck was strongly in favor of continuing the movement of the army in the direction of Culpeper and Gordonsville and my own plan was as strongly adhered to by me," although Halleck only admitted that "I refused to give any official approval of this deviation from the President's instructions until his assent was obtained." General Haupt, well aware of the rickety state of the Orange and Alexandria Railroad, which would serve as the main supply line for a thrust toward Culpeper and Gordonsville, energetically supported Burnside's plan, while General Meigs simply stated that he had no serious objections to the proposed operation. Both of these department heads viewed a drive from Fredericksburg toward Richmond as a relatively safe, manageable enterprise which offered a reasonable prospect of supplying and feeding the now enormous *Army of the Potomac* as it lurched southward. On the other hand, the Orange and Alexandria Railroad had few sidings and switches, few readily available depots for wood and water, and a high vulnerability to Rebel cavalry raids. Thus Burnside had gained two crucial allies in the strategic debate.

Burnside was extremely anxious to secure official approval for his plan as he telegraphed Halleck on Thursday night, only hours after he had left Warrenton, "If possible, can you send me tonight a definite answer with my plans of operations?" Staff officers spent the early hours of Friday morning putting together tentative plans for the change of base and in a dramatic example of the acceleration of communications allowed by the telegraph, by 1100 on Friday the wires from Washington to Warrenton carried the message from Halleck. "The President has just assented to your plan. He thinks that it will succeed if you move very rapidly; otherwise, not." Hours later, the controversial Fredericksburg campaign was fully underway.

Burnside organized the massive **Army of the Potomac** *into four* **Grand Divisions** *for the Fredericksburg operation. Burnside and his four commanders were depicted in* **Harpers Weekly** *for December 13, 1862.*

The new commanding general's first significant activity was to reorganize the huge army that would now be marching eastward. The Union army was now so large that Burnside decided to form it into a command structure that resembled the army groups used later in the European Theater of Operations during World War II. The general ordered six of the frontline army corps combined into three grand divisions, essentially self-contained armies of 32,000 to 41,000 men. The *II* and *IX Corps* became the *Right Grand Division* under Edwin V. Sumner, the *I* and *VI Corps* became the *Left Grand Division* under William Franklin, and the *III* and *V Corps* became the *Center Grand Division* under Joseph Hooker. When this reorganization was completed, Sumner commanded two brigades of cavalry, fourteen batteries of artillery, and two infantry corps under Orlando Willcox and Darius N. Couch; Franklin could deploy a brigade of cavalry, 22 batteries of artillery, and the infantry corps of John Reynolds and William F. Smith; and Hooker fielded a brigade of cavalry, 17 artillery batteries, and two corps under George Stoneman and Daniel Butterfield. Above and beyond this imposing force of 119,000 men, Burnside could also deploy a *Reserve Grand Division* of 28,000 men from *XI* and *XII Corps* and draw additional troops from the 52,000-men garrison of the Washington defenses. Altogether, the new commander of the *Army of the Potomac* could field an immensely powerful army of 199,000 men supported by just under 800 guns against a Rebel army that would be fortunate to oppose him with one third as much strength. If Burnside could actually steal a march on Lee and confront the Rebels before they could fully prepare for battle, there seemed to be a good chance that the Federals might be able to force their way into Richmond and, perhaps, force the Confederates to attack them under conditions that heavily favored the Yankee army. However, this scenario would only become possible if the Unionists were able to get across the Rappahannock River before Robert E. Lee's outnumbered but confident graycoats could spread out along the heights above Fredericksburg to stop this onrushing blue move.

Ambrose Burnside Before Fredericksburg

Ambrose Everett Burnside was born in Liberty, Indiana on May 23, 1824. Burnside's father had been a slaveholder in South Carolina before moving to the midwest. Ambrose was apprenticed as a tailor but became bored with his career prospects and used his father's political influence to secure an appointment at West Point. He graduated 18th in a class of 38 in 1847 and spent most of his first year in the service on garrison duty in the closing stages of the Mexican War. After the war ended, he was involved in a campaign against hostile Apaches where he was wounded in a skirmish.

By the early 1850s, Burnside was restless over the slow promotion structure of the peacetime army and in 1853 he resigned to go into private business in Bristol, Rhode Island. Burnside soon developed a revolutionary new breech-loading rifle that could use metallic cartridges, but the weapon was initially too fragile for heavy combat use and while he was attempting to improve the gun, his new company went bankrupt. In the spring of 1858, Burnside was without any real source of income and he was forced to approach his old army comrade, George McClellan, for a job with the Illinois Central Railroad. McClellan was serving as president of the railroad and generously offered to share his house in Chicago with Burnside while the former gun developer took a job as a cashier.

In early 1861, Burnside's fortunes dramatically improved even as the Union disintegrated. The secession of the Southern states prompted the War Department to begin ordering the manufacture of Burnside's new rifle while the Rhode Islander himself was given command of the *1st Rhode Island Volunteer Infantry*. While Burnside had been living in Chicago, he had become friendly with Abraham Lincoln, and despite the new colonel's Democratic party affiliation the new chief executive took an active interest in his career. Although Burnside's performance at the Union disaster at Bull Run had been less than spectacular, he was soon given a choice assignment of command of an expeditionary force charged with capturing New Bern and Roanoke Island in North Carolina. Burnside's force won a number of modest but highly publicized battles in the Tar Heel state, and by March of 1862 the former railroad cashier was a major general who enjoyed the friendship of both Lincoln and McClellan.

When McClellan began his operations on the peninsula of Virginia, Burnside was given command of *IX Corps* of the *Army of the Potomac* and the Rhode Island general turned in solid performances during the next several battles. By the time of the Antietam campaign, Burnside commanded a wing of McClellan's army and was charged with responsibility for crossing Antietam Creek below Sharpsburg and outflanking the right end of the Confederate line. Burnside stumbled badly in this operation as he insisted on capturing a well-defended bridge across the creek when it was obvious that almost undefended fords were available further upstream. The Rhode Islander's caution allowed Confederate reinforcements to shore up the wavering Rebel line and permitted Lee's army to escape destruction, a situation that dramatically strained the friendship between Burnside and McClellan. Thus when Burnside rather reluctantly accepted command of the *Army of the Potomac* in November of 1862, he had already exhibited a very mixed record of success.

Edwin Sumner (1797-1863)

One of Ambrose Burnside's most loyal subordinates during the Fredericksburg campaign was General Edwin Vose Sumner. Sumner was the oldest active corps commander in the Civil War and a member of one of the earliest families to settle Massachusetts. He never attended West Point but was commissioned in the army in 1819. Sumner was captain of dragoons by 1833, promoted to lieutenant colonel during the Mexican War, and became commanding officer of the elite *1st Cavalry Regiment* in 1855. By the outbreak of the Civil War, he was one of only three brigadier generals in the entire United States army and while he remained personally loyal to the Union he watched two of his sons-in-law side with the Confederacy. One became Stonewall Jackson's chief of artillery at Fredericksburg and then served as a general under Joseph Johnston to whom he was related.

Sumner's seniority in the pre-war army virtually guaranteed him a high rank in the new volunteer army, and George McClellan quickly gave him command of *II Corps* which he led in the Peninsula campaign. The Massachusetts native was wounded twice during this campaign and promoted to major general while receiving extensive praise for his gallantry and energetic leadership. These traits did not serve him as well at Antietam as he personally led a charge by one of his units while failing to ensure that other divisions were actually engaged in the battle.

Sumner clearly favored the appointment of Burnside over Hooker in the fall of 1862, but became somewhat annoyed at the new commander when the Rhode Islander restrained him from capturing the town of Fredericksburg before the bulk of the Confederate army arrived. When Hooker finally succeeded to command in January of 1863, Sumner asked for a transfer to the Department of the Missouri, but he died in Syracuse, New York, en route to his new position. Despite Sumner's rather advanced age, he generally was regarded as an energetic, considerate field commander who was an asset to the Union cause.

Joseph Hooker (1814-1879)

While Ambrose Burnside had a number of close friends in the Confederate army, perhaps his most bitter enemy was a fellow Union general, Joseph Hooker. Hooker was one of the most colorful, controversial generals of the Civil War. The grandson of a Revolutionary War officer, Hooker was born in 1814 in Hadley, Massachusetts, and attended Hopkins Academy before enrolling in West Point in 1833. After graduating in the middle of his class in 1837, Hooker served in the Seminole War before being named to General Zachary Taylor's staff at the outbreak of the

Mexican War. Hooker was transferred to General Winfield Scott's staff for the Mexico City campaign and ended the war as a brevet lieutenant colonel in the Division of the Pacific.

It is possible that, like Ulysses S. Grant, Hooker experienced problems with alcohol abuse during peacetime, as he resigned his commission in 1853 to become a marginally successful farmer in California and according to one account, "descended almost to the level of a beachcomber." At the beginning of the Civil War, Hooker was virtually penniless, but his previous military record earned him command of a California militia regiment.

The former Mexican War hero decided to go to Washington to secure a more active command and apparently his newly vocal abolitionism and new-found Republican allegiance gained him notice in an army filled with generals who had mainly Democratic leanings. Hooker was almost immediately appointed a brigadier general of volunteers and by the Peninsula campaign he was a division commander in Samuel Heintzelman's *III Corps*. During one of the battles in this campaign, a press release reading "Fighting-Joe Hooker" was sent to dozens of Northern newspapers and a rather unwanted nickname was born.

After a solid showing in the disastrous Union defeat at Second Bull Run, "Fighting Joe" was promoted to major general and given command of *I Corps*. He was wounded fairly early in the battle of Antietam. Hooker used his recuperation in Washington to excellent advantage as he developed a close personal relationship with Secretary of the Treasury Salmon Chase. When Lincoln decided to relieve George McClellan, many

Radical Republican senators and congressmen proposed this apparently abolitionist general for command of the *Army of the Potomac*; but the president decided to name Burnside due to his friendship with McClellan. Hooker's tenure under Burnside as commander of the *Center Grand Division* was extremely contentious and the Massachusetts general took every opportunity to inform political leaders of Burnside's incompetence.

When Lincoln finally decided to promote Hooker to command of the army, after accepting Burnside's resignation, Hooker initiated a highly successful series of reforms which dramatically improved morale in the Union army. Hooker's plan for the Chancellorsville campaign came much closer to succeeding than Burnside's Fredericksburg operation and he very nearly trapped Lee's army in an untenable position. However, Hooker's nerve failed at a crucial moment in the battle and the Confederates scored a major victory.

After the battle of Chancellorsville, Hooker developed a running feud with Secretary of War Edwin Stanton and Commanding General Henry Halleck regarding the defense of Washington during Lee's new offensive, and in exasperation he asked to be relieved almost on the eve of the battle of Gettysburg. However, the Union disaster at Chickamauga prompted the War Department to give Hooker command of a relief force consisting of the *XI* and *XII Corps* of the *Army of the Potomac* that was moved by train to support the Federal troops beseiged in Chattanooga.

"Fighting Joe" became a national celebrity in November when his troops won a spectacular victory on Lookout Mountain in "The Battle

Above the Clouds" even though the battle itself was not particularly large. Several months later, during Sherman's Atlanta campaign, Hooker fully expected to be promoted to command of the *Army of the Tennessee* when that army's commander, James McPherson, was killed in action. Sherman bypassed Hooker to name his subordinate Oliver O. Howard as the new commander, and the Massachusetts general promptly resigned from the Western army. Hooker was given departmental command in the Northern Department during the remainder of the war and the Department of the East after the war. He retired as a regular major general in 1868. Hooker died in Garden City, New York in 1879, lauded by many of the men who served under him but derided as an incompetent by Grant and Sherman.

William B. Franklin (1823-1903)

One of the generals who emerged from the Fredericksburg campaign with a badly tarnished reputation was William Buel Franklin of York, Pennsylvania. Franklin was the top graduate in the West Point class of 1843 and a classmate of the eventually far more successful Ulysses S. Grant. During the Mexican War Franklin won a brevet promotion for gallantry at the battle of Buena Vista, and afterward obtained the choice assignment of supervising the construction of the new Capitol dome and the addition to the Treasury building in Washington, D.C.

Shortly after the surrender of Fort Sumter, Franklin was appointed commanding officer of the regular *12th United States Infantry Regiment*, but three days later he was pulled from this assignment and promoted to brigadier general of volunteers. After the Union disaster at Bull Run, Franklin was appointed to command a division in the reorganized *Army of the Potomac* and when McClellan embarked on the Peninsula campaign, the York native was a corps commander and a member of McClellan's inner circle. Franklin performed well in Virginia as commander of *VI Corps* but during the Antietam campaign his hesitation in capturing Crampton's Gap against a vastly inferior force of Confederate defenders helped allow Lee to concentrate his army around Sharpsburg.

The removal of McClellan in favor of Burnside hardly injured Franklin's career as the new commanding general named the Pennsylvanian as a *Grand Division* commander along with Edwin Sumner and Joe Hooker. Franklin emerged from the Fredericksburg disaster with a tarnished reputation as he appeared to bungle the whole operation against Stonewall Jackson's defenders. The *Grand Division* commander then earned the hostility of Burnside by conspiring against the army commander with a number of his subordinate generals. When Abraham Lincoln removed Burnside, he relieved Franklin as well, but the Pennsylvanian had enough political influence to secure a new command in General Nathaniel Banks's Department of the Gulf. Franklin commanded *XIX Corps* in the disastrous Sabine Pass and Red River operations and was badly wounded in the latter campaign.

While Franklin ended the war as a rather unsuccessful commander, his post-war career was far more profitable. He became general manager of the fast growing Colt Fire Arms company; supervised construction of the Connecticut capitol; was a presidential elector in the 1876 election; and was commissioner of the United States exhibit at the Paris Exposition of 1888. William Franklin was a classic example of a general who may have been a competent brigade or division commander but who was promoted far above his abilities.

CHAPTER IV

Race for the Rappahannock

*U*nlike Vicksburg, Atlanta, or Richmond, neither the Union nor Confederate government believed that possession of Fredericksburg was vital to the outcome of the war. The picturesque town of 5,000 people did have historical significance since George Washington, John Paul Jones, and James Monroe had all owned homes in the region, but Fredericksburg itself was not a vital military target. The town's location halfway between Richmond and Washington put the community into the middle of the surging and ebbing tides of war, and by 1865 Fredericksburg would change hands between Rebels and Yankees seven times. However, most of the time neither government thought the place was important enough to station more than a token force in the community. Yet in December of 1862 this quaint riverfront town would become the focal point for one of the largest concentrations of soldiers in the history of North America.

On Friday, November 14, 1862, General Ambrose Burnside held a meeting of his senior commanders and then sat for a series of photographs with several of his generals. Early the next morning, General Edwin "Bull" Sumner's *Right Grand Division* of the *Army of the Potomac* marched out of its camps near Warrenton, Virginia, and headed toward the north bank of the Rappahannock River. The blue-coated soldiers, who were used to the leisurely pace of marching ordered by George

McClellan, suddenly found themselves being pushed to the limits of their endurance at a rate that even Stonewall Jackson would have approved. By noon on Monday a powerful force of 30,000 Federal soldiers was deploying in the north shore town of Falmouth and cavalry scouts were soon probing on the south bank near Fredericksburg. The men of the *II* and *IX Corps* had accomplished a significant feat; they had stolen a march on Robert E. Lee and for a brief moment Lincoln's appointment of Ambrose Burnside appeared to be inspired genius. However, within hours after the arrival of the Yankees, the Federal plan began to unravel.

Edwin Sumner now had 30,000 troops encamped only a short distance from the town of Fredericksburg that at this moment held only a few companies of Confederate troops. The *Right Grand Division* commander was so ecstatic about his accomplishment that he begged Burnside for permission to push part of his army across the Rappahannock at several fords upstream from Fredericksburg and then march overland and occupy the town and the high ground beyond it. Sumner's

This photograph taken from the Union positions shows the extent of the town of Fredericksburg and the high ground beyond.

plan would have dramatically changed the course of the campaign and put the Federal army in command of the vital heights that dominated the area. However, Burnside refused to grant permission for his subordinate's bold idea. The new commanding general had seen his predecessor allow the *Army of the Potomac* to be divided by a river at least twice during the Peninsula campaign of the previous spring and each time the Federal army had narrowly avoided disaster. In late May, the Yankee army was caught on opposite sides of a flooding Chicahominy River when Confederate General Joseph Johnston launched an offensive that resulted in the battle of Fair Oaks. A month later Johnston's successor, Robert E. Lee, caught the Union army in a similar predicament at the beginning of the Seven Days battles. In each case stubborn Yankee fighting and poorly coordinated Rebel attacks allowed the Federals to escape with a drawn battle, but Burnside was afraid that a third roll of the dice might not be nearly so lucky. Burnside's caution threw away his best chance at securing a significant tactical advantage on his adversary, but left a small window of opportunity for victory if every element of the Rhode Islander's campaign plan came together. Unfortunately for the Union cause, this was not to be the case.

Ambrose Burnside's plan of operations was not based on the prospect of occupying the high ground around Fredericksburg and fighting a battle on the Rappahannock. The new commanding general saw Fredericksburg only as a rear supply base for his enormous army as it thrust deeper into Virginia and attempted to get between Lee's army and the Confederate capital. If the Union army was going to conduct an extensive campaign deep in enemy territory, it would have to have a secure line of supply all the way back to Aquia Creek and the Potomac River. Therefore, if Burnside's plan of deep penetration was going to succeed, two major logistical challenges would have to be surmounted; a reliable supply line would have to be established between the Potomac and the north bank of the Rappahannock, and a series of bridges would have to be constructed to allow men and supplies to move to the south shore of the river and on into enemy territory.

The first challenge confronted Henry Haupt, the director of the U.S. Military Railroad. When Haupt arrived at Aquia Creek landing shortly after Sumner's troops marched into Falmouth, he quickly saw that the Confederates were not about to make his task an easy one. Rebel forces had temporarily gained control of this area a few weeks earlier and when they withdrew, Lee had ordered the wharves burned and the rail line from Aquia Station to Fredericksburg torn up along with the destruction of the railroad bridge over the Rappahannock River. The Yankee railroad czar quickly put into operation a massive repair effort, but he informed Burnside that it would take three days to repair the docks and an additional five days to put the rail line back in working order. If Burnside was going to thrust into enemy territory before Lee knew what had happened, he was going to have to march with the supplies he already had on hand. However, even these supplies would be useless until the destroyed Rappahannock River bridge could somehow be replaced.

This second challenge would eventually fall into the hands of Major Ira Spaulding and a regiment of New York engineers. The destruction of the railroad bridge at Fredericksburg was a major barrier to a Federal advance, but this barrier could be surmounted with the use of the *Army of the Potomac*'s extensive supply of pontoon trains. After the battle of Antietam, most of the bridging equipment in the Union army had been shipped to Berlin, Maryland, to allow McClellan to push southward over the Potomac River in pursuit of the Confederate army. Since most of the pontoons could easily be floated down the nearby Chesapeake and Ohio canal the entire 50 miles to Washington, General Burnside assumed the bridging equipment could be shipped to Falmouth almost as fast as his soldiers marched to the same destination. When the commanding general wired a request to the War Department on November 12 that he would require extensive bridging equipment delivered to Falmouth as soon as possible, he expected that the pontoons would probably be waiting when Sumner's troops arrived. Unfortunately for Burnside, this expectation was soon shown to be a fantasy.

Where bridges did not exist or had been destroyed the Union army could deploy pontoons. The presence or absence of pontoons at various stages of the Fredericksburg campaign had a decisive influence on the outcome.

When General Burnside's message reached the War Department, the pontoon equipment was even closer to Falmouth than he had expected. At almost exactly the same time as the general's report was transmitted, an unknown functionary in the War Department bureaucracy had decided that the bridging equipment was no longer needed at Berlin, and ordered Major Ira Spaulding's *50th New York* engineers to transfer the pontoons to Washington. Spaulding and 76 pontoons arrived in the capital the next afternoon, but the major's superior, General Daniel Woodbury, had never been informed of Burnside's report. The pontoons were duly ordered into storage and Spaulding was told to dismantle the equipment and then enjoy himself in the city. On November 15, as Sumner's troops force marched toward the north bank of the Rappahannock the vital bridging equipment was being dismantled.

The pontoon fiasco rolled into an even higher gear the next day when a routine inquiry by one of Burnside's staff officers revealed that no bridging equipment was on its way to Falmouth. Spaulding was hurriedly located at a Washington hotel, and a flustered War Department officer cut orders to send half the pontoons by water to Belle Plain, Virginia, and the other half on an overland wagon train. The overland journey descended into near farce when 40 teamsters were roused from near stupors in local saloons to handle teams of horses that had never been used to haul wagons. As the tipsy drivers and their balky horses streamed out of Washington, torrential rain fell in sheets and the roads south to the Rappahannock turned into quagmires. Meanwhile, the steamboat that had been assigned to tow the water-borne segment of the pontoons promptly developed engine trouble and then ran aground on the river. For the next five days two parallel trains of pontoons inched toward Burnside's army while Robert E. Lee discovered the Yankee intentions and sprang into action.

When Robert E. Lee was informed of the change in command of the *Army of the Potomac*, he told his subordinates that he regretted to part with McClellan "for we always understood each other so well." Some of his generals insisted that Burnside was far less competent than his predecessor, but Lee retorted, "I fear they may continue to make these changes till they find someone whom I don't understand." The Virginian now commanded over 78,000 men in an army that artillerist E. Porter Alexander considered the most powerful force that Lee ever put in the field, since Confederate numbers would never again reach this total and the men were at a peak of confidence in their ability to defeat the Yankees. However, this impressive force had to be prepared to meet an offensive by Burnside from at least four possible directions.

Lee considered it possible that his new adversary might continue McClellan's operation of moving south from Warrenton toward Longstreet's corps deployed around Culpeper Court House. A second possibility was a lunge westward through the Blue Ridge Mountains in an attempt to hit Stonewall Jackson's four divisions in the Shenandoah Valley before Longstreet could arrive to reinforce his colleague. A third possible avenue of approach might be McClellan's old route from Norfolk up the Peninsula toward Richmond. Finally, Burnside could cross the Rappahannock somewhere from Fredericksburg on downstream and march toward the Confederate capital using the series of rivers in that region as supply lines secured by the Federal navy.

The commander of the Army of Northern Virginia took each of these threats quite seriously but he felt confident that his army could handle any of these challenges. In case of a Federal thrust toward Culpeper, Lee relied on Jackson's "Foot Cavalry" to tear at his adversary's flank and rear before he could get into position to seriously threaten Longstreet. If the Rhode Islander lunged toward Jackson, "Old Pete" would shift westward and link up with his eccentric colleague in the Shenandoah Valley. An amphibious landing at Norfolk would be delayed by local garrisons until Lee arrived to attempt a repetition of the Seven Days offensive, possibly this time resulting in the annihilation of the *Army of the Potomac*. Finally, a Yankee move across the Rappahannock offered the possibility of springing a trap on the Federal army about 25 miles south of Fredericksburg along the North Anna River.

Lee was in his usual aggressive mood in the early winter of 1862 and he saw each potential Federal operation as an opportunity to badly hurt his Yankee opponents. However, early and accurate intelligence of Burnside's actual intentions were vital if the Confederate general had any hope of reuniting his divided army and ending the 1862 campaign season with a spectacular victory. J. E. B. Stuart's cavalry soon gave the Virginian the vital information he needed. On Monday, November 17, a scouting force of graycoat cavalry operating downstream on the Rappahannock River discovered that Federal gunboats and transports were gathering at Aquia Creek. The next morning, another unit of Rebel horse soldiers found that the Yankees were no longer camped near Warrenton. Lee could now see Burnside's plan begin to unfold and he took immediate steps to challenge the bluecoat advance.

General Longstreet was ordered to send one division to Fredericksburg to hold the town and delay a Union advance beyond the Rappahannock. However, the commander of the Southern army initially had no intention of seriously challenging his adversary near the picturesque colonial town. Lee's attention was focused 25 miles below Fredericksburg along the banks of the North Anna River. Lee was confident that as long as he could unite his two corps on the heights above Fredericksburg, he could repulse almost any force that Burnside threw at him. However, both Lee and Stonewall Jackson agreed that any victory at Fredericksburg would provide few long-term benefits. The Yankee-occupied north bank of the Rappahannock contained much higher ground than the south shore. Thus even if Burnside's army was decimated in a frontal assault, it would be almost impossible to launch a counterattack at the retreating bluecoats. When the hard charging Rebels poured down from the heights onto the plain below to chase the Federals, Union artillery on Stafford Heights would simply pulverize the Confederate regiments and turn the battle back into a bloody draw. If the year was to end on a more spectacular triumph, Burnside had to be enticed to fight the climactic battle further south.

Lee and his corps commanders knew that their opponent had been placed in charge of the *Army of the Potomac* on the assumption that he would be far more offensively oriented than McClellan. If Burnside was determined to attack under almost any circumstances, a confrontation along the North Anna offered far more inviting opportunities for the South. Lee was particularly intrigued by Stonewall Jackson's plan to entice Burnside into a dangerous trap. Stonewall insisted that the North Anna River was the ideal place to confront the Yankees since the north bank offered no advantage of high ground, unlike the Rappahannock. The Virginia corps commander proposed that Confederate engineers should build strong fortifications along the south bank of the North Anna while Lee's army staged a slow retreat down from Fredericksburg. When the Confederate withdrawal suddenly screeched to a halt at the North Anna, Burnside would obligingly attack a powerful Rebel position. Unlike the Rappahannock line, the alternative position offered enormous possibilities for a counteroffensive. The Union attackers would have almost no protection on their flanks as they charged forward, and once the assault had run its course, the exhausted bluecoats would be wide open to a powerful counterattack by fresh Confederates held in reserve. Then, as the Yankees retreated northward, Rebel cavalry units would swoop down and destroy the bridges over the Po and Rappahannock Rivers to the north. At this point Burnside would be trapped against largely unfordable rivers and in real danger of losing his army.

The plan proposed by Jackson, and supported by Lee, was a bold gamble that had an enormous potential payoff. However, before the trap could be set in motion, political pressures in Richmond ensured that the great battle would be fought along the Rappahannock. Jefferson Davis spent most of his presidency deriding the idea of voluntarily surrendering any Confederate territory to the invading Yankees. In the fall of 1862, as it became obvious that the *Army of the Potomac* was determined to launch an end-of-the-year offensive, Davis emphasized that he refused to give up large sections of Virginia even if it was a temporary loss in order to spring a decisive trap. Lee's complex relationship with the Confederate president seldom allowed him to directly challenge his superior on a major issue, and in this case it was the general who obediently complied with the chief executive's wishes. As Lee explained, "My purpose was changed, not from any advantage in the position, but from an unwillingness to open more of our country to depradation than possible and also with a view to collecting such forage and provisions as could be obtained in the Rappahannock Valley."

Once Lee reluctantly discarded his plan to challenge Burnside along the North Anna River, the Southern commander began directing his energies toward seizing the high ground behind Fredericksburg before the Union army could pour across the Rappahannock. An emotional race now began that affected Rebels, Yankees, and civilians alike. On Thursday evening, November 20, General Lafayette McLaws's division began occupying the heights beyond Fredericksburg while Burnside once again rejected Edwin Sumner's request to establish a beachhead on the south bank before the Rebels arrived in force. When Confederate snipers began blazing away at the Yankees from the cover of houses and outbuildings, the

As a Mexican War veteran and former secretary of war, Jefferson Davis felt himself qualified to intervene in the day-to-day operations of the Confederate armies.

frustrated *Right Grand Division* commander sent a courier across the river to demand the surrender of the town or face massive bombardment. Sumner insisted that if the town had not surrendered by 0900 the next morning, massed artillery on Stafford Heights would open fire. At this point General Longstreet arrived in town with additional units, and he authorized the town's mayor to promise that Fredericksburg itself would not be used for military purposes if the Federals suspended their threat of bombardment. Sumner agreed to at least postpone any action, but when Lee arrived, he advised civilians to vacate the town.

Most of Fredericksburg's citizens took Lee's advice seriously and soon a steady stream of old men, women, and children filed out of town clutching whatever possessions they could carry. Colonel E. Porter Alexander insisted that "it was pitiful to see the refugees endeavoring to remove their possessions and encamping in the woods and fields for miles around during the unusually cold weather which followed." Colonel James Nance of the 3rd South Carolina Regiment observed the exodus with rising emotions and noted that "there were doubtless many cases of suffering and trial with these good women. I understand many of the ladies have camped in the woods and crowded together in mean houses to escape the danger which threatens the city and its inhabitants. Army wagons and ambulances are employed in hauling away the people and their effects." The colonel affirmed that "no more loyal town honors Virginia and no people in her borders are more hospitable and virtuous."

While Lee oversaw the civilian evacuation of Fredericksburg and the deployment of his newly arrived divisions, his Northern counterpart fumed at the logistical failures of his army and tried to develop an alternative plan that would meet with Lincoln's approval and offer a reasonable chance of success. As Burnside studied his maps and discussed plans with his generals, the president asked the Rhode Islander to make the short trip to Aquia Creek to discuss possible strategies.

Burnside and Lincoln spent two days aboard the steamer *Baltimore* and then continued their discussions two days later in Washington and the summit meeting produced mixed results. The president offered to transfer 15,000 men from the capital's garrison to the field army which combined with the

Abraham Lincoln appointed and dismissed a succession of supreme commanders, but generally left the actual operations of the Union armies to the military leaders.

three *Grand Divisions* and Franz Sigel's reserve force could provide over 16,000 bluecoats for a Union offensive. Lincoln suggested that Burnside place 25,000 men downriver at Port Royal and an additional 25,000 troops on the north bank of the Pamunkey River. With these two major forces advancing to threaten Lee's flanks and rear, the main army might cross the Rappahannock successfully at Fredericksburg. If all three columns could then converge, they might have the choice of either marching to Richmond with minimal opposition or turning to annihilate Lee's heavily outnumbered army. At this point Burnside and Henry Halleck joined forces to insist that there were too many logistical difficulties to allow the plan to work and the president reluctantly relented.

The president deferred to his two generals and told Burnside that he need not launch an offensive until he was fully prepared, but it was also obvious to the new commander that Lincoln could have kept McClellan in command if he simply wanted a general who could lead his men into winter quarters. Burnside insisted to his superior that "the army is in good spirit, good condition and good morale and fully prepared to cross the river in face of the enemy and drive him away." While Lincoln accepted his general's evaluation of his army, he was already wondering whether his replacement of McClellan was actually going to reap any dividends. He informed one of his political allies, "I certainly have been dissatisfied with the slowness of Buell and McClellan, but before I relieved them, I had great fears I should not find successors to them, who would do better, and I am sorry to add, that I have seen little since to relieve those fears." At least one Union officer empathized with Lincoln's dilemma as he exclaimed, "All theories seem to be upset and our generals groping in the dark until some master mind can discover the principles which should regulate warfare." At that moment one of the "groping generals" was certainly Ambrose Burnside as he searched desperately for a strategy that would gain a substantial edge on Robert E. Lee.

The appearance of increasing numbers of Confederate soldiers on the south bank of the Rappahannock River initially encouraged the Union commander to consider some

Thaddeus Lowe developed his own balloons and equipment and made numerous innovations in aerial observation and artillery spotting. He and his balloonists made a considerable contribution to the Union army during the first half of the Civil War.

form of wide flanking movement that would allow the Federal army to cross well below Lee's heaviest defenses. One plan envisioned throwing a large force across the Rappahannock opposite the town of Port Royal, 17 miles south of Fredericksburg. This might disrupt Lee's line of communications to Richmond and force him to pull at least part of his army from its position on the heights above Fredericksburg. This plan was complicated by the fact that the river was over a half mile wide at this point and would be very difficult to bridge with available pontoon equipment. However, Burnside was serious enough about this option that he dispatched two of Professor Thaddeus Lowe's observation balloons on a reconnaissance mission. The Yankee aeronauts reported that at least part of D. H. Hill's division was deployed along the riverbank while it was quite possible that even more Confederates were concealed by the dense woodlands a short distance in from the Rappahannock.

The Union general then shifted his attention to Skinker's Neck, a point five miles upstream from Port Royal and twelve miles downstream from Fredericksburg. A young Federal engineering officer had quietly crossed the river to examine the south bank for possible pontoon bridgeheads and he reported that few Rebel troops were in the vicinity. However, by the time the plodding Union general carefully considered this landing site, Stonewall Jackson's corps had arrived on the scene and crusty acting-division commander Jubal Early had deployed several thousand graycoats right where the Yankee engineers had planned to span the river. As a rainy and cold November turned into a snowy and frigid December, General Ambrose Burnside was moving rapidly toward a decision that would lead to one of the most lopsided Confederate victories of the entire Civil War.

Jefferson Davis's Impact on the Fredericksburg Campaign

While the president of the Confederacy was hundreds of miles from Virginia during the battle of Fredericksburg, Jefferson Davis still exercised significant influence on the unfolding of the campaign. Davis believed that his service as a regimental commander in the Mexican War and secretary of war under Franklin Pierce qualified him to be an actively involved strategist in the Confederate war effort. Abraham Lincoln never hesitated to make suggestions to his field commanders but he would also generally defer to generals if they explained their reasoning. The Confederate president went much further than Lincoln in developing strategy, and in late 1862 much of this strategy was based on a reluctance to abandon even one square mile of Southern territory. Ideally, Davis would have preferred that the Army of Northern Virginia confront the Yankees along the line of the Potomac River on the opposite bank from Washington, D.C. The Confederate president reluctantly tolerated Lee's withdrawal further into Virginia after the bloody standoff at Antietam, but made it clear that a withdrawal even further south to the North Anna River was politically unacceptable. Thus Lee was forced to suppress his own, and Stonewall Jackson's, desire to spring a trap on the North Anna where an initial defensive victory could be turned into the possibility of annihilating the Yankee army.

Ironically, while the Fredericksburg campaign was largely fought by Davis's ground rules, several months later the tables would be turned when Lee prepared an invasion of Pennsylvania. In June of 1863, when the Confederate president wanted to shift a large part of the Army of Northern Virginia westward to prevent a Union capture of Vicksburg, Lee largely ignored Davis's arguments and went ahead with plans that would eventually result in the Confederate disaster at Gettysburg. Thus if the situation was exactly reversed, if Lee had won approval for his North Anna campaign and if Davis had insisted on utilizing Army of Northern Virginia units to relieve the crisis in the West, the course of the war might have been very different.

Fredericksburg Before the War

Fredericksburg, Virginia, was a relatively modest-sized community in 1862, but the town had enormous historical importance. Fredericksburg had become an important river port for the lucrative tobacco trade of 18th-century Virginia, and the town reflected the prosperity of its bustling commerce. Streets of substantial brick and wood residences included the homes of Revolutionary naval hero John Paul Jones and President James Monroe. The north side of the Rappahannock included an estate where George Washington spent much of his youth, while Old Ferry plantation had been the home of Washington's mother during the last years of her life. One of the community's most prominent citizens during the early 1770s had been Dr. Hugh Mercer, owner of a prosperous apothecary shop and one of Virginia's leading physicians who became a close personal friend to George Washington. Dr. Mercer became General Mercer during the War of Independence and his life ended at the point of British bayonets only moments before Washington's decisive victory over the redcoats at Princeton, New Jersey.

The Longstreet-Jackson Team at Fredericksburg

One of the ironies of the Civil War is that the battle of Fredericksburg was the only engagement in which James Longstreet and Stonewall Jackson actually worked as an official team of corps commanders in the Army of Northern Virginia. During Second Bull Run and Antietam, Lee gave the two generals unofficial command of two provisional corps, but in both of these battles the men were still officially only division commanders, since the Confederate Congress had not yet authorized the rank of lieutenant general. The battle that followed Fredericksburg, the engagement at Chancellorsville, found the Confederate team split as Longstreet and much of his command was involved in operations in southern Virginia and unable to return to Lee in time to affect the outcome of the battle. Any opportunity for reuniting Lee's two premier subordinates disappeared when Stonewall Jackson was mortally wounded by friendly fire during the evening of the first full day of the battle of Chancellorsville.

Robert E. Lee seemed at the peak of his confidence in his ability to defeat the enemy when he had his two favorite lieutenants each commanding a wing of the Army of Northern Virginia, and this presumption of success was very evident during the Fredericksburg campaign. Longstreet enjoyed fighting on the defensive in carefully prepared positions and viewed the high ground outside of Fredericksburg as an ideal place to fight a battle. Jackson's defensive posture always seemed to be a preparation for a spectacular counterpunch that just missed occurring at Fredericksburg. Despite these significant differences in tactics and personality, the Confederate corps commanders actually got along quite well together and respected each other's attributes and skills. The dramatic alteration of this winning combination after the Fredericksburg campaign would put the Confederate army at a severe disadvantage in the battles from Gettysburg to Appomattox.

CHAPTER V

The Battle for the Bridgeheads

On the cold, snowy evening of November 29, 1862, a 39-year-old general wearing a battered felt hat and a gray coat that was too short for him politely knocked on the pole of the headquarters tent of Robert E. Lee and announced that the Second Corps of the Army of Northern Virginia was present and available for action. Lee eagerly shook hands with Thomas J. "Stonewall" Jackson and congratulated his lieutenant on marching four divisions of almost 35,000 men 175 miles through alternating snowstorms and downpours to reach the Confederate camp near Fredericksburg. The commander of the Southern army now had his entire nine divisions available to defend the south bank of the Rappahannock River and Ambrose Burnside would soon be forced to radically alter his plans for conducting a fall campaign against the Confederacy.

By early December of 1862, 78,000 gray-coated soldiers were in position along a 20-mile stretch of the Rappahannock River and capable of challenging a Yankee crossing at almost any point along this stretch of water. James Longstreet's First Corps of 35,886 men in five divisions was deployed between a bend of the Rappahannock River just above Fredericksburg called Beck's Island and Deep Run Creek, about two miles below the town. The divisions of Richard H. Anderson, Lafayette McLaws, Robert Ransom, George Pickett, and John Bell Hood were positioned along a series of ridges that fea-

This picture of the road through Fredericksburg to Marye's Heights shows clearly the muddy and broken nature of the ground.

tured two prominent landworks, Marye's Heights and Telegraph Hill. Marye's Heights rose up behind the Marye family mansion called "Brampton" and stretched from Taylor's Hill near the Rappahannock bend to Hazel Run Creek which originated near the lower end of Fredericksburg. On the other side of Hazel Run was a relatively new highway leading out of town called Telegraph Road which ran past a 90-foot elevation called Telegraph Hill.

These various elevations were anywhere from a half mile to a mile beyond Fredericksburg and rose fairly abruptly from what seemed to be a featureless stretch of flat ground. However, as many Yankee soldiers would soon discover to their dismay, this alternating muddy and snowcovered plain was not quite as unbroken as it first seemed. Two ravine-like obstacles stretched between the town and the ridge line beyond. The barriers to potential attackers were a canal which looped from near Beck's Island to the edge of town and a wide, muddy ditch that forked off from the canal and ran over to the local paper mill. Any mass of bluecoats charging across the plain would have to negotiate both of these impediments in the face of Confederate fire from the heights. Another important feature that Burnside and his generals could not easily detect from the far side of the river was that a stretch of Telegraph Road was actually below the surface of the adjoining fields as it ran past Marye's Heights. The side of the road facing Fredericksburg also featured a four-foot-high stone wall that could easily be turned into an almost impregnable fortification with relatively minor work by Confederate soldiers.

While Longstreet's men were deployed in a fairly compact line that ran for about five miles from left flank to right flank, the 33,692 men that made up Stonewall Jackson's Second Corps were stretched out for almost 15 miles until the actual day of the battle of Fredericksburg. Jackson placed one of his four divisions along the wooded heights of Prospect Hill, a 40-foot elevation that overlooked the tracks of the Richmond, Fredericksburg and Potomac Railroad line as it approached the important road and rail junction of Hamilton's Crossing. General William Taliaferro's division was deployed four miles further down the rail line at Guiney Station, which became Jackson's temporary headquarters. General Jubal Early, temporarily in command of Richard Ewell's division, blocked Federal access to the Rappahannock at Skinker's Neck, while Jackson's brother-in-law Daniel Harvey Hill was even further downstream at Port Royal.

Lee considered this deployment of his men to be the best possible arrangement until his opponent tipped his hand. If Burnside tried to cross the river at Skinker's Neck or Port Royal, which the Confederate general thought likely, Jackson's units were mobile enough to concentrate at the Yankee bridgehead. On the other hand, if the Federal general decided to lunge directly at Fredericksburg, Longstreet's men would be waiting to mow down the attackers from almost impregnable positions. Lee's position was so strong that his western counterpart, General Joseph Johnston, exclaimed, "I wish someone would attack me in a position such as this!"

By early December, most generals in the *Army of the Potomac* would have agreed with Johnston's reasoning. The two preferred avenues of advance, Skinker's Neck and Port Royal, had been blocked by the arrival of Jackson's troops.

Now the only remaining options seemed to be either a withdrawal of the army into winter quarters, with the hope that a new opportunity would turn up by spring, or a very dangerous all out attack on Fredericksburg itself. Burnside was probably tempted to end the campaign season and hope for better luck in 1863, but he also realized that Abraham Lincoln had not given him the largest field army in American history to send them into the same winter quarters that McClellan would have ordered. The president may have been cordial and diplomatic with his new commander, but it was clear that Lincoln expected another major confrontation with the Rebels before winter had fully taken hold of the Virginia countryside.

Ambrose Burnside now faced the cruel irony of commanding the most powerful military force in his nation's history while facing an enemy that held one of the most formidable defensive positions of the 19th century. The new commander's predecessors in the *Army of the Potomac*, Irvin McDowell and George McClellan, had confronted the Rebels in the open fields of Manassas, the Peninsula, and Sharpsburg with less than spectacular results for the Union cause. In fact, the only one-sided Yankee victory had occurred at Malvern Hill where Lee was foolish enough to attack the Federals on high ground where their massed artillery blasted the Rebels to pieces. Now, it was Lee who held the high ground and yet Burnside's superiors in Washington expected the bewhiskered general to come up with some fantastic plan that could turn what looked to be a certain defeat into a spectacular victory.

Burnside now admitted that the campaign was moving rapidly away from the plan he had submitted to Halleck and Lincoln a month earlier.

> It is very clear that my object was to make the move to Fredericksburg very rapidly, and to throw a heavy force across the river before the enemy could concentrate a force to oppose the crossing, and supposed the pontoon train would arrive at this place nearly simultaneously with the head of the column. Had that been the case, the whole of General Sumner's column—33,000 strong—would have

crossed into Fredericksburg at once over a pontoon bridge in front of a city garrisoned by a small squadron of cavalry and a battery of artillery which General Sumner silenced within an hour of his arrival. Had the pontoon bridges arrived on [November] the 19th or 20th, the army could have crossed with trifling opposition.

However Burnside felt that, through no fault of his own, his superiors had failed to provide the absolutely essential bridging equipment on time and now "the opposite side of the river is occupied by a large Rebel force under General Longstreet with batteries ready to be placed in position to operate against the working parties building the bridges and the troops in crossing." The Union general had originally intended to use Fredericksburg as a base of operations for a confrontation with the Rebel army on open ground somewhere south of the Rappahannock where the huge Federal manpower advantage could be used to maximum effect. Now a campaign that was only supposed to begin at Fredericksburg looked increasingly like it would climax with a battle in or around the historic town and Ambrose Burnside began looking desperately for some way to escape this tactical dead end.

By Monday, December 8, General Burnside knew that most of Longstreet's corps was deployed along the high ground beyond the town of Fredericksburg and at least part of Jackson's corps was blocking a crossing attempt at Skinker's Neck or Port Royal. The Union commander now became increasingly intrigued with the idea of getting the *Army of the Potomac* between those two Rebel units and then threatening either Longstreet's or Jackson's flanks. As a battle plan began to take shape, Burnside became increasingly fascinated with the fact that because a frontal assault against Marye's Heights seemed completely impossible, Lee would never imagine that his adversary would ever be stupid enough to attempt such an attack. As the Federal commanding general ruminated over those two ideas, the plan that was to result in the battle of Fredericksburg began to take shape.

On that Monday afternoon, Burnside sat in his headquar-

William Franklin had important responsibilities at Fredericksburg but, as a McClellan loyalist, was preoccupied with internal rivalries in the **Army of the Potomac.**

ters in the Phillips house behind Stafford Heights and began to finalize his operational plan. First, he decided to construct pontoon bridges where Lee would least expect them, right in front of Fredericksburg itself. Then while Edwin Sumner's *Right Grand Division* stormed across the bridges and seized the town, William Franklin's men would advance over other pontoons downstream and capture the vital crossroads of Hamilton's Crossing. Franklin would then have the option of either turning east to smash into Stonewall Jackson's scattered divisions or advance westward and roll up Longstreet's right flank. Meanwhile, Joe Hooker's *Center Grand Division* could either support Sumner in an attack on Marye's Heights if Lee stripped that position to challenge Franklin, or "Fighting Joe" could support Franklin if the Confederate commander kept his men on the Heights at full strength. Burnside's plan had much in common with British General William Howe's plan to fight the colonists at Bunker Hill 87 years earlier. Both plans assumed that the defenders couldn't stop threats to their lines from two very different directions, and that as soon as the enemy commander stripped one position to strengthen another point, the attackers would swarm in and overwhelm the weakened spot. Neither of these assaults were supposed to be mindless attacks in the face of massed muskets and cannons, and yet just as Sir William's plan unraveled into disaster on that hot summer day in 1775, Ambrose Burnside's plan would soon suffer the same fate in the winter of 1862.

Once Burnside began to formalize his attack plan, he began to query his generals for their opinions about the operation's prospects for success. The response of his senior officers was hardly enthusiastic. Joe Hooker saw himself as the legitimate successor to George McClellan and he and Burnside made no secret of their personal loathing for one another. "Fighting Joe" was convinced that the only reasonable hope for Union success was to cross the Rappahannock upstream and get at Lee from above, a tactic he would use with initial success at Chancellorsville six months later. He believed that Burnside's plan was preposterious and made it clear to his confidant Secretary of War Edwin Stanton that his rival's plan was doomed from the beginning, an opinion he freely shared with the commanding general when his advice was sought.

General William Franklin was on much better personal terms with Burnside than Hooker but the *Left Grand Division* commander was very cautious by nature and was also closely watching a court-martial trial that was about to destroy one of his closest friends, General Fitz John Porter. Porter, who had probably been George McClellan's closest friend in the army, was currently on trial for his professional life as he was accused by blustering John Pope of refusing to launch an ordered attack with his corps during the battle of Second Bull Run. Franklin, like Porter and McClellan, was a strong supporter of the Democratic Party and the *Left Grand Division* commander now believed that the Radical Republicans were looking for any excuse to purge the *Army of the Potomac* of Democratic generals. Therefore, the man who would command one of the most vital operations of the Union assault was convinced that the best plan for his professional survival was simply to keep his head down and offer virtually no strong opinions to anyone, including Burnside.

An elderly commander with a long career behind him, Edwin Sumner supported Burnside's tactical decisions against his better judgment.

Edwin Sumner, who was to command the desperate assault against Marye's Heights, was the only *Grand Division* commander who gave Burnside his full support. "Bull" Sumner was 20 years older than most of his colleagues and believed in a chain of command where his commanding general deserved unquestioning support. Therefore, the *Right Grand Division* commander merely assured Burnside that he would energetically carry out any operation that the Rhode Islander wished to attempt and promised that his men would be right behind him in the charge against the enemy lines.

Burnside received such lukewarm support from his *Grand Division* commanders that he soon began to solicit the opinions of corps and division commanders, perhaps hoping that more of these men would offer a solid note of confidence. On Tuesday night, December 9, the army commander rode over to General Sumner's headquarters at the Lacy House and met with the *Right Grand Division*'s senior generals. Darius Couch, commander of *II Corps* recalled later, "The result was a plain, free talk around in which words were not minced, for the conversation soon drifted into a marked disapprobation of the manner in which Burnside contemplated meeting the enemy." Couch insisted that Edwin Sumner felt badly that his generals refused to endorse Burnside's plans and the commanding general himself became increasingly annoyed as General Winfield Scott Hancock kept challenging the workability of the operation. The Pennsylvanian kept reminding Burnside that "he had no animosity against the general but he knew there was a line of fortified heights on the opposite side that it would be pretty difficult for us to go over there and take them!" Couch, who admitted that he had been as vocal a critic as Hancock, finally agreed that he would give Burnside the benefit of the doubt and insisted, "If I had ever done anything in any battle, in this one I intended to do twice as much."

On Wednesday morning, December 10, Burnside had either convinced himself that he had swung his subordinates over to his views or simply ignored their objections and finalized his battle plan. Each *Grand Division* commander was brought into headquarters for verbal orders which were followed up with written orders later that afternoon. Edwin Sumner was told that "your first corps, after crossing the Rappahannock, should be protected by the town and the bank of the river as much as possible until the second corps is well closed up and in the act of crossing; after which you will move the first corps directly to the front with a view to taking the heights that command the plank road and the Telegraph road, supporting it by your other corps as soon as you can get it over the river." William Franklin was told that "after your command has crossed you will move down the old Richmond road in the direction of the railroad, being governed by circumstances as to the extent of your movements." Finally, Joseph Hooker was instructed "to hold yourself in readiness to support either General Sumner or General Franklin" and "should we be so fortunate as to dislodge the enemy, you will pursue him by the two roads." Each *Grand Division* commander now had his orders, and on this brisk December night, the first stage of the battle of Fredericksburg lurched into motion.

Soon after sunset on December 10, the stillness of the frigid winter night was pierced by several Union regimental bands that formed up along the Rappahannock and began to serenade soldiers on both side of the river. Tunes such as "Hail

Columbia" and "The Star Spangled Banner" brought little response from the south bank, but when a rousing version of "Dixie" began, gray-coated soldiers let out cheer after cheer. However, while most of the Rebel soldiers concentrated on listening to the music, at least one Confederate general quickly became suspicious of the timing of the nighttime concert. General Lafayette McLaws, commander of the division responsible for defending both Marye's Heights and the town of Fredericksburg, firmly believed that the Yankee serenade was designed to cover major movements on the part of the Federal army and he began to closely inspect the Southern defenses in the colonial community.

McLaws had assigned General William Barksdale's brigade the task of challenging a Federal thrust across the Rappahannock into Fredericksburg and the colorful Mississippian assured his superior that the Yankees would pay dearly for every yard of the town they captured. Barksdale chose the 17th Mississippi Regiment, three companies of the 18th Mississippi and the 10 best sharpshooters from the 13th Mississippi to deploy in the houses and outbuildings nearest the banks of the Rappahannock, and harass the Yankee engineers when they began to construct their pontoon bridges. Most

Lafayette McLaws was an able Confederate division commander. His later Civil War career was marred by controversies, but he was highly effective at Antietam and Fredericksburg.

William Barksdale led Mississippi troops in numerous gallant actions early in the Civil War, but was killed on the second day at Gettysburg.

of the rest of the brigade was positioned in rifle pits and houses further in from the river with orders to contest each street in a determined rear-guard action as the Federals advanced through the town.

At about 0200 early on the morning of December 11, 1862, engineers of the *Army of the Potomac* began dragging their bridging equipment down to the frigid water of the Rappahannock. An hour later, as a dense fog enveloped the entire area, the sounds of pounding hammers echoed through the still night and men on both sides of the river began to realize that a major battle was approaching. Burnside's engineers had enough pontoons to construct five bridges. Two spans were to be built leading to the upper part of Fredericksburg at the foot of Hawk Street; a middle bridge was ordered about a half mile downstream near the remains of the destroyed railroad bridge; and another pair of pontoons were to be erected a mile farther down the Rappahannock near the mouth of Deep Run Creek. While riflemen had been assigned to provide covering fire for the engineers at each of these three construction points, the main deterrent to Rebel challenges was expected to be the 147 artillery pieces that General Henry J. Hunt had deployed along Stafford Heights. The energetic and talented Federal artillery commander had positioned artillery battalions at four key points to provide overlapping cannon fire anywhere the engineers ran into serious resistance. A right wing group of 40 guns, deployed from Falmouth to just above the upper pontoon site, was designed to silence Confederate artillery on the opposite heights. A right center battalion of 38 pieces would cover the engineers as they reached the opposite side of the river and support Federal infantry regiments when they pushed into Fredericksburg. A left center group of 27 cannons was positioned between the middle bridge and the lower bridge and was ordered to discourage the Rebels from concentrating for a counterattack while Federal troops tried to organize a bridgehead between Deep Run and Hazel Run Creeks. Finally, a left battalion of 42 guns would cover Union troops as they streamed across the lower bridges and discourage a Rebel attack on the extreme left flank of the Yankee bridgehead. Burnside was highly impressed with this level of firepower, but Hunt repeatedly warned his superior that while his guns could challenge enemy artillery fire from the opposite heights and counter an enemy counterattack on the bridgeheads, his batteries would have a very difficult time protecting the engineers from enemy marksmen concealed in the town's hundreds of buildings. The Yankee construction crews would learn this unfortunate truth very soon.

As the Federal engineers pushed the expanding pontoon bridges ever closer to the south shore of the Rappahannock, Lafayette McLaws sent a message to General Barksdale to wait until the engineers were about halfway across the river and then order his men to fire even if it was still too dark to distinguish individual targets. At about 0430, several dozen of the Rebel riflemen cocked their muskets and opened fire into the darkness in the general direction of the slowly advancing pontoons. While the fog and the darkness provided a measure of cover for the New York engineering unit, random shots still frequently found their mark and men either dropped to the floor of the bridge or fell into the frigid waters of the Rappahannock as their comrades watched in horror. Finally, as a pale winter sun began to dissipate the fog, Confederate snipers began to see much more clearly and the toll among the blue-coated engineers rose alarmingly. Several regiments of Massachusetts and Michigan infantry were deployed along the north shore to provide covering fire, but they could do little to help their engineering comrades. As a captain in the *19th Massachusetts* insisted, "on our arrival at the river at daylight we found but a very small section of the bridge laid in consequence of the commanding position which the enemy held on the right bank of the river, secreted as they were behind fences made musket-proof by piling cord-wood and other materials against them." Major Spaulding's engineers soon developed an uncomfortable routine of hammering a few more feet of pontoons into place and then running back to the north bank minus a few more casualties as Union riflemen poured largely ineffective volleys toward the opposite shore. Finally after at least nine of these costly work sessions had dramatically whittled down the number of unwounded engineers, the whole operation threatened to grind to a halt. One of Spaulding's officers noted that "the bullets of the enemy rained upon my bridge, they went whizzing and spitting by and around me, puttering on the bridge, splashing in the water and thugging through the boats."

Fredericksburg is bombarded while Union engineers construct a pontoon bridge under heavy fire.

As Ambrose Burnside watched in horror from Stafford Heights while his plan rapidly unraveled, the *Army of the Potomac* commander sent word to his artillery chief to begin a massive bombardment of Fredericksburg. At this relatively early point in the Civil War, an intentional bombardment of a major town was still a real rarity in most battles and observers on both sides of the Rappahannock were awestruck by the destructive capabilities of large numbers of cannons firing on a population center. Henry Hunt had just over 100 guns emplaced in positions that could directly fire on Fredericksburg, and at just past 1000, battery after battery let loose with every gun that could fire. General McLaws, watching the bombardment from Marye's Heights, was shocked at the devastation that such concentrated fire could cause.

It is impossible fully to describe the effects of this iron hail hurled against the small band of defenders and into the devoted city. The roar of the cannons, the bursting shells, the falling of walls and chimneys and the flying bricks and other materials dislodged from the houses by the iron balls and shells added to the fire of the infantry and the smoke from the guns and the burning houses made a scene of indescribable confusion, enough to appall the stoutest hearts.

Confederate artillerist E. Porter Alexander was torn between the horror of the bombardment and a professional gunner's interest in the power of the massed cannons.

The spectacle was one of the most magnificent and impressive in the whole course of the war. The city, except its steeples, was still veiled in the mist which had settled in the valleys. There soon rose three or four columns of dense black smoke from houses set on fire by the explosions. The atmosphere was so perfectly calm and still that the smoke rose vertically in great pillars for several hundred feet before spreading outward in black sheets. The opposite bank of the river for two miles to the right and left was crowned at frequent intervals with blazing batteries, canopied in clouds of white smoke. The earth shook with the thunder of guns and high above all, a thousand feet in the air, hung two immense balloons. The scene gave impressive ideas of the disciplined power of a great army and of the vast resources of the nation which had sent it forth.

Within Fredericksburg itself, Barksdale's determined defenders and the small number of civilians who refused to evacuate their homes had a less philosophical approach to the bombardment than Colonel Alexander. One woman who remained in her home during the shelling noted that "the shricking of those shells, like a host of angry fiends rushing through the air, the crashing of the balls through the roof and upper stories of the house were indescribable at the time. I could not even pray, but only cry for mercy." As Robert E. Lee watched the opposite shoreline blaze with fire and shells cascade into the town where he had first courted his wife, he vented his increasing rage by condemning the Yankees' actions in front of his aides. In a rare burst of public anger at the enemy, he exclaimed that "those people delight to destroy the weak and those who can make no defense; it just suits them!"

On the north side of the Rappahannock the men of the *Army of the Potomac* were just as awed by the power of the bombardment as their adversaries. A Union battery commander insisted to his sister that "I have just seen a new phase of military operations, that of shelling a city. It has been the most severe artillery fire I have ever seen. Judging from the fires in the city and its general appearance the city must be nearly or quite ruined." A Federal surgeon agreed that the spectacle was one of "awful grandeur. The bursting bombs, the great tongues of flame from the burning building and the shock of the artillery which shook the earth made up one of the most terrifying yet magnificent of scenes."

The bombardment of Fredericksburg was one of the most dramatic visual events of the entire Civil War, but General Henry Hunt suspected that the more than 5,000 shells his men

Above are some of the houses damaged in the shelling of Fredericksburg in December, 1862. Private houses had not normally been bombarded during the Civil War prior to Fredericksburg. Although some of the houses were being used by snipers, the bombardment shocked the Confederates and even some Unionists.

had lobbed into the blazing town still wouldn't make the task of the engineers any easier. His cannons could pulverize buildings, but he knew that the Confederate defenders would have taken cover in cellars that would suffer relatively little damage in even the most powerful bombardment. As the Union artillery chief predicted, within moments after the bombardment ceased and blue-coated engineers gingerly inched forward on the pontoon bridges, Rebel marksmen dusted the debris from their clothes and resumed firing from fences and upper story windows.

Ambrose Burnside was now visibly shaken by the disruption of his plans and he quickly approved Henry Hunt's proposal to break the deadly stalemate. Hunt contacted the commander of one of the covering brigades of infantry, Colonel Norman Hall, and asked him if some of his men would volunteer to cross the river in pontoons and dislodge the Rebel marksmen in order to enable the engineers to complete the bridges while there were still enough engineers left standing to accomplish the task. Several of the pontoon builders were quickly recruited as temporary oarsmen, and volunteers from the *7th Michigan, 19th Massachusetts,* and *20th Massachusetts* clambered aboard the improvised landing craft and pushed out into the frigid Rappahannock. As chunks of ice drifted past the fragile pontoon boats, Confederate marksmen blazed away and picked off several of the almost helpless bluecoats.

Colonel Hall, who was riding in one of the lead pontoons, wisely ordered the polemen to maintain a widely dispersed formation to provide less inviting targets to the Rebel snipers. Most of the Yankee volunteers survived the harrowing water journey and soon were climbing out of the makeshift landing craft and scrambling up the river bank that fronted the streets of Fredericksburg. Private Josiah Murphy of the *20th Massachusetts* was still out in the river when the first pontoons hit the beach and he watched as men jumped out and waded to the land. When it was Murphy's turn to wade ashore, he noticed that the men who had landed earlier had already rounded up about 20 Confederate prisoners and were rapidly establishing a beachhead.

The Yankee assault force was soon able to force the relatively thin screen of Rebels on the waterfront to withdraw up into the main part of town, but as the bluecoats advanced up further from the Rappahannock they encountered growing Confederate resistance. When Colonel Hall formed several companies of men and led them up Fauquier Street, hundreds of concealed Mississippians calmly loaded their muskets and waited for the Yankees to get within range of their hiding places. When the Federals advanced to within 75 yards of one group of houses and fences the Rebels unleashed a withering sheet of fire. According to Private James Dinkins of the 18th Mississippi Infantry, "as if by common impulse, a volley rang out from the rifle pits on the cold air which sounded almost like one gun, and hundreds fell dead in their tracks. The front line of the enemy, paralyzed and dismayed by the shock, fell back in confusion. In the meantime, the Mississippians were firing on them as they ran. It was a dreadful slaughter which might have been considered a retaliation for the dreadful bombardment of two hours before." Private Murphy, who was on the receiving end of this fire, admitted that the Confederates badly mauled his company: "As soon as we came in sight of the rebels who were concealed in every house and behind every fence, they opened a terrible fire on us at short range and our men began dropping at every point; those stricken in the vital parts dropping without a sound, but those wounded otherwise would cry out with pain as they limped to the rear. But despite this terrible fire we pressed up the street."

Up to this point in the war, the men of the *Army of the Potomac* and the Army of Northern Virginia had mainly faced each other in fields or woodlands, but this engagement was rapidly developing into one of the largest street battles of the Civil War. Hundreds of blue-coated soldiers were splashing ashore and then entering a deadly contest with Southern adversaries who seemed to fire from every window and every fence in Fredericksburg. Large numbers of Mississipians remained concealed in cellars until Union companies had marched up the street and then emerged to fire into the Yankees' rear before the Federals knew what hit them. Captain H. G.Weymouth of the *19th Massachusetts* agreed that Barksdale's men richly deserved the nickname of "Confederate Hornets" given to them by General Longstreet and these hornets were proving to be a deadly menace to dozens of bluecoats. As Weymouth admitted:

It was now apparent that our thin line could not make any farther advance against the formidable barricades the enemy had erected on the south side of Caroline Street, consisting of barrels and boxes filled with earth and stones, placed between the houses, so as to form a continuous line of defense and the left of our line was forced to fall back down Fauquier Street fully one half the distance from Caroline Street.

As men from Massachusetts and Mississippi blasted at one another from behind fences and upper story windows, one of the confrontations turned very personal. One of Barksdale's company commanders was a graduate of Harvard,

Union soldiers advance into Fredericksburg during the height of the fighting. The white Zouave leggings on these troops possibly identify them as the **114th Pennsylvania.**

and he spotted one of his classmates swinging a sword and leading a charge of New Englanders against the Confederate position. When the regimental commander sent a message that his company was being surrounded and it was time to fall back, the young Mississippian had become so engrossed in the personal nature of the contest that he refused to retreat. Finally, in desperation, Barksdale ordered the young officer arrested and virtually carried out of harm's way before his unit was overrun by the far more numerous Yankees.

The onset of darkness on this grim winter afternoon found the street battle in Fredericksburg gradually shifting in favor of the Federals. However, Colonel Hall admitted, "platoon after platoon was swept away," while a Union sergeant insisted "the Rebels opened on us from windows and doors and from behind the houses. After losing half our company, we made a rush for the houses and broke in doors." In a gruesome struggle that previewed on a smaller scale the carnage between Germans and Russians in World War II battles such as Stalingrad, bluecoats and Rebels fought by the light of burning buildings and struggled for control of houses that were now only shells. General Barksdale at first ignored McLaws's orders to fall back to Marye's Heights and his men tenaciously hung on to every building they could still occupy. However, slightly more than 1,000 Mississippians were now rapidly being engulfed by huge numbers of Yankees, who were swarming across the completed pontoons, and their commander finally ordered a fallback to the stone wall fronting Telegraph Road. The *Army of the Potomac* could now lay claim to Fredericksburg, but a small force of determined Rebels had dismantled Ambrose Burnside's entire attack plan.

Lafayette McLaws (1821-1897)

Lafayette McLaws, the nephew of Mexican War hero Zachary Taylor, was born in Augusta, Georgia, and graduated from West Point in 1842 along with future corps commander James Longstreet. McLaws served in relatively minor capacities in the pre-war army until he resigned in March of 1861. His fortunes improved dramatically in the Confederate army as he was almost immediately commissioned as colonel of the 10th Georgia Infantry. During the campaigns of 1862, McLaws enjoyed a steady series of promotions so that by the time of the Fredericksburg campaign he was a major general and division commander in the Army of Northern Virginia's First Corps.

McLaws was responsible for key segments of the Confederate line during the battle and he continued to be viewed as a solid, reliable division commander until Longstreet's disastrous assault on Fort Sanders in Knoxville in the autumn of 1863. This was one of the most one-sided Confederate defeats of the war, and Longstreet charged that McLaws was responsible for the failure of the attack against Burnside's defenses. The division commander was fully exonerated by Jefferson Davis, but when Longstreet threatened to resign in protest, McLaws agreed to a transfer to Joseph Johnston's army charged with the defense of Atlanta. McLaws served with Johnston until the end of the war and then held appointments as revenue collector and postmaster for the city of Savannah, Georgia. Despite the acrimony over Fort Sanders, McLaws was generally viewed as a highly competent division commander who received frequent commendations by his superiors.

William Barksdale (1821-1863)

William Barksdale was born in Smyrna, Tennessee, in 1821. He attended the University of Nashville, studied law in Columbus, Mississippi, and then became editor of the Columbus *Democrat*. He served as both an enlisted man and officer in the Mexican-American War and soon after the conflict ended was elected to the United States Congress. During his tenure in Washington, Barksdale emerged as a member of the extreme states'rights wing of the Democratic party and was a vocal opponent of any abolitionist organization. While in Congress, Barksdale also was named quartermaster general of Mississippi's militia units, but when the state seceded the lawmaker quickly maneuvered to secure a more active command.

At the battle of First Bull Run, Barksdale commanded the 13th Mississippi Regiment with some distinction and he was soon promoted to brigadier general and participated in every major battle of 1862 except for Second Bull Run. Barksdale's superiors acknowledged him as one of their most reliable brigade commanders and his stubborn defense of Fredericksburg during the Yankee crossing of the Rappahannock made him one of the heroes of the battle and a favorite of Robert E. Lee. On the second day of Gettysburg, Barksdale led one of the most dramatic assaults on the Union position near the Round Tops and he was severely wounded and captured by the Federals. He died the next day in a Union hospital.

CHAPTER VI

A Fatal Interlude

*B*y 1900 on the frosty Thursday evening of December 11, 1862, Union soldiers finally controlled a town that could have been captured effortlessly about three weeks earlier. William Barksdale's Mississippians had pulled back to Marye's Heights and five newly completed pontoon bridges were now available to transport the *Army of the Potomac* to the south bank of the Rappahannock River. However, while Ambrose Burnside now held Fredericksburg, he had just made a monumental tactical error and was on the verge of making an even bigger mistake in the next few hours.

Burnside's whole command style during this campaign had been a curious mix of aggressiveness and caution, and this fatal combination was emerging again. While Yankee engineers and infantrymen had fought a desperate battle to build and secure the upper and middle bridges opposite the town of Fredericksburg, the construction of two downstream bridges had proceeded with minimal enemy resistance. A foul up in delivery of construction materials to the river bank had delayed the onset of laying the downstream pontoons but by midmorning on Thursday, Federal engineers were pushing the twin spans rapidly toward the southern shore near Deep Run Creek. A combination of extremely dense fog and the fact that Confederate defenders were deployed much further from the river than in Fredericksburg itself allowed the Union work-

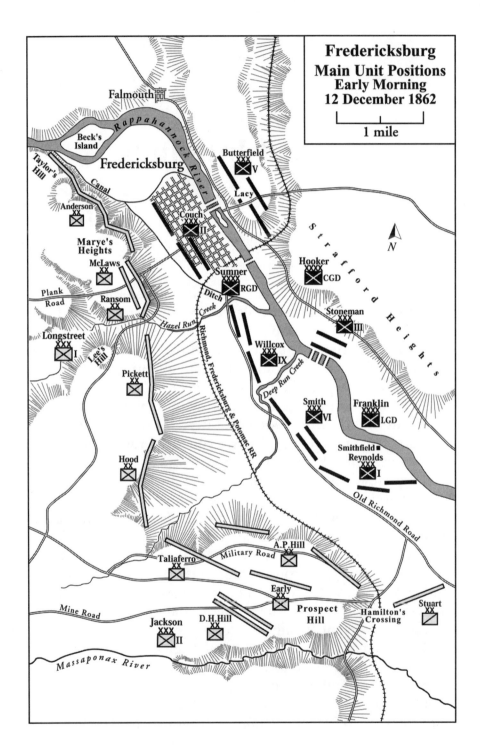

Fredericksburg
Main Unit Positions
Early Morning
12 December 1862

1 mile

ers to practically finish the bridges before the Rebels fully understood what had happened. Just as a mixed force of Mississippi riflemen and John Bell Hood's hard-fighting Texans rushed to the riverbank, a large force of Yankee infantrymen swarmed across one of the newly completed pontoon bridges and established a secure bridgehead. At noon, while Hunt's artillery was still bombarding Fredericksburg to clear the way for the upstream bridges, several regiments of Union soldiers were already safely across the river at Deep Run and eagerly awaiting orders to advance. Burnside now had a golden opportunity to initiate a sweeping flank attack into the town, which would catch the Mississippians in a giant pincers in which only retreat or surrender was possible. Meanwhile, plenty of other Federal troops were available downstream to push rapidly inland and effectively cut off Stonewall Jackson's corps from Longstreet's men. However, the same Burnside who had convinced his superiors in Washington of his aggressiveness and then refused to allow Edwin Sumner to cross the

Fredericksburg appears deceptively calm in this print of Union troops crossing the Rappahannock on the night of December 11, 1862. In fact the burning town was being looted by Union soldiers and sporadic rifle and artillery fire was being exchanged.

Union troops engage in some of the Civil War's first street fighting. As with most of artist Alfred Waud's eyewitness drawings, this print was developed over the following two weeks from a rough sketch made on the spot.

Rappahannock until the rest of the army joined him, now suffered the same burst of panic and refused to order Franklin to cross his entire *Left Grand Division* until the upstream bridges were completely secure.

Ambrose Burnside was now exhibiting an obsession with orderly advances. The commander of the *Army of the Potomac* could only envision his entire army crossing the Rappahannock at once, even if this removed the opportunity for Franklin's divisions to seriously threaten Lee's defense line. The Rhode Islander then proceeded to compound this error by granting his adversary a stunning present of a full extra day to concentrate a still scattered Confederate army. The bridging of the Rappahannock and capture of Fredericksburg had taken far longer than Burnside originally expected. However, once the bridges and town were secure, it was still quite possible to push a large portion of the *Army of the Potomac* over to the south bank before Stonewall Jackson's four divisions were given time to fully concentrate. At 1900 on Thursday evening two of Jackson's divisions were still far downstream and a third division was 10 miles to the southeast. A rapid transfer of William Franklin's *Left Grand Division* to the south bank of the river during Thursday night and Friday morning would have allowed the Yankees to seize much of the high ground around Hamilton's Crossing and make it difficult for Lee to unite his whole army. Any serious engagement on December 12 would have left almost 25,000 Confederate infantrymen off the chessboard of battle, and would have created a serious threat to Lee's not yet completed right flank. However, in yet another of a long string of disastrous mistakes, Burnside made no attempt to insist that his army cross the bridges all night and decided that Saturday morning was early enough for the planned Union assault.

Much of the Union army spent most of Friday engaged in violent activities, but unfortunately for the Federal operation, very few of them were directed at Confederate soldiers. As thousands of bluecoats marched over the pontoons into Fredericksburg, large numbers of men began looking for souvenirs in the historic town. What began as a relatively harmless activity quickly degenerated into pillage and looting as the hunt for booty became more violent. As soldiers carted clothing, blankets, jewelry, and small pieces of furniture out of homes, other men picked fights in the streets to gain possession of the best items. Then contests began to see who had the most original technique to destroy many of these things. Several disgusted Union officers likened the scene to the sack of a medieval city as books, antique colonial furniture, and other heirlooms were tossed into the snowy streets and then smashed or ripped to pieces by gangs of soldiers. Paintings were slashed with bayonets or smeared with ink; glasses and dishes were dropped from upper story windows and then the windows themselves were smashed. The few provost marshals on duty tried to intervene and then quickly backed off as they began to fear for their lives. Several officers insisted that this wanton destruction never would have been allowed when George McClellan was in command and viewed the looting as a sign that Burnside had lost control of the army.

A major in the *108th New York Infantry* likened the scene

around him to something out of Dante's *Inferno*. He noted that "dead rebels were lying around promiscuously with their ghostly gaping death wounds as monitors of what might be in store for us." Meanwhile, very live Yankees ignored the grisly scene and concentrated on pillaging the town.

> The boys came with silver pitchers, silver spoons, silver lamps etc. Great three story brick houses were broken into and their contents scattered over the floors and trampled by the muddy feet of the soldiers. Splendid alabaster vases and pieces of statuary were thrown at $60 and $700 mirrors. Closets of the very finest china ware were broken into and their contents smashed onto the floor and stamped to pieces. Finest cut glass goblets were hurled at plate glass windows. Beautifully embroidered curtains were torn down. Rosewood pianos were piled in the street and burned or soldiers would get on top of them and dance and kick the keyboard and internal machinery to pieces. Wine cellars were broken into and the soldiers would drink all they could and then open the faucets and let the rest run out. The soldiers seemed to delight in destroying everything. Libraries worth thousands of dollars were overhauled and thrown on the floor and in the streets.

A lieutenant in another New York regiment noted with disgust that even officers seemed to join in the pillaging and admitted that he was not sure whether to be disgusted or merely curious about what he called a "boisterous sport." "Very soon the streets were filled with a motley crowd of men, some of them dressed in women's clothes, others with tall silk hats. Some carried pictures, one man had a fine stuffed alligator and most of them had something." This officer was convinced that the senior generals in the army tolerated and even encouraged such behavior to keep the soldiers' minds off the coming assault on Marye's Heights. "No attempt was made by the officers to interfere, their minds were thus distracted until summoned to fall in for the storming of the heights." A correspondent for a Northern newspaper considered the level of looting tolerated by Burnside as "disgusting" and insisted "this pillaging is fit for the French Revolution and a disgrace to the Union army. Houses were burned down, furniture scattered in the streets and men are pillaging in all directions."

While much of the *Army of the Potomac* was tearing Fredericksburg apart, the commanding general was shuttling between opposite sides of the Rappahannock trying to conjure up a plan that would have some reasonable chance of defeating Lee. Burnside seems to have spent most of Friday with only the vaguest idea of where Stonewall Jackson's divisions were deployed, yet he admitted that control of the Confederate right flank would probably determine the outcome of the battle. By afternoon the Rhode Islander was closeted with his *Left Grand Division* commander and Franklin's two corps commanders, John Reynolds and William "Baldy" Smith, and the four generals debated the best way to turn Lee's formidable line. As the short winter day neared sunset, this group of blue-coated generals reconnoitered much of the south bank of the Rappahannock and returned to Franklin's headquarters with the semblance of an operational plan.

Burnside and his subordinates all agreed that while two of Joe Hooker's divisions took responsibility for keeping the downstream bridges in Federal hands, Franklin's entire *Left Grand Division* would form up on the Richmond Stage Road and launch an overwhelming assault on what seemed to be the right flank of the Confederate line. Their prize was the new military road that Southern engineers had constructed along seven miles of ridges to connect the left, center, and right of Lee's lines. Now, Burnside proposed to use this road as an avenue to roll up the Rebel army brigade by brigade until Lee was forced to pull large numbers of troops from Marye's Heights to meet this new threat to his flank. At this point, "Bull" Sumner's *Right Grand Division* would lunge forward from the streets of Fredericksburg and assault the Confederate flank just as it was being stripped of defenders. Meanwhile, most of Joe Hooker's men would wait until the pattern of the battle developed and then add a powerful punch to either Sumner's or Franklin's assaults. If all went well, by Saturday evening Lee's army would be pushed from the high ground and streaming southward towards Richmond with Burnside's victorious army snapping at their heels.

A detailed examination of Burnside's battle plan reveals that it wasn't quite the mindless frontal assault for which he has received such long-term condemnation. While the plan itself had some merit, it was badly weakened in practice by two enormous errors by the commanding general. First, Burnside was developing an attack plan with almost no idea of the location of half of the enemy army. When the general ordered Franklin's *Left Grand Division* to attack Lee's right flank from the Richmond Stage Road, the Yankees would first have to get over Prospect Hill before they could do any real damage. Unfortunately, the Union commander didn't seem to know whether Stonewall Jackson had 30 or 30,000 men deployed on the hill—he just ordered Franklin's troops to advance regardless of the enemy numbers. By the morning of the attack the number of Rebel defenders would actually be more like 30,000 than 30 yet Burnside made no real allowance for this contingency. While McClellan made many of his plans based on the inflated numbers he thought he was facing, Burnside simply seemed to ignore enemy numbers completely as though the Union army was the only force on the field.

The second fatal flaw in Burnside's plan was the timing of the attack. If the Union general had accelerated the river crossing and attacked even as late as early afternoon on Friday, he would have had about 112,000 Yankees facing about 55,000 Confederates, a better than two to one advantage. Now that the attack had been postponed, it was clearly in Burnside's best interest to suspend an assault until Franz Sigel's 28,000-man *Reserve Grand Division* and the 15,000 troops transferred from the Washington garrison reached him. This would have given the Union army another two to one advantage over Lee's 78,000 defenders. However, Burnside chose the worst of both worlds; he decided to schedule the attack after all of Lee's divisions had concentrated and before significant reinforcements could reach his own army. The Union commander had now given his opponent even more gifts of strategic and tactical advantage than Lee usually received in a battle and the Federal army would soon pay dearly for this "generosity" in their commanding general.

While Burnside spent most of this chilly Friday attempting to cobble together a workable attack plan, his Southern counterpart was dealing with a different tug of emotions. The Yankee bombardment and pillaging of Fredericksburg had deeply disturbed him and gave an ominous hint of a much more total war in the months or years to come. Despite the heavy casualties in Lee's engagements with George McClellan, the two adversaries had developed a tacit understanding that noncombatants would be kept out of the line of fire as much as possible. When McClellan emphasized that he would only make war "on the highest standards of Christian civilization," he was very much speaking Lee's language. The only major exception to this tacit understanding had occurred when John Pope had taken command of the newly constituted Union *Army of Virginia* and threatened to call down a "hard war" upon the Rebels. In turn, much of the Second Manassas campaign had been an attempt by Lee to "suppress" a man he considered to be a major aberration from the rules of civilized warfare. Once Pope had suffered a humiliating defeat on the old Bull Run battlefield and was packed off by Lincoln to fight Indians in the West, Lee and McClellan resumed their more gentlemanly contest of the war.

Now, with the replacement of McClellan with Burnside, Robert E. Lee faced a new and more complicated ritual of warfare. Unlike Pope, Ambrose Burnside seemed to harbor no ill will against Southern civilians and had been known as a chivalrous officer in the pre-war army. However, even though he did not exhibit the blustering threats of Pope, Burnside had directed his artillery arm to bombard a large Southern community on December 11 and now a day later, was allowing his men to pillage one of the most historic communities in America. Lee was genuinely shocked at this escalating level of warfare and began to wonder if a similar fate was in store for other Virginia cities if the Federal army penetrated deep into the Old Dominion.

Robert E. Lee usually left troop dispositions to the discretion of his corps commanders, but the massive numbers of Union troops at Fredericksburg led him to personally supervise the more threatened portions of the Confederate line.

While Lee was deeply distressed at the plight of noncombatants in Fredericksburg, he realized that the looting of the town would delay any serious attempt to attack the Confederate army for at least 24 hours. The Southern general began to appreciate the fact that his opponent actually intended to throw virtually his entire army at a series of positions that were already formidable and would become almost impregnable if he could concentrate all nine divisions of his army in an extended line along the high ground south of Fredericksburg. As J. E. B. Stuart's cavalry scouts attempted to confirm the intentions of Franklin's *Left Grand Division* as the bluecoats took position south of the Rappahannock, Lee took the first step in concentrating his army by ordering A.P. Hill up from Yerby's Farm and William B. Taliaferro over from Guiney Station in order to protect the right flank of Longstreet's Corps.

James Longstreet was now convinced that he could stop almost any thrust against the five miles of defenses that Lee entrusted to his care. He described his position in some detail:

The plain on which Fredericksburg stands is so completely commanded by the hills of Stafford (in possession of the enemy) that no effectual opposition could be offered to the construction of the bridges or the passage of the river without exposing our troops to the destructive fire of his numerous batteries. Positions were therefore selected to oppose his advance after crossing. The hills occupied by the Confederate forces, although overcrowned by the heights of Stafford, were so distant as to be outside the range and effective fire by the Federal guns and with the lower receding grounds between them, formed a defensive series that may be likened to natural bastions. Taylor's Hill, on our left, was unassailable; Marye's Hill was more advanced toward the town and of less height than the others and we considered it the point most accessible and guarded it accordingly. Lee's Hill [Telegraph Hill] near our center, with its rugged sides returned from Marye's and rising higher than its companions was comparatively safe.

James Longstreet fully expected Burnside to attack early on Friday morning, and when the assault failed to materialize, the burly Georgian worked energetically to enhance his

James Longstreet commanded the most heavily engaged Confederate positions on Marye's Heights. While his troops took only modest casualties, they worried that there might be more Northerners than they had bullets.

As a talented artillery commander, Edward Porter Alexander was present at most of the important engagements of the Civil War. His memoirs are one of the most complete accounts of the war from the Confederate side.

already formidable position. The Confederate corps commander rode and walked over a five-mile stretch of ground and conferred with each of his division commanders. Richard Anderson's men occupied the extreme left flank of the Rebel line in positions near Taylor Hill; Robert Ransom's troops concentrated on defending the ground around the Marye House; Lafayette McLaws was given responsibility for the sunken part of Telegraph Road; George Pickett secured the area on the west side of Deep Run Creek; and John Bell Hood's men deployed between the east bank of that stream and the extreme left flank of Stonewall Jackson's corps. At one point in his tour of positions, Longstreet was accompanied by fellow Georgian, E. Porter Alexander, one of the Confederate army's senior artillery officers. Alexander had deployed a number of guns in reserve positions to be wheeled out just as the expected Federal attack reached its crescendo. When his corps commander remarked that one particular cannon seemed to be too far to the rear to be of much use, Alexander retorted, "General, we cover that ground now so well that we will comb it as with a fine tooth comb. A chicken could not live on that field when we open on it."

While General Lee was confident that Longstreet's men were deployed in almost impregnable positions, he was somewhat more uncertain about the strength of his right flank. When Burnside started pushing his men across the Rappahannock on Friday morning, the Confederate army commander still had a nagging belief that all of this activity was merely a ruse to cover a Union thrust at Skinker's Neck or Port Royal. The Virginian now mounted the crest of Telegraph Hill, which would soon be renamed Lee's Hill, and peered intently through his field glasses as he tried to discern exactly how much of the enemy army was really deployed around Fredericksburg itself. At about noon, Stonewall Jackson joined Lee, and the two generals discussed the issue of whether the divisions commanded by Harvey Hill and Jubal Early should remain downstream to counter a Yankee push from that direction or be ordered back toward Fredericksburg to strengthen the main Confederate lines. A few minutes later, Major von Borcke, a German volunteer serving on J. E. B. Stuart's staff, rode to Telegraph Hill with important news. The Prussian cavalryman insisted that he and Stuart had just been on a scouting patrol within a few hundred yards of the bluecoat lines and they returned convinced that the Yankees were deploying to launch a major attack on the high ground around Hamilton's Crossing. Lee and Jackson quickly mounted their horses and accompanied the huge German horseman to a barn near the Union picket lines. The three Confederate officers then crept forward along a ditch that led them to a small hill dominated by two old gateposts. The two generals quickly adjusted their field glasses and were soon able to distinguish the features of the Northern soldiers who were less than 400 yards away. The two Virginians were now very close to the downstream Federal pontoon bridges and they saw seemingly endless streams of Yankee soldiers tramping across one span while supply wagons and artillery caissons created a 19th-century version of a traffic jam as they crept across a parallel bridge. The army commander and his lieutenant noted that Federal soldiers were using picks and shovels to construct rifle pits along the riverbank, and the generals counted 32 field guns already in position with more cannons in the process of being unlimbered. The two gray-coated leaders were so intent on their observations that they became less and less cautious about their own security and von Borcke asked himself what would happen to his adopted cause if two of the most important men in the Confederate army were killed or captured. Finally, as the German major breathed a sigh of relief, the two generals agreed that they had seen enough to convince them that Burnside intended to attack here, not further downstream and Jackson and Lee hurried back to Telegraph Hill to issue orders to concentrate the Confederate army.

Couriers quickly mounted horses and galloped downstream to inform D.H. Hill and Early to gather every soldier who could carry a musket and move upriver as rapidly as possible. About midway between Port Royal and Fredericksburg the residents of a local plantation were about to see the results of Lee's orders first hand. The mistress of Moss Neck plantation, Roberta Cary Corbin, had a husband serving with a Virginia cavalry regiment, and on this frigid early winter Friday, Mrs. Corbin rode over to the home of her father-in-law to seek news of her spouse. As she started back toward Moss Neck near evening she encountered thousands of Rebel soldiers crowding the roads. The sight was both uplifting and a little disconcerting to the patriotic mistress of the plantation.

> Toward twilight, as we returned to Moss Neck, we met many Southern soldiers on the way to whom we gave a nod and a smile. As we drew near home, uniforms became more numerous and presently a fine looking officer said in a courteous tone "ladies, you are about to meet several regiments, indeed, a whole division is coming." While he was speaking, we saw long lines of soldiers opening ranks before us to leave the road clear. [When Mrs. Corbin and her sister-in-law arrived home] we found the whole place occupied by troops so dense that we were compelled to dismount and creep in through the back way into our own house. Yards, stables

and all the place had become one moving mass of soldiers—on foot, on horseback, with wagons, ambulances and artillery pieces all moving as nearly as possible in a bee line, removing obstacles such as fences and making short cuts through the fields.

These thousands of Rebel troops were answering a summons to march with all possible speed to reinforce the right flank of the Confederate defense line. The focal point of their march was an elevation overlooking Hamilton's Crossing called Prospect Hill, and Jackson was determined to make this two-mile-long ridge a nearly impregnable bastion. Thirty-five hundred yards of fields and woods were now being packed with Southern troops as most of four divisions, nearly 35,000 men, were filing into a series of positions that stretched up and over Prospect Hill and continued down to the fields behind. Jackson planned to support his riflemen with a formidable array of cannons that included 14 guns overlooking Captain Hamilton's house, 12 pieces north of the Richmond, Fredericksburg and Potomac Railroad line, and 21 additional cannons concealed in the woods 200 yards beyond the tracks. While Longstreet's men held five miles of lines, Jackson's men were concentrated along only two miles of wooded ridges. Ambrose Powell Hill's division formed in two lines along the woods of Prospect Hill with William Taliaferro and Jubal Early close behind in support. Daniel Harvey Hill was posted just south of Mine Road in case any Yankees somehow got around Jackson's flank.

By midnight on this frigid Friday evening, Robert E. Lee had deployed 78,000 confident Confederate soldiers along some of the most advantageous ground of the entire Civil War. From Richard Anderson's riflemen positioned at the bend of the Rappahannock above Fredericksburg to J. E. B. Stuart's troopers screening the Rebel right flank on the Massaponax River, men in gray and butternut uniforms waited with rising expectations for the dawn and the Federal attack. Lee had purposely minimized the construction of field works, hoping to entice Burnside to attack a position that looked just vulnerable enough to attempt an assault. On the north side of the Rappahannock, the object of Lee's attention, Ambrose Burnside, picked up a pen and began to write the orders that would set in motion one of the most disastrous operations of the entire Civil War.

The "Valley Forge" of the Army of the Potomac

The Union army under Burnside's command not only suffered one of its most one-sided defeats at the battle of Fredericksburg, it also endured a level of privation that would mark this period as the low point of the *Army of the Potomac*'s entire existence. Ambrose Burnside had become a popular general in the period before the Fredericksburg campaign by his careful attention to the needs of the men under his command. However, during the late fall and winter of 1862-63, Burnside became so focused on strategic and tactical issues that he largely ignored the physical well-being of his soldiers.

Most of the Fredericksburg campaign was fought within 60 miles of the national capital, but Burnside seems to have make little effort to ensure that adequate supplies were shipped from Washington to the Rappahannock area. The Fredericksburg campaign was conducted during a period that included frequent snowfalls and a number of exceptionally cold early winter days when the temperature flirted with single digits, yet there were frequent complaints from Union soldiers of a shortage of blankets, gloves, winter headgear and similar items. While Union supply officers provided adequate rations of hardtack, almost every other type of food seemed to be in short supply at just the point when the onset of winter made foraging much more difficult. Compared to McClellan, before him or Grant after him, Burnside failed miserably in the effort to provide Union soldiers with fresh meat, vegetables, and even to some extent that staple of the Yankee soldier's diet, coffee. The lack of vegetables was so widespread that scurvy and similar diseases began

sweeping the Federal camps, and for one of the only times of the war, blue-coated soldiers began to suspect that their gray-coated adversaries were actually better fed.

The meager diet under Burnside's command might have been supplemented by utilizing the services of the sutlers who operated around the periphery of the army camps, but, in one of the embattled general's most serious mistakes of his tenure, he failed to make provisions for paying his troops. During the Fredericksburg campaign, hundreds of Union soldiers complained that paymasters seemed to have almost disappeared from the *Army of the Potomac* camps. Soon, morale was plummeting as soldiers were unable to supplement their boring diet with the delicacies that sutlers's wagons always seemed to display. Not only had the men lost their access to extra food, they began to worry about the survival of their families back home. As one Union colonel insisted, "the men are discouraged that their families are in want and of course have no heart to work or fight; if the government would only pay the troops, all would be right."

By the time of Burnside's resignation in late January of 1863, Union morale had plummeted to one of the low points of the war. However, enthusiasm rose quickly with the appointment of Joseph Hooker. "Fighting Joe" ensured that the men received their back pay; supervised the construction of dozens of bakeries to provide fresh bread; ordered supply officers to provide much larger quantities of fresh meat and veg-etables, and completely transformed the fighting spirit of the army. "Valley Forge" ended only when Ambrose Burnside relinquished his command.

E. Porter Alexander (1835-1910)

The battle of Fredericksburg was one of the high points for the Confederate artillery arm during the Civil War, and one of the major architects of this success was E. Porter Alexander. Alexander was born in Washington, Georgia, in 1835 and graduated from West Point in 1857. After resigning from the United States Army in May of 1861, he was commissioned as a captain of engineers in the Confederate forces. Alexander played an important role in detecting Irvin McDowell's plan of attack at First Bull Run when he observed the deployment of key Union formations from a signal station, but was eventually transferred to an artillery battalion.

Alexander was heavily involved in the deployment of James Longstreet's artillery batteries in the vicinity of Marye's Heights, but during the battle of Gettysburg, Union and Confederate roles were largely reversed and the Georgian was charged with the daunting task of eliminating Yankee cannons trained on the approach route to George Pickett's assault on Cemetery Ridge. Alexander was transferred west as Longstreet's chief of artillery for the Chickamauga campaign but was back in Virginia at the start of Grant's spring, 1864 offensive. After receiving a severe wound during siege operations around Petersburg, the artillerist returned to the army in time to take part in the retreat to Appomattox. When Lee requested opinions concerning acceptance of Grant's surrender terms, Alexander suggested continuation of the war through guerrilla tactics and only reluctantly accepted the capitulation of Confederate forces.

After the war, Alexander prospered as a professor of engineering, railroad president, and political leader. His memoirs of the war were considered one of the most authoritative accounts of the conflict by a general in either army. Alexander lived long enough to see the long-term efforts of the Federal victory in the Civil War and insisted in his memoirs that the conflict had ultimately forged an unbreakable union that would become the envy of the world in the 20th century.

CHAPTER VII

The Duel for Hamilton's Crossing

The early morning hours of Saturday, December 13, brought a cold and biting wind over the Rappahannock River and in both Union and Confederate camps men shivered and counted the hours until dawn. Most of the fields around Fredericksburg were covered with a coating of snow, and in the town itself soldiers slipped and stumbled on icy streets. Just before sunrise, the wind died down and was replaced by a freezing fog that rose from the unmelted snow and dropped visibility to less than 50 yards in any direction. On the heights above the town, Robert E. Lee stood on the summit of Telegraph Hill and adjusted his field glasses in an attempt to get at least a glimpse of the Federal army that was massing against him. The Southern commander could not see his opponents, but he could hear drums rolling, bugles sounding, and officers shouting orders. As he lowered his glasses, he remarked to an aide, "I shall try to do them all the damage in our power when they move forward." The Virginian had concentrated one of the most powerful forces that the Confederacy would field in the entire Civil War and now 78,000 men in gray and butternut uniforms were insisting to one another that no army in the world could push them from this position against their will.

Lee was soon joined on Telegraph Hill by three other senior Confederate generals, James Longstreet, J. E. B. Stuart, and Stonewall Jackson, and for a moment the grimness of the

The greatest danger faced by the Confederates at Fredericksburg was being out-flanked by the numerically superior Union army. J. E. B. Stuart's cavalry tirelessly screened the flanks of Lee's army throughout the battle.

upcoming battle was relieved by Jackson's stunning new uniform. Up to this point in the war, the eccentric VMI professor had gone into battle wearing a battered cadet's cap with a broken visor and an ill-fitting coat missing several buttons. Stuart had secretly engaged a tailor to create a whole new uniform for the new lieutenant general, and on this frosty morning the somewhat embarrassed Jackson wore his new outfit for the first time. While Longstreet, Stuart, and even Lee smiled at the dramatic transformation of their colleague, a nearby private muttered, "Old Jack will be afraid of his clothes and will not get down to work!" The bantering among generals continued as Longstreet asked Jackson about his opinion of the power of the enormous Union army arrayed against them. "General, do not all those multitudes of Federals frighten you?" Jackson replied sternly, "We shall see very soon whether I shall not frighten them!" When the Georgian pushed harder for Stonewall to explain how he would deal with the enemy, Jackson answered, "Sir, we will give them the bayonet."

While Lee continued to attempt to penetrate the fog with his field glasses, Jackson and Stuart tried to convince their commander that this was a perfect time to strike the Yankees before they could launch their attack. The two generals emphasized that the last thing that Burnside would expect at this moment was a Rebel offensive and they believed that the low hanging fog would largely negate the power of the Union batteries deployed along Stafford Heights. Lee politely thanked his generals for their advice and then insisted that he preferred to open the battle by letting Burnside's larger army smash itself unit by unit against the Rebel defenses. Then, if it appeared that the cohesion of the Yankee army was disintegrating, he would consider ordering a Confederate counterthrust. The Southern commander had seen a similar scenario develop a few months earlier at Second Bull Run when John Pope had frittered away entire Union regiments in futile attacks on Confederate positions. The Yankee army had barely escaped a rapidly closing Rebel pincers and Lee had at least some hope that Burnside wouldn't be as lucky.

On the north side of the Rappahannock River, Lee's counterpart snatched a few hours sleep and then rose well before dawn to set in motion the advance of the largest army in the history of the American republic. At 0555 the first order to a

Stonewall Jackson was unhappy with his defensive role at Fredericksburg, feeling that the Confederates should launch an aggressive counter-attack.

Grand Division commander went into the field from Burnside's headquarters. William Franklin was informed that "the general commanding directs that you keep your whole command in position for a rapid movement down the old Richmond road and you will send out at once a division at least to pass below Smithfield to seize, if possible, the heights near Captain Hamilton's on this side of the Massaponax, taking care to keep it well supported and its line of retreat open." Burnside then informed Franklin that his operation would advance in conjunction with an offensive by General Sumner to seize the heights near Plank Road and Telegraph Road further upstream. Franklin was assured that "holding those two heights with the heights near Captain Hamilton's will compel the enemy to evacuate the whole ridge between those points."

A few minutes later at 0600, a letter from "Headquarters Army of the Potomac" to General Sumner was dispatched to the commander of the *Right Grand Division*. Sumner was informed that "the general commanding directs that you extend the left of your command to Deep Run, connecting with General Franklin, and extend your right as far as your judgement may dictate." Burnside then ordered his subordinate to "push a column of a division or more along the Plank and Telegraph roads with a view to seizing the heights in the rear of the town." This movement was "to be well covered by skirmishers and supported so as to keep a line of retreat open." Finally, an hour later at 0700, a much briefer message was sent to Burnside's archenemy in the *Army of the Potomac*, Joseph Hooker. The commander of the *Center Grand Division* was merely directed, "that you place General Butterfield's corps and Whipples' division in position to cross at a moment's notice at the three upper bridges in support of the other troops over the river while the two remaining divisions of General Stoneman's corps are to be in readiness to cross at the lower ford in support of General Franklin."

Ambrose Burnside commanded the most powerful army on the continent of North America but these orders had defeat written all over them. They were vague and indecisive and fully committed only two of eighteen Union combat divisions

Some of the magnetism of Ambrose Burnside's personality comes across in this photograph. Despite criticism of his military abilities he was very popular both during and after the Civil War.

to an engagement with the Confederates. Commanders of tens of thousands of men were told more about keeping lines of retreat open than exactly what they were supposed to do once they had achieved their objectives. The orders also contradicted much of the verbal direction that Burnside had given his generals the afternoon before. On Friday afternoon Generals Reynolds, Smith, and Franklin had assumed that their superior had authorized all six divisions of the *Left Grand Division* to assault Stonewall Jackson's position around Hamilton's Crossing, while Joe Hooker took responsibility for the security of the pontoon bridges in case of a surprise Confederate offensive. Now Franklin and his corps commanders had no specific assurance that "Fighting Joe" would hold the bridges and only one division, not six, was specifically ordered to attack the Confederate right flank. Instead of an order to "carry the heights at Captain Hamilton's at all hazards," Burnside seemed to be directing the already cautious Franklin to try a low risk operation with a relatively small force that would constantly be looking backwards to ensure that it could retreat at a moment's notice. Even if this stripped down assault force actually succeeded in pushing the Confederates from

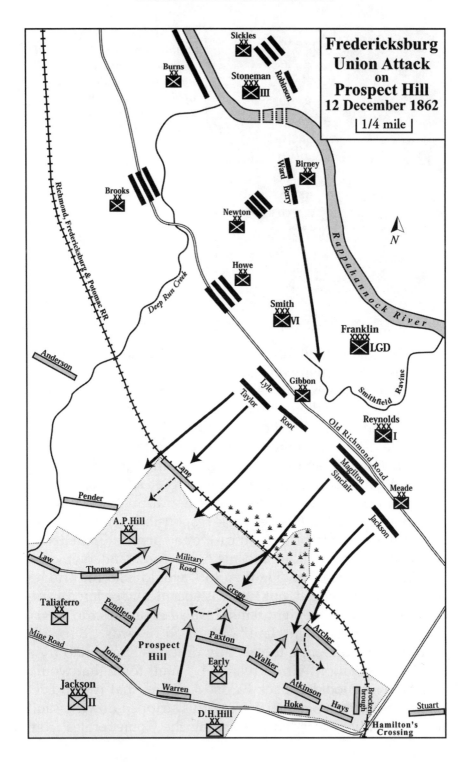

Fredericksburg
Union Attack
on
Prospect Hill
12 December 1862

| 1/4 mile |

the high ground, there was very little direction about what the victorious troops were expected to do next.

If Ambrose Burnside's timid orders initiated the unraveling of the assault on Hamilton's Crossing, William Franklin's equally cautious interpretation of these orders almost guaranteed a Yankee disaster. For reasons that have never been fully explained, Franklin chose the smallest division in the *Army of the Potomac* to challenge the power of Stonewall Jackson's corps on this winter morning. While William "Baldy" Smith's three oversize divisions of the *VI Corps* provided security along the Rappahannock bridges, George Meade's small division of 4,500 Pennsylvanians earned the dubious honor of spearheading the Union attack. Meade was an experienced division commander leading excellent troops, and he would be supported by the divisions of John Gibbon and Abner Doubleday, but the inescapable fact was that about 17,000 Union soldiers were being ordered to carry a position defended by 34,000 Confederate infantrymen backed up by 7,000 Rebel horse soldiers. As these men from John Reynolds' *I Corps* formed into a series of attacking columns 300 yards apart, more than one of these bluecoats must have wondered what the nearly 100,000 other men in the *Army of the Potomac* would be doing

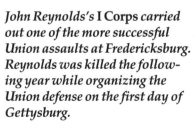

John Reynolds's I Corps carried out one of the more successful Union assaults at Fredericksburg. Reynolds was killed the following year while organizing the Union defense on the first day of Gettysburg.

to support them as they encountered Stonewall Jackson's confident men deployed along the wooded ridges of Prospect Hill.

As the assault troops of *I Corps* started to march across the snowcovered fields that led to the Richmond Stage Road, the fog that had shrouded the area began to lift rapidly and a startling panorama was revealed. Union artillerymen on Stafford Heights and Confederates on Marye's Heights could suddenly view over 100,000 Federal soldiers forming on the plains between them. Tens of thousands of Yankee cavalrymen, gunners, and riflemen almost magically appeared as if a curtain had just risen on a play. Thousands of bayonets glinted off the mid-morning sunlight while dark blue coats contrasted sharply with the white of snowcovered fields. However, in the first act in this unfolding drama, the men in the three divisions of John Reynolds' corps would be the only significant Union players while the rest of the Yankee host would serve as little more than emotionally charged spectators.

As Reynolds' men scrambled around Smithfield Ravine and pushed through the fields toward the Richmond Stage Road, a young Alabama artillery officer attached to Stuart's cavalry shadowed the bluecoats from behind a series of hedges. Major John Pelham, a blond 22-year-old graduate of West Point, had already attracted the attention of senior officers during J. E. B. Stuart's raid into Pennsylvania in October. Now the young gunner was stalking the advancing Yankees with a strike force of exactly one 12-pounder cannon. One of the artillerists in Pelham's tiny command noted later "beyond the hedge we could hear the Federal infantry maneuvering, distinguishing a medley of voices, but we could not see them. Then the fog commenced to lift and as we peered through the hedge we saw a grand spectacle of marshalled soldiers spread out in vast proportions on the level plain in our immediate front. With alertness and yet fearing annihilation at their hands in such close range of their infantry, we opened fire."

A single Confederate artillery officer was now taking on the firepower of three divisions of Federal soldiers and yet, for some time, the Rebel gunner was winning the duel. In or-

Major John Pelham's contribution to the Confederate victory at Fredericksburg and his lasting fame were out of all proportion to his rank and the single cannon he commanded.

der to get past Bowling Green Road, the Yankees had to scramble up and over a number of ditches and hedges and as they clambered over these barriers, Pelham's cannon shells began dropping in their midst. One Pennsylvania corporal noted:

> A shot whizzed high in the air passing over our heads from left to right along our line. The order was given "down" when from the force of the custom we fell face downward, I suppose the whole line did so excepting the field and some of the line officers. I had no time to notice who remained standing, being naturally engaged in pressing down hard, bearing on and flattening out that I might not interfere with any of the flying iron. [As the shaken Federal soldier admitted] this single gun soon got the range when his shells exploded overhead and on the flanks of some regiments. Moving his gun slightly to the left he planted at least two solid shot or unexploded shells in the prostrate ranks immediately in our front.

As the single gun stopped the Union advance in its tracks, Pelham was reinforced with a second cannon, a long-range British Blakely gun and soon, twice as many shells were exploding in the bluecoat lines. Federal infantry officers began shouting for Union artillery support, and within a few minutes five batteries totaling 20 cannons were pouring their lethal fire in the direction of the Confederate-held hedges. A rain of shells quickly knocked out the Rebel Blakely gun, but the 12-pounder simply wouldn't go away. From his command post on Telegraph Hill, Robert E. Lee watched the unequal artillery duel with growing fascination and was increasingly moved by the exploits of a single Confederate officer. The Virginia general exclaimed, "it is glorious to see such courage in one so young," and called the Alabama artillerist "the gallant Pelham." Finally, with more and more Yankee cannons being trained on the single Rebel gun, Pelham began considering a fallback. One of his gunners noted, "We were commanded to cease fire and lie flat on the ground. While in this position a shot struck squarely the head of one of our men and decapitated him. The rain of shot and shell was terrific both from the Field Batteries at close range and also from their big guns on the north bank of the river." Three separate times J. E. B. Stuart sent messages to Pelham ordering his withdrawal but the artillerist seemed determined to hold the Yankees at bay indefinitely. However, when a blue tide of Union infantry surged toward the bridges, the single gun was wheeled out of position and pulled back to the safety of the Confederate cavalry regiments.

Pelham's spectacular duel had not only delayed the Union advance on Hamilton's Crossing by almost an hour, it had also significantly whittled down the power of the Yankee assault. A combination of the Alabaman's audacious fire and the menace of Stuart's troops hovering near the Massaponox encouraged John Reynolds to order Abner Doubleday to concentrate his division as a screening force against Rebel artillery or cavalry flank attackers, thus leaving only two divisions to lunge at Jackson's men on Prospect Hill. Now, only about 11,000 bluecoats would be available to assault a powerful Rebel position that held three times as many men. As Yankee assault troops under Gibbon and Meade streamed over the Richmond Stage Road and advanced toward the looming railroad embankment that ran in front of Prospect Hill, their only direct support from the main part of the Union army was the artillery fire that soared over their heads into the wooded ridge. Stonewall Jackson had plenty of his own cannons prepared to welcome the bluecoats with a torrent of steel, but he was reluctant to give away the positions of his batteries until the full effect of their fire could be directed at the Federals. One Confederate company commander hunkered down in the woods with his men was less than enthused about Stonewall's tactics. He insisted that the Yankee artillery support was nerve-wracking as "the shells were of enormous size and tearing through the tree tops above us brought down huge limbs which was trying to the men. Soon a total of 67 guns were directed on this front, but there was nothing to do but to lay still and take it. The gun redoubts offered little protection. Some of the men lay flat on the ground and some hugged the trunks of the large trees, which was all right but for the limbs which came down from above."

More than a few Rebel troops were probably cursing their corps commander at this point, but Stonewall Jackson was an old artillerist who wanted to get the maximum effect from the guns that he had so expertly positioned. At about 1130, lead units of Gibbon's and Meade's divisions had advanced to within about 800 yards of the railroad embankment and as the Yankees surged past this imaginary line, Stonewall gave the order for every available battery and musket to open fire. One Confederate officer was startled by the effect as "spaces, gaps and wide chasms instantly told the tale of a most fatal encounter. Volley after volley of small arms continued the work of destruction while the artillery kept up a withering fire on the lessening ranks. Then the enemy wavered, halted and finally retreated."

As the short winter day reached its midpoint, the Union attack on Lee's right flank had degenerated into a stalemated

Like a number of Confederate generals, Ambrose Powell Hill was eccentric and temperamental, but an aggressive and effective commander. He was the general mentioned by Robert E. Lee in his dying words.

duel between Rebel and Yankee sharpshooters as not one Federal unit could pass safely through the curtain of steel blasting from Prospect Hill. Union artillery commander Henry Hunt spent the next hour positioning every gun he could find for a spectacular covering fire that would hopefully allow Gibbon's and Meade's men to push from the open fields into the wooded ridge line. At about 1300, the two division commanders decided to try another advance and this time, despite horrendous casualties, the Yankees pushed over the railroad tracks and began scrambling uphill through the woods. Now, for a brief moment, fortune smiled upon the Federals.

When Stonewall Jackson began deploying his men on the Confederate right flank between Deep Run Creek and Hamilton's Crossing, he had assigned the men of Ambrose Powell Hill's division to position themselves as the first line of defense. At the time of the Fredericksburg campaign the two Virginia generals were engaged in one of their periodic feuds regarding their very different interpretations of insubordination to a superior officer and apparently the men were barely speaking to one another. When Hill deployed his brigades, Stonewall Jackson was at best only vaguely informed of their disposition. In a spirit of creative deployment of battle lines, amazingly similar to Union General Daniel Sickles's seven months later at Gettysburg, A. P. Hill positioned his units in a way that would ignite controversy for decades to come. He anchored the left of his line with Dorsey Pender's North Carolinians, but then stationed the next brigade, under General James H. Lane, about 150 yards closer to the railroad than Pender's Tar Heels. Lane not only had no friendly troops on his immediate left, he was even more vulnerable on his right. When Hill had surveyed the ridge along Prospect Hill, he encountered a 600-yard-wide stretch of swamps and bogs that he was convinced could never be crossed by advancing Yankees. Therefore, he simply left a yawning gap in this line and positioned his next unit, James J. Archer's brigade, on the right side of the swamp. Then, almost as an afterthought, he deployed a brigade of South Carolinians under General Maxcy Gregg well back in the woods beyond the swamp. Now, as happened so often during the Civil War, an attacking army was about to gain an enormous advantage from the sloppy actions of an enemy general.

When the six brigades of Yankee soldiers under John Gibbon and George Meade poured over the Richmond, Fredericksburg and Potomac Railroad line and climbed up the wooded banks of Prospect Hill they were still being met by powerful Rebel musket and artillery fire. However, Gibbon's bluecoats managed to slice between Pender's and Lane's defenders and the two Rebel brigades were badly positioned to support one another in a crisis. Over 200 men in gray or butternut were quickly captured and large numbers of Confederates were forced deeper into the woods. Then, as the Southern line began to come unhinged, George Meade's Pennsylvanians charged over the "impassable swamp" and threatened to annihilate several Rebel regiments.

Meade's men met stiff resistance on their flanks but as the Pennsylvanians pushed deeper into the wooded ridgeline they began to realize that they were beginning to split a sizeable portion of Stonewall Jackson's corps in two. Confederates from the right flank of Lane's brigade and the left flank of Archer's brigade had watched in startled amazement as the Yankees poured right through the "impenetrable" bog separating them and now these men were becoming part of the jetsam of the battle as they were in danger of being cut off from the rest of the Rebel army. One Tennessee regimental officer insisted

The extreme left of one brigade and the extreme right of another brigade believing they were about to be surrounded, gave way, yet their comrades on the right, unaware of the condition of affairs, were amazed at this confusion. Their officers and men on the right were enraged at what seemed to them dastardly cowardice and rushing toward their broken lines, officers and privates stormed at, shouted at and threatened them as base cowards. Officers leveled their pistols and, with many privates, fired into these fleeing comrades and broken ranks.

Suddenly, the reason for the wild retreat toward the rear became more apparent to men in these units as the graycoats saw Yankee soldiers rushing furiously into the woods and pushing toward the top of the ridge line. General Maxcy Gregg's South Carolinians, who had been deployed beyond the area of the swamp, assumed that because they were officially in the second line of defenders there must be some other unit between them and the railroad tracks. Thus, when they saw fast charging soldiers making their way through the woods, most of them assumed they were merely fellow Confederates who were withdrawing from a Yankee attack forming beyond the railroad embankment. Gregg's men were so sure that the "distant" fighting didn't affect them that they had stacked arms and were sprawled around their campsites when the first soldiers came into view. A few South Carolinians grabbed muskets and began shooting at the charging figures but other men screamed for them to stop firing, as they thought they were shooting at friends.

As comrades argued over the identity of these oncoming strangers, General Gregg mounted his horse and shouted for his men to cease fire because they were firing at friends. A moment later, a Yankee bullet tore into Gregg's spine, inflicting a fatal wound, but the general's men still couldn't tell friend from foe. One perplexed corporal admitted "far up to the right we could see our men jumping up and seizing their guns. Many were firing and loading as fast as they could, others stood irresolute as many officers in front tried to keep the men from firing." Some of Gregg's men were convinced they were confronting the enemy shouting, "they are Yankees, I see the blue coats" while others insisted, "they couldn't be Yankees, there's a North Carolina brigade out front and its been there all the time."

This delay in recognition of the true identity of Meade's men was fatal for dozens of South Carolinians. A few officers formed their men and according to one participant, "down the slope we went, firing and driving whoever they were." But the South Carolinians were now effectively surrounded and large groups of them either surrendered or ran further into the woods. As one officer admitted, "we were broken, slaughtered and swept from the field." According to General Reynolds's post-battle report, at this point, "Meade's division had successfully carried the wood in front, crossed the railroad, charged up the slope of the hill and gained the road and edge of the wood, driving the enemy from his strong positions in the ditches and railroad cut, capturing the flags of two regiments and sending about 200 prisoners to the rear." Meanwhile, Gibbon's men "crossed the railroad and entered the wood, driving back the first line of the enemy and capturing a number of prisoners." However, the very nature of the woods that had allowed the Yankees to pounce on Gregg's men before they were even aware they were being attacked now prevented the Federals from following up their initial success.

John Gibbon and George Meade had attempted to coordinate their attack on a two division front, and as they swept over the railroad embankment the tactic was working. However, as the two forces pushed further and further into the dense woodlands that dominated so much of Prospect Hill, the units became separated and what had been a division level fight was now rapidly developing into a pitched battle between individual Union and Confederate regiments and companies. A Rebel formation that was four lines deep must have increasingly appeared endless to the now panting and exhausted

The Union artillery was a highly proficient branch of service, but the relative altitude of the Confederate positions at Fredericksburg considerably reduced their effectiveness.

bluecoats as they groped their way through the woods. The men were thrilled with the excitement of watching their enemies flee in front of them but in this dense woodland it was now becoming increasingly difficult to see any friends as well. Just as Yankee units were splitting off into smaller and smaller segments dozens of fresh Confederate regiments were pushing through the trees to seal off the Union threat.

George Meade was viewed by many of his colleagues as an ill-tempered, cantankerous officer. He was balding and so nearsighted that he could barely see without his thick spectacles. Unlike the more handsome, more cordial generals such as McClellan, Burnside, and Hooker, many of the Yankee soldiers saw Meade as "a damned goggle-eyed snapping turtle." However, in the early afternoon of December 13, Meade had every right to be in a foul temper. His Pennsylvanians, after suffering heavy casualties, were threatening to split the enemy army in two and yet they seemed to be doing this vital job virtually by themselves. Meade's men had now largely lost contact with their comrades in Gibbon's division and not one of the other 100,000 soldiers in the *Army of the Potomac* seemed to be coming to their support as they pushed deeper into the heart of the Confederate lines. No one from Meade on down yet thought of retreating from this hard won ground, but the bluecoats were realistic enough to realize that Stonewall Jackson was not about to let them slice his corps into pieces without a major struggle.

Jubal Early was probably one of the few officers in the pre-war army who could match George Meade's reputation for being cantankerous, but now the foul-talking Virginian was commanding a division for Stonewall Jackson and was doing everything in his power to stop his former colleague from Pennsylvania in his tracks. Early left one of his brigades in place to handle any other unexpected Yankee breakthrough and formed his remaining three brigades into a powerful strike force to push the bluecoats clear out of the woods and hopefully back to the Rappahannock.

One of Early's most dependable units was a mixed brigade of men from Alabama, Georgia, and North Carolina commanded by Colonel Robert F. Hoke. Hoke's regiments had been deployed directly behind Maxcy Gregg's South Carolinians when the Federals had broken through and now Early intended to use this brigade to turn the advancing Yankees in the opposite direction. A sergeant in the 15th Alabama Infantry insisted that this was one of the most emotional moments for many of his men.

> My brigade was directly in the rear of General Maxcy Gregg's South Carolinians and they were attacked with such overwhelming numbers that caused them to fall back. Colonel Hoke called us to attention and ordered us to fix bayonets as a perfect stream of wounded was passing to our rear. The cheers of the advancing Yankees could be plainly heard. They were following the South Carolinians with perfect joy but the poor fellows did not know what they were soon to meet!

William C. Oates, an Alabama regimental commander who would soon duel with Colonel Joshua Chamberlain for possession of Little Round Top at Gettysburg, had just ordered his men to raise the Rebel Yell and launch a bayonet charge after firing a volley of musketry. One participant in the charge noted of Meade's men:

> They could not stand. They were not expecting such a deadly volley. They broke and we ran after them down the hill to the cut in the railroad where we overhauled a goodly number of them crouched down waving white handkerchiefs to surrender. Our troops on the right and left charged simultaneous with us and had the same success. The railroad made a curve at this place and as far as I could see to the right and left there were Yankees and our men all mixed up together.

A captain in one of Hoke's Georgia regiments emphasized the bloody chaos of the battle around the embankment after Colonel Hoke ordered the charge. "We went into the railroad cut capturing many prisoners. I emptied my self-cocking Colt as we advanced. I ran up in front of my men and jumped into the cut, landing on a big captain's head, ramming it down in the mud. The men piled in after us and seeing that we were outnumbered were inclined to be rough but we stopped them as the Yankees wanted to surrender."

The Confederates now had the advantage of momentum and soon the men from Gibbon and Meade's divisions were retreating across the fields that separated the railroad line and the stage road. The bluecoats were beginning to run out of ammunition and dozens of Union troops began surrendering rather than subjecting themselves to the Rebel fire now pouring out of the woods. Then as the Union line began to unravel, Yankee reinforcements rushed across the fields from the Richmond Stage Road.

In one of the few examples of good timing in the Union army on this bloody Saturday, Joe Hooker had pushed several regiments of David B. Birney's division across the Rappahannock and ordered the general to support Reynolds's men. Birney, who was the son of an Alabama planter who had become an abolitionist, led his men across fields that were now turning into slush and mud as the temperature soared towards 60 degrees in a sudden afternoon thaw. These welcome reinforcements quickly collided with Confederate General Alexander R. Lawton's Georgians in the fields between the stage road and the rail line, and the battle surged back and forth between these two boundaries. This part of the battlefield would soon acquire the grisly title of the "Slaughter Pen" by men on both sides, but despite heavy casualties, the Union regiments were able to fight their way back to the railroad embankment by about 1400. The men of Gibbon's, Meade's, and Birney's divisions now held a precarious toehold on Prospect Hill, but as both William Franklin and Stonewall Jackson considered their next moves, the focal point of the battle of Fredericksburg shifted upstream to a confrontation between Edwin Sumner and James Longstreet. As the struggle for Hamilton's Crossing ground into a stalemate, Yankees surging out of the streets of Fredericksburg and Confederates lining Marye's Heights would now determine the course of the battle.

Confederate Arms, Equipment, and Uniforms During the Fredericksburg Campaign

The Fredericksburg campaign probably marked the closest level of parity between Yankees and Rebels in arms, equipment, and supplies of any point in the Civil War. Earlier in the war many Confederate units had been handicapped in battle when they were forced to fight with large numbers of short-range smoothbore muskets often manufactured as far back as the War of 1812. Later in the war, the Southern army would be at an increasing disadvantage as more and more Yankee regiments were supplied with fast firing breech-loading rifles. However, during this confrontation along the Rappahannock most Confederate infantrymen were on equal terms with their Union adversaries as they were equipped with imported British Enfield rifled muskets, Confederate made versions of the same weapon, or Springfield muskets that had been captured by the thousands during Rebel victories.

During the fall of 1862, Lee's army was also fortunate to be deployed in a position that could easily be supplied by a railroad line coming up from Richmond. At this point in the war, when the Federal blockade was not yet at full force, relatively little Confederate territory was occupied, and the rickety Southern rail network was still more or less functioning, a reasonable supply of rations, blankets, and other equipment was reaching the soldiers along the Rappahannock.

If the Confederate soldiers were relatively well-armed and supplied with at least a tolerable level of rations during the campaign, their clothing was already looking more like rags and less like uniforms every week. In theory, each regiment's home state was expected to provide a continuous supply of new uniforms for the men, but while most men may have marched off to war fairly well dressed, replacement clothing barely trickled into the camps. Some states failed to provide adequate transportation for new uniforms, other states held most uniforms for regiments that were actually deployed in the state, and other states simply had incompetent quartermasters. The result was that by late 1862 a typical Confederate regiment was decked out in a bewildering variety of outfits ranging from battered gray coats to patched butternut jackets to flannel hunting shirts. Officers, who tended to buy their own uniforms, were somewhat better dressed but still reflected the individualism of the Confederate army with a variety of hats and coats that suited personal tastes.

Union Arms, Equipment, and Uniforms During the Fredericksburg Campaign

The Federal army that took the field along the Rappahannock River in the autumn of 1862 was somewhat different in appearance than the earlier version of the army that fought along Bull Run Creek 17 months earlier. By the time of the Fredericksburg campaign the vast majority of Yankee soldiers were wearing blue coats, unlike the first battle at Manassas when significant numbers of Union troops fought for the American flag wearing gray uniforms. On the other hand, the men who fought under Burnside still wore much more varied outfits than most armies in 20th century wars. A number of regiments marched into battle wearing variations on the Zouave uniforms sported by troops in French North Africa. They wore exotic headgear including turbans and fezzes, baggy trousers, and other colorful features. Yankee soldiers who had enlisted in the new rifle regiments being organized by Colonel Hiram Berdan were outfitted in bottle-green coats and pants in order to reduce their visibility in the woods. Even in the more conventionally uniformed regiments, headgear was far from uniform. While the more or less official kepi cap was more often seen than in the Western armies, it was far from universal as some enlisted men and a large number of officers purchased a variety of slouch hats that did a better job of protection from sun, rain, and snow. A few of the better equipped regiments were even provided with fur hats for winter campaigning while other soldiers tied scarves around their heads to keep out the cold during this relatively unusual campaign.

Most regiments in Burnside's army were now equipped with the standard Springfield model 1861 rifled musket which was the most commonly used Union weapon of the Civil War. This weapon was the most technologically advanced and the last of the muzzle-loading weapons. It was fairly reliable, had excellent range, and was cheap to produce, but was still fairly cumbersome and had only the same rate of fire¾two or three shots a minute¾that muskets in the Revolution featured. A few regiments were still stuck with a variety of inferior foreign muskets, notably Belgian and Austrian weapons that had a high rate of mechanical failure. On the other hand, some more fortunate regiments had either purchased themselves, or induced their states to purchase, the new breech-loading rifles manufactured by the Colt, Henry, Spencer and other firearms companies. At this point in the war most of the available breechloaders were single-shot weapons that could fire about 10 rounds a minute, but a small number of repeating rifles were starting to appear in the *Army of the Potomac* camps and these guns could produce 10 times the firepower of the muzzleloaders.

Jubal Early (1816-1894)

One of the most controversial, contentious generals in Lee's army was fellow Virginian Jubal Early. This cantankerous officer graduated from West Point in 1837 and served with some distinction in the Seminole War. However, Early resigned his commission to become a successful attorney in Rocky Mountain, Virginia, and was soon elected as a member of the state legislature. Early took a leave of absence to serve as a major of volunteers in the war with Mexico and then returned to legislative duties where he was viewed as a strong Unionist in a very divided Old Dominion. During the state's secession convention in 1861, Early continued to oppose separation from the Union but, like Stonewall Jackson and Robert E. Lee, accepted a commission in the state forces when it became obvious that Virginia would side with the Confederacy.

While Early was quickly given command of the 24th Virginia infantry, the lawyer's sloppy appearance and profane language did not allow him to fit in well with the more aristocratic officers of many Confederate units. Despite this handicap, Early rose from brigade to division command and during the Fredericksburg campaign he performed outstanding service in holding the right flank of the Confederate army. After significant roles at Chancellorsville and Gettysburg, Early was given temporary command of A. P. Hill's corps and by the end of the Wilderness campaign had been promoted to lieutenant general. When Hill returned, Early was given command of Richard Ewell's corps which quickly turned into an independent command when Lee ordered him to launch offensive operations in the Shenandoah Valley in an attempt to force Grant to abandon his siege of Petersburg.

Early enjoyed significant success at the beginning of the campaign, defeating Union General David Hunter and then engaging future *Ben Hur* author Lew Wallace at Monocacy, Maryland on July 11, 1864. The Virginian's force was able to advance as far as the fortifications outside Washington and actually brought Abraham Lincoln under fire, but Grant had rushed the Union *VI Corps* northward and Early was forced to withdraw. Grant then appointed General Philip Sheridan to chase Confederate forces out of the northern regions of the Shenandoah Valley, and Early was badly defeated at the battles of Winchester and Fisher's Hill. The Confederate general recovered to launch a brilliant surprise attack at Cedar Creek but the offensive faltered and Early's command gradually disintegrated during the winter of 1864-65.

At the end of the war Early feared arrest as a high ranking Rebel officer and escaped in disguise to Mexico. He eventually returned to practice law in Lynchburg, Virginia, and became the first president of the Southern Historical Society while engaging in emotional feuds in print with James Longstreet over the causes of Confederate defeat.

John Reynolds (1820-1863)

One of the most promising Union generals to be killed in action was John Reynolds of Pennsylvania. Born in Lancaster, Pennsylvania, about 50 miles from Gettysburg, Reynolds attended Lancaster County Academy and entered West Point in 1837. He graduated from West Point in 1841 and was promoted to brevet major for his gallantry in the war with Mexico. During the next 10 years he took part in various campaigns against Plains Indians and the Mormons in Utah and by the eve of Fort Sumter he was commandant of cadets at West Point with the rank of lieutenant colonel. When war broke out Reynolds was given command of a brigade of Pennsylvania volunteers and his first star.

During McClellan's invasion of Virginia in 1862, Reynolds's brigade was ordered to cover the retirement of the Union army's right flank near Boatswain's Swamp during the Seven Days battles and during the retreat the general was cut off from his unit and captured. After being exchanged a few weeks later, Reynolds commanded a division at Second Bull Run where he again successfully covered the retreat of the Union army. He was promptly promoted to major general and, at the request of Governor Curtin of Pennsylvania, was placed in charge of all Keystone State militia units during Lee's first invasion of the North. When Joseph Hooker was promoted to *Grand Division* commander by Burnside, Reynolds took over *I Corps* which he led at Fredericksburg and Chancellorsville. Reynolds had a number of admirers in the War Department and was considered for command of the army after the removal of McClellan, Burnside, and Hooker. However, the Pennsylvanian insisted that he would only accept the command of the army if he was given a much freer hand to develop strategy than Lincoln was willing to allow. When Meade assumed command in late June of 1863, Reynolds was assigned to take *I, III,* and *XI Corps* into Pennsylvania to counter Lee's threat. He was achieving considerable success in challenging the Confederate attacks of July 1, 1863, when he was killed by a sniper. Many Union officers viewed his death as one of the most grievous blows to the *Army of the Potomac* during the war.

CHAPTER VIII

A Winter Harvest of Death

As Yankees and Rebels surged back and forth over the woods and railroad embankment near Prospect Hill, an even more spectacular drama was unfolding further up the icy Rappahannock River. Ambrose Burnside had originally envisioned the Federal army engaging in a series of coordinated attacks in which rapidly increasing pressure on Stonewall Jackson's lines would force Lee to strip troops from Marye's Heights just as Edwin Sumner's bluecoats poured out of Fredericksburg and sprinted toward the ridge. However, as Franklin's drive against the Rebel right flank gradually sputtered into a stalemated engagement, the Union commander began shifting his attention to Longstreet's part of the Confederate line in the desperate hope that massive attacks in that direction would weaken the defenses along Prospect Hill and allow the Yankee *Left Grand Division* to roll up the graycoats from east to west. Unfortunately for the Federals, Burnside had now essentially abandoned his original battle plan and set the stage for one of the most disastrous assaults of the Civil War.

As thousands of blue-coated soldiers fanned out from the streets of Fredericksburg into the open fields facing Marye's Heights, Robert E. Lee could not believe his enormous good luck in having his adversary attack him at his strongest point in the line. The Confederate general initially was convinced

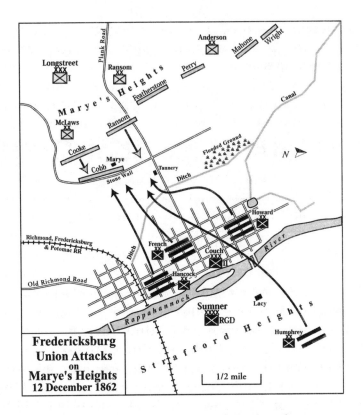

Fredericksburg Union Attacks on Marye's Heights 12 December 1862

that the highly visible massing of Federal troops was a smokescreen intended to draw his attention away from a surprise Union thrust further upriver, which might get around the extreme left flank of the Rebel lines and threaten to roll up Longstreet's divisions from west to east. However, it gradually became apparent that Burnside was simply going to throw brigade after brigade against Marye's Heights in an operation that prompted one Confederate officer to exclaim "if we couldn't whip the Yankees under these conditions, we couldn't whip anything and had better give up the war."

Burnside's loyal *Right Grand Division* commander, Edwin Sumner, had given General Darius Couch's *II Corps* the dubious honor of undertaking the initial assault against the Confederate defenses looming on the ridge just under a mile from the streets of Fredericksburg. Couch had been one of the most vocal critics of Burnside's battle plan and he was convinced that the attack would be a fiasco. As the corps commander sat in his makeshift headquarters in the Fredericksburg Court House, a messenger arrived with Sumner's orders.

> You will extend your right so far as to prevent the possibility of the enemy occupying the upper part of the town. You will then form a column of a division for the purpose of pushing in the direction of the Plank and Telegraph roads for the purpose of seizing the heights in the rear of the town. This column will advance in three lines, with such intervals as you may judge proper; this movement is to be covered by a heavy line of skirmishes in front and on both flanks. You will hold another division in readiness to advance in support of this movement to be formed in the same manner as the leading division. Particular care and precaution must be taken to prevent collision with our own troops in the fog.

Since Ambrose Burnside spent most of the day in his headquarters on the far bank of the Rappahannock and the commanding general ordered Sumner to remain in his north bank headquarters as well, Darius Couch now became, in effect, the officer in charge of implementing a battle plan in which he had virtually no faith. While Robert E. Lee was very much on

Darius Couch may be best known for leading Pennsylvania militia units during the Gettysburg campaign, but he played a major role at Antietam, Fredericksburg, and earlier battles of the **Army of the Potomac.** *He spent the latter part of the Civil War with the Western armies.*

the scene of the battle from his post on Telegraph Hill, he was now basically engaged in a duel with only a third-tier Federal general who had been given very little leeway to alter plans during a sudden change in the course of battle.

Darius Couch commanded nine brigades of assault troops who would largely decide the outcome of the battle of Fredericksburg. Whatever order of attack Couch decided upon, the first major problem for the attackers was to move from the streets of Fredericksburg to the foot of Marye's Heights over a series of fields that offered little protection from enemy fire. Burnside had assumed that Franklin's attack on Prospect Hill would force Lee to shuffle at least some brigades from his left flank to right flank, but now that the *Left Grand Division* assault had sputtered to a halt, Couch's men would have to face the full fury of one of the most impressively deployed defensive forces of any battle of the Civil War.

At about 1100, as Franklin's men were dodging Pelham's well-placed shells, orders went out to William H. French's division to form up for the assault on Marye's Heights. It took almost an hour to get three brigades of assault troops organized along the narrow streets of Fredericksburg, but just before noon, a covering force of skirmishes sprinted out of town and occupied the few houses and outbuildings that lined the approach to Marye's Heights. As the skirmishers and a picked group of sharpshooters opened fire from the windows of these buildings, French's men marched over Hanover and Princess Anne streets and emerged into the open country beyond the town limits. The men of the lead brigade, under the command of General Nathan Kimball, stayed in good formation until they reached the runoff ditch that snaked out from the nearby canal. Two small bridges provided crossing points for the ditch, but the Confederates had removed most of the planking which forced some bluecoats to walk gingerly over the stringers while their more daring comrades waded through frigid, knee-deep water in the ditch itself. As the Yankees clambered over or through the ditch, Confederate gunners made their final calculations and prepared to send a lethal salvo against the oncoming Federals.

The Marye house was a central feature of the Fredericksburg battle. The house itself escaped damage but the grounds were extensively dug up for Confederate artillery and infantry positions.

Confederate artillerist Colonel E. Porter Alexander was fully prepared to challenge the Yankee assault, but was shocked at the lack of imagination in the Federal operation. He was convinced that Burnside would throw his assault force at the extreme left of the Confederate line, where the graycoat defenders were almost all within range of the massive Union batteries on the opposite shoreline. As the Georgian insisted "it was a fatal mistake. The most obvious and proper attack for the Federals was one turning the Confederate left along the very edge of the river above Falmouth supported by artillery on the north bank which could enfilade and take in reverse the Confederate left flank." Instead, Burnside was ordering his men to attack in a direction where a combination of excessive distance and fear of hitting their own men severely limited the supporting role of the North's most powerful arm. While Union guns would play relatively little role in covering the Yankee assault, Confederate artillery would play one of its most important roles of the war.

Longstreet and Porter Alexander had supervised the deployment of 22 cannons around the Marye mansion while other powerful batteries, including a pair of huge 4,200-pound

Parrott guns firing 29-pound shells provided massive support for the Rebel infantry. One of the most powerful artillery units on this December afternoon was the famous Washington Artillery of New Orleans which deployed four 12-pounder cannons, two 12-pounder howitzers, and three 10-pounder rifles in the front yard of the Marye house. Around noon the men of this battalion, which included numerous society figures in the Crescent City, were sitting in the yard munching on a lunch of hardtack and bacon and smoking pipes when a lookout shouted that the Yankees were advancing from Fredericksburg. One battery commander, Lieutenant William Owen, agreed with his men that the shouts of the advancing bluecoats seemed very different from the famous "rebel yell" but were just as spirited and awe inspiring. Just as the Unionists scrambled across the ditch, "our guns began their deadly work with shells and solid shot" and dozens of bluecoats dropped on the newly thawing ground. One Rebel gunner remarked, "how beautifully they came on! Their bright bayonets glistening in the sunlight made the line look like a huge serpent of blue and steel. The very force of their onset leveled the broad fences bordering the small fields and gardens that interspersed the plain. We could see our shells bursting in their ranks making great gaps but they came as though they would go straight through us and over us."

The advancing blue line that seemed so irresistible to the Rebel gunners seemed far less formidable to the men who formed the assault force. The commander of the *8th Ohio Infantry*, Colonel Franklin Sawyer, insisted that his men were being cut to pieces before they could even clear the ditch. "As we came to the slight fall in the street as it approached the canal, a terrible fire from sharp shooters and several shells struck the head of the column. Over twenty officers and men fell but our step was not even checked as the men rushed down to the bank." Another participant in the attack noted that once across the ditch new impediments awaited the men. "As soon as we rose over the bank, the missiles came upon us spitefully and the air was full of exploding shells. The fences had to be pushed or cut down and there were several extremely bad bogs or holes taking the men in a half leg deep." As the men of the *4th Ohio* reached the ditch they encountered a combination of artillery and musket fire and "just as we were in the very act of climbing up the embankment we could plainly see the rebels upon redoubts on Marye's Heights move rapidly to and fro when there is a puff of smoke on the Heights and two men fall; immediately several more cannon belch forth fire and sixteen more men fell. Hundreds who had watched our advance had seen the batteries open on us and the men falling right and left . . . they thought we had been annihilated."

As the attacking bluecoats pushed through this gauntlet of fire they reached a part of the field that offered welcome protection. Part way between the ditch and the sunken portion of Telegraph Road was a slight dip or swale that was difficult to hit from the Confederate lines. As units reached this part of the field they were able to catch their breath and reorganize before they made the final 300 yard rush to the stone wall and the heights beyond. When the lead regiments reached this dip and prepared to sprint toward the heights, their attention was focused on the cannons and riflemen clearly visible on the ridge above. However, the most significant threat actually came from the sunken stretch of road that fronted the high ground.

General Longstreet quickly realized that the key to the defense of Marye's Heights was the sunken stretch of the Telegraph Road that was flanked by a stone wall about four feet high. This presented enormous possibilities for defenders, and the Confederate corps commander deployed 2,500 men under General Thomas R. R. Cobb in the sunken road. Cobb deftly placed his troops in four mutually supporting firing ranks that would allow men to fire and reload in relays and provide almost continuous fire along the length of the stone wall. Now, as the Federals advanced from the top of the swale, the men in the front rank rested their muskets on the wall and carefully took aim at the approaching Yankees.

As Nathan Kimball's men sprinted across the soggy fields and closed on Marye's Heights, they were subjected to one of the most fearsome shocks of the entire war. At a single command, hundreds of Georgians cocked their rifles, glanced for an instant along their barrels, and opened fire on the massed bluecoats. Then, just as the Federals were reeling from the initial shock of the riflemen, the gunners on the heights above rammed canister shells into their barrels and sent tens of thousands of deadly pellets smashing into the shocked Yankees. Kimball had led his men into battle with the optimistic cry, "cheer up men, remember this brigade has never been whipped —don't let it get whipped today!" However, no one, from the Mexican War veteran brigade commander to the newest recruit, could have imagined the concentrated firepower that would be arrayed against them behind the stone wall and the heights above. The four ranks of Georgians quickly developed a deadly routine of leaning on the stone wall, firing a shot, and then falling back to allow another rank to fire while they reloaded. These 2,500 men were producing an almost continuous sheet of flame that prevented any attacker from even closely approaching the stone wall let alone charging up the heights to overrun the batteries on the crest. Once Kimball went down with a serious wound in the thigh, almost all cohesion was lost and more and more bluecoats withdrew to the relative safety of the swale or dodged the rain of shells and bullets as they sprinted back to the cover of the streets of Fredericksburg. In a very few moments of action 520 Federal soldiers from Indiana, Ohio, New Jersey, and West Virginia had been killed or wounded and not one foot of the Rebel line had been seriously threatened.

As the survivors of Kimball's brigade either hugged the ground or streamed back to town, the men of John Andrews's brigade swung into position, stepped gingerly over the bodies of their comrades, and took their turn in the sights of the Rebel guns. Andrews's collection of regiments from Delaware, New York, and Pennsylvania hoped that the enemy would have to take a few minutes to reorganize after beating back the first assault, but they quickly discovered that the Confederates were fully prepared to meet a new threat. One of the survivors of Kimball's assault watched in horror as the new brigade was cut to pieces.

The second brigade crossed the ravine, came up the slope, dropped down at the crest and joined the general fusilade against the stone wall. They rushed over the plain over the dead, wounded or dying, closing up the gaps while the showers of lead and iron left the field more difficult to cross because of the increased number of mangled remains that must be trampled into the earth. Thousands of men came over the slope and got down at the crest with us before the heights while hundreds of the bleeding and mangled were dragging themselves . . . wounded men fell upon their dead and the mangled while overhead is a pandemonium of shrieking missiles.

A Confederate gunner watching the attack from the yard of the Marye house noted "the advance, although passing the point reached by the first column and doing and daring all that brave men could do, recoiled under our canister and the bullets of the infantry in the road and fell back in great confusion." Andrews's men had lunged a little closer to the enemy lines than their predecessors but at no point had they penetrated the Confederate defenses and in perhaps 10 minutes, an additional 340 blue-coated soldiers were lying sprawled in the grass.

As the wave of bluecoats that was Andrews's command receded, Oliver Palmer's brigade began forming ranks at the main Fredericksburg railroad station for their turn at this deadly contest. Major Francis Pierce of the *108th New York Infantry* insisted that almost as soon as his men began marching down the railroad line toward the open fields, a hurricane of enemy fire smashed into them: "It was an awful place going up that railroad. Shell, solid shot, pieces of railroad iron and minnie balls came down the railroad in a perfect storm. Grape, cannister and minnies were poured into us from the front and from the right shells were thrown into us, raking us and exploding in our ranks fearfully. How any man went up and back again alive is more than I can imagine."

Darius Couch, watching Palmer's men attack from his observation post, was shocked at the severe losses in so short a time: "As they charged, the artillery fire would break their formations and they would get mixed; then they would close up, go forward, receive the withering infantry fire, and those who were able would run to the houses as best they could. As each unit came up in succession, they would do their duty and melt like snow coming down on a warm ground."

The men in Palmer's regiments had already had a shattering experience with an earlier Confederate-held sunken road. These bluecoats had lost over 500 of their comrades in a wild charge at Bloody Lane at the battle of Antietam and now, less than three months later, they were facing an equally well-defended road. As one officer recalled, "I don't see how a worse place could by any means have been made. We got to the bottom of a little ridge this side of the batteries and could go no farther it was so awful. Regiments would start ahead and before going half the distance would come back shattered and broken—half of their men behind them." Another 300 Federal troops were either writhing on the ground or beyond any movement at all in a far more futile attack than the assault at Sharpsburg in September.

General William French's division of Union soldiers was now a shattered unit that had lost nearly 1,300 men while producing almost no threat to the Confederate defense line. Now it was the turn of Winfield Hancock's men to test their endurance. Hancock was undoubtedly one of the most talented generals in the *Army of the Potomac* and would achieve lasting fame for his heroic role in stopping Lee's army on the hills around Gettysburg, Pennsylvania, the following summer. However, at this moment the Pennsylvanian was caught in the dilemma of attempting to show enthusiasm for an attack which he had violently opposed in earlier conferences with Burnside. Hancock had insisted to his superior that virtually no force of Federals, no matter its size, could successfully overrun the formidable defenses that Lee had placed in front of them on the outskirts of Fredericksburg. Now, on this relatively mild winter afternoon, Hancock was about to lead just over 5,000 men into a field that would become the final resting place for scores of them.

Winfield S. Hancock played a major role in the **Army of the Potomac** *from Gettysburg to Appomattox. At Fredericksburg, as with most Union officers, he could only carry out assaults he knew to be hopeless as effectively as possible.*

As Hancock watched French's men being cut to pieces, one of his aides stood beside him and uttered a sarcastic analogy to the fate of Roman gladiators as he intoned, "Hail Caesar, we who are about to die salute you." Several officers agreed that the approach to Marye's Heights reminded them of a Roman amphitheater and also commented on the large number of obstacles that would slow down the advancing soldiers and give the Confederates that much more time to shoot them. In essence, these unlucky Federal troops had been ordered to advance through a large-scale shooting gallery in which it would be almost impossible for Rebel marksmen to miss their targets.

Hancock's men would be facing an even tougher approach than their predecessors, as Confederate division commander Lafayette McLaws had begun funneling men from Robert Ransom's brigade down into the sunken road to back up Cobb's Georgians, while an additional regiment of North Carolinians was deployed part way up the slope behind the road to add another tier of riflemen to the already potent defenses. The first brigade to encounter these expanded obstacles to a successful assault was a mixed force of men from Connecticut, Delaware, New York, and Pennsylvania under the command of General Samuel Zook. The Pennsylvania native insisted that the only hope for success was to push his men across the field at top speed and launch the assault "like a catapult." Hancock accompanied his brigade commander on a rapid march through the ranks of French's retreating bluecoats and the two generals then led the men "at great speed" over the ground between the crest of the swale and the stone wall. A Georgia sergeant standing securely behind that wall marveled at the rapid marching pace of the advancing Yankees but insisted that his men were more than ready to meet the challenge: "We waited until they got within about 200 yards of us and rose to our feet and poured volley after volley into their ranks which told a most deadly effect. They soon began to waver and at last broke from the rear as only a few rounds from our brave and well tried men was necessary to tell them that they had undertaken a work a little too hard. I have been in many engagements before but I never saw in my life such slaughter!" This sheet of flame quickly cut down all but two of Hancock's personal staff and the general himself was grazed in the abdomen while attempting to rally his men. Some of Zook's survivors were able to build a crude barricade back at the swale which would enable them to provide covering fire for the next assault brigade, but 527 men were dead or wounded, and the offensive operations of yet another brigade of Yankees was over for the day.

As Zook's remaining marksmen blasted away at the stone wall, a huge green flag with a gold harp emblazoned in the center announced the arrival of the next attack unit, the mostly Celtic members of the famed *Irish Brigade*. This collection of Hibernians from New York, Massachusetts, and Pennsylvania was largely the creation of one of the most colorful officers in the *Army of the Potomac*, Colonel Thomas F. Meagher. After narrowly escaping a British hangman in an Irish uprising, Meagher had escaped to America and used his brilliant speaking abilities to recruit men for the Union cause. The colonel wore a magnificent tailored green coat with a yellow silk scarf

Thomas F. Meagher's **Irish Brigade** *made one of the most famous of the doomed charges at Fredericksburg. The unit had considerably more success at Antietam and Gettysburg.*

across his chest to complete a uniform that one soldier insisted was "a picture of unusual grace and majesty." Every man in the brigade wore a sprig of evergreen in his cap and some of the best singers and musicians in the Union army called the *Irish Brigade* their home.

Hancock's most famous unit was so well-trained and so enthusiastic that even some of the men from the already repulsed regiments began to hope that this force could turn the tide of the battle in the Union's favor. The Irishmen threw away their knapsacks, overcoats, and almost anything else that would encumber them, and trotted at a rapidly quickening pace toward the ominous wall fronting Telegraph Road. Colonel Meagher ordered two companies of the *69th New York* to cover his right flank in a loose skirmish formation while the rest of the brigade swept forward at right shoulder arms jogging toward the stone wall and its bristling muskets. Artillery fire immediately blew large gaps in the ranks of the Irishmen but the brigade swarmed forward as officers and men dropped even more frequently.

As the Hibernians closed on the stone wall, even the Confederate defenders paid grudging tribute to the kind of men that were engaged in this attack. General George Pickett wrote to his fiancee, "your soldier's heart almost stood still as he watched those sons of Erin fearlessly rush to their deaths. The brilliant assault on Marye's Heights of their Irish brigade was beyond description. We forgot they were fighting us and cheer after cheer at their fearlessness went up all along our lines!" A correspondent for the *London Times* insisted that "never at Fontenoy, Allevera or at Waterloo was more abundant courage displayed by the sons of Erin than those frantic dashes which they directed against the almost impregnable positions of their foe." The incredible panorama of one of the most courageous charges of the day was one of the key actions that led Robert E. Lee himself to remark as he watched from Telegraph Hill, "it is well that war is so terrible lest we grow too fond of it."

The Rebel troops may have admired their adversaries, but they had no intention of allowing these Irishmen to overrun the Confederate line. Colonel Robert Nugent of the *69th New York* quickly went down badly wounded, the color sergeant of the *116th Pennsylvania* was shot six times before he fell in a bloody heap alongside his flag, and Major William Horgan of the *88th New York* was killed as he launched a final sprint at the stone wall. However, despite the carnage, the Irishmen had advanced closer to the Confederate line than any other unit and for a brief moment they threatened to pour into the sunken road. At this moment of crisis, General Cobb, who had been actively directing the fire of his men, suddenly slumped forward with a mortal wound, and, as he was carried unconscious from the field, the morale of the Georgians began to slip.

As Meagher's men threatened to penetrate the Rebel line another Irishman, Confederate Colonel Robert McMillan, stepped in to turn the tide back in the Southerners's favor. McMillan commanded a Georgia regiment that was almost as Celtic in origin as the Yankees attacking them and the Rebel colonel ordered his enthusiastic men to collectively hold their fire until the main body of Federals had closed almost to the wall. At this moment, McMillan ordered every man in the regiment to fire at once, and the effect was staggering. As one of these Irish Confederates noted, "Meagher met his match at Fredericksburg against another gallant son of the Emerald Isle as the assault was repulsed with tremendous slaughter." When the smoke cleared, Colonel Richard Byrnes of the *28th Massachusetts* could find only 12 men still capable of continuing to attack while other units were at least temporarily in a similar condition. As the Federals tried to organize for one final lunge at the wall, General John R. Cooke led two regiments of North Carolinians into the sunken road to reinforce the Georgians. Cooke, a Harvard graduate, was the son of Union General Philip St. G. Cooke and brother-in-law of J. E. B. Stuart, and the general's Tar Heels were a welcome addition to the defenders behind the stone wall. Cooke and McMillan quickly organized a sequence of volley firing that was six men deep and provided a volume of fire that was almost impenetrable. Within minutes, 545 Irishmen lay sprawled around the fields in front of the stone wall and some Federal companies were fighting with only eight or nine men still on their feet. As Meagher's survivors withdrew away from this hellish scene, Hancock's last brigade swept forward in a vain hope to locate a weak point somewhere in the wall of muskets that faced them.

General John Curtis Caldwell, a 29-year-old graduate of Amherst College, now commanded the largest brigade in Hancock's division. Caldwell was considered one of the most brilliant young officers in the *Army of the Potomac* and he was confident that his men could find a vulnerable point in the enemy line. Caldwell ordered one of his equally gifted young regimental commanders, Colonel Nelson A. Miles, to use his specially equipped *64th New York Infantry* to provide massive covering fire while the remaining regiments sprinted toward the stone wall. Miles, who had vowed that he would come back from this attack as a general or a corpse, commanded a unit armed with special long range Austrian sniper rifles, and as the rest of the brigade charged toward Telegraph Road, his men were able to pick off some of the men behind the stone wall and even some of the Rebel artillerists on the ridge above. Unfortunately, Confederate snipers were quickly focusing on this new threat and within minutes, Miles was sprawled on the ground with blood gurgling out of a serious throat wound and a moment later Caldwell himself was also grievously wounded leading the assault regiments across the field. Two of Hancock's most energetic officers were out of the battle in the space of a few minutes and the result was distressingly predictable.

Colonel Edward Cross of the *5th New Hampshire* now attempted to restore the faltering momentum of this latest Yankee charge. Cross who had been a journalist, newspaper editor, and soldier of fortune in the Mexican army, now faced his most significant challenge. He recounted that "I passed along the ranks and spoke to the officers and men; told them it was to be a bloody strike; to stand firm and fire low; to close on the colors and be steady." A moment later, "the regiments rose up as one man and started forward in complete order." As the bluecoats advanced, a shell exploded in the air and fragments slammed into Cross' chest, jaw, and eye. As the colonel drifted in and out of consciousness he watched his men stagger into a lethal crossfire that left virtually no senior officer standing. Not only had the men of Caldwell's brigade failed to get as far as many of their predecessors, they had lost an incredible 952 men, the worst loss of any Federal unit. The stunned survivors now retreated from the seemingly impregnable stone wall and waited to see which Federals would now take their place in the killing fields.

Darius Couch had now fully followed his superiors's orders and sent about 9,000 bluecoats crashing against Telegraph Road and its lethal stone wall. Almost half of these men had been killed or wounded as Couch admitted "the musketry fire was very heavy and the artillery fire was simply terrible." The corps commander had been holding his third division, commanded by General Oliver Otis Howard, in reserve to exploit any Federal breakthrough but no breakthrough had occurred and Howard's men were the last fresh troops in Couch's corps. Their role as reserves was now about to end.

Howard and his brigade commanders had been watching the assaults by the men of French and Hancock's divisions and they had been appalled at the number of men who had been lost at such little advantage in the battle. When Colonel Joshua Owen moved his brigade up to support the other divisions he was shocked by their losses and sent a dispatch back to Howard exclaiming, "I was sent out here to support General Hancock's division but there is not much left of it to support." Howard's main hope was that he would be able to throw his men against the Confederate defenders of that portion of the Telegraph Road that was not covered by the stone wall and then roll up the Georgians and Carolinians defending the wall from the flank. However, as these latest regiments of bluecoats attempted to shy away from the menacing barrier in front of them they confronted an unexpected obstacle. Water seeping from the drainage ditch near the canal had created a large stretch of swampy ground that impeded any advance against the part of Telegraph Road that wasn't protected by the stone wall. As men from Howard's brigade desperately searched for firm ground from which to launch an attack, they found themselves drifting back within range of the marksmen behind the wall. As regiments ran out of room to maneuver, they lunged toward the stone wall in mounting frustration and soon another 1,000 Federal soldiers were sprawled dead or injured in the fields approaching Marye's Heights, while Confederate defenders calmly prepared to meet further attacks.

By the middle of this bloody winter afternoon, the men of the *Army of the Potomac* found themselves in a situation very similar to the plight of the British units assigned to drive the colonialists from the high ground near Boston that collectively became known as Bunker Hill. On that hot, sultry June afternoon in 1775, General William Howe had thrown regiment after regiment of elite British troops against American defended high ground and had lost almost half of his army in the process. However, just as it appeared that the British army was about to suffer a humiliating defeat, a change of tactics by Sir William and a series of crucial mistakes by the colonialists turned a looming British disaster into a narrow victory for His

Majesty's forces. Now, Ambrose Burnside was in much the same position as William Howe. The Union general now had about two hours of daylight remaining with which to turn the battle of Fredericksburg into a hard fought Yankee triumph or see the *Army of the Potomac* suffer one of the most humiliating defeats in its history.

Darius Couch (1822-1897)

One of the most outspoken critics of the entire Fredericksburg campaign was General Darius Couch, commander of the Union *II Corps* during the battle. Couch was born in Putnam County, New York, in 1822 and attended local public schools. He entered West Point at the age of 20, and graduated in the class of 1846 along with George McClellan, Stonewall Jackson, and 16 other classmates who would become generals during the Civil War. Couch saw almost immediate action in the war with Mexico and was commended for gallant and meritorious conduct. After serving eight years as an artillery lieutenant, he resigned to enter his father-in-law's copper manufacturing business in Taunton, Massachusetts.

By the outbreak of the Civil War, Couch was an influential businessman in the Bay State and he was quickly offered command of the *7th Massachusetts Regiment*. Couch's active Civil War career began when his classmate George McClellan took command of the *Army of the Potomac* in August of 1861. The regimental commander was quickly promoted to brigadier general and given command of a brigade. During the Peninsula campaign, McClellan promoted Couch to division command in the *Army of the Potomac*'s *IV Corps* with appointment to major general on July 4, 1862. Couch contracted a number of illnesses during that summer and actually tendered his resignation at one point, but he recovered enough to perform well at Antietam. When McClellan finally began his halting fall offensive, Couch was promoted to commander of *II Corps* and he remained in this position during both the Fredericksburg and

Chancellorsville campaigns. Couch was extremely critical of the leadership skills of both Burnside and Hooker, particularly the latter, and after the debacle near the Chancellor mansion, he resigned from the *Army of the Potomac*, expecting to be transferred to another theater.

The Confederate invasion of Pennsylvania prompted the War Department to transfer Couch to command of the Department of the Susquehanna which included responsibility for defense of the Keystone State. The former *II Corps* commander organized the Pennsylvania militia in the defense of Harrisburg. After Gettysburg, Couch requested assignment to a more active theater and was rewarded with command of the second division of *XXIII Corps* which participated in a number of Western campaigns. He distinguished himself in the Union victory at Nashville and played a fairly prominent role in the final campaign against Joe Johnston in North Carolina before tendering his resignation on May 26, 1865.

After the war, Couch became a political ally of his old friend George McClellan but failed in a bid to win the governorship of Massachusetts. President Andrew Johnson named him as Collector of the Port of Boston but after a brief term in this office Couch moved to Norwalk, Connecticut, where he became a successful businessman and served in high positions in the ranks of the state militia. During this time he wrote extensively about his experiences in the war and continued to criticize both Burnside and Hooker, while in turn being accused of inflating his own abilities and accomplishments. He died in 1897.

Winfield Scott Hancock (1824-1886)

Winfield Scott Hancock was born on the outskirts of Norristown, Pennsylvania, on February 24, 1824, along with a twin brother. Hancock's father, a prominent Norristown attorney, secured admittance for Winfield to the United States Military Academy in 1840 where he became the youngest member of the entering class. The young lieutenant saw extensive service in the war with Mexico and then served in frontier posts in Kansas and Utah before he was transferred to the Department of the Pacific. At the outbreak of the Civil War, Hancock was a quartermaster officer in the sleepy town of Los Angeles but was viewed as a valuable commander by George McClellan and brought east to receive a brigadier general's commission.

Hancock led a brigade of Maine, New York, Pennsylvania, and Wisconsin regiments during the Peninsula campaign, and when General Israel Richardson was killed at Antietam, the Pennsylvanian was promoted to command of the first division of *II Corps* with the rank of major general. This unit was viewed as one of the better performing divisions during the Fredericksburg debacle, and when he played a prominent role in covering Joseph Hooker's retreat during Chancellorsville, Hancock emerged as a major figure in the *Army of the Potomac*.

Hancock's most prominent role in the war occurred during the battle of Gettysburg, when new commander George Meade dispatched his fellow Pennsylvanian to the scene of the battle erupting at Gettysburg with the discretion to either hold the ground near the town or order a retreat to Pipe Creek, Maryland. Hancock quickly realized the importance of holding Cemetery Ridge and anchored the Union line there while advising Meade to send the rest of the army to support him. On July 2, Hancock commanded the left wing of the army that successfully repulsed the assaults of Longstreet's corps and the following day the Pennsylvanian was a key figure in the repulse of Pickett's charge. However, Hancock was severely wounded when a bullet carried a nail and bits of wood from the pommel of his saddle into his thigh and groin and he never fully recovered from the injury.

Hancock returned to the army to command an enlarged *II Corps* during the Overland campaign of 1864 and he played a prominent role in almost every battle of that spring and summer. However, soon after the siege of Petersburg began, Hancock's wound reopened and he occupied administrative positions for the remainder of the war. After the war, Hancock was rewarded with a major generalship in the regular army and was appointed commander of the Department of the East while also receiving a significant number of votes for his presidential candidacy in the Democratic national convention of 1868. Twelve years later, during the Democratic convention in Cincinnati, Hancock received the presidential nomination and lost the national election by a narrow margin to James A. Garfield. The candidate still held his military command of the Department of the East and died at his headquarters in New York in February of 1886. Hancock emerged as one of the most talented generals in the Union army after the Fredericksburg campaign and, along with George Meade, was probably the person most responsible for the Federal victory at Gettysburg.

Thomas F. Meagher (1823-1867)

General Thomas Meagher's feats during the battle of Fredericksburg were lauded by both Yankees and Confederates and he soon came to symbolize the bravery yet hopelessness of the Union assaults on Marye's Heights. Meagher was born in Waterford, Ireland, in 1823, the son of a wealthy Catholic merchant. Meagher lived an extremely privileged life for a Catholic but was shocked by the poverty and misery of most of his co-religionists under British rule. By the age of 26, he was a leading figure in plots to overthrow British occupation of Ireland and he was eventually captured and banished to the Australian province of Tasmania. Three years later, Meagher managed to escape to the United States and he quickly emerged as an influential leader in the growing Irish-American community of New York.

The outbreak of the Civil War gave Meagher and fellow Irish immigrants the chance to demonstrate their loyalty for their adopted country while gaining fighting skills that might someday be used against the British. Meagher was quickly commissioned to organize a company of volunteers in the *69th New York Regiment* and by the time of Bull Run he was a major and executive officer of the regiment. President Lincoln encouraged the organization of an "Irish brigade" during the winter of 1861-62 and Meagher soon emerged as the senior officer with a rank of brigadier general. While this unit fought in most of the major battles of 1862, the charge at Marye's Heights gained the most public attention and made Meagher a national celebrity. However, the Irish native soon had a series of conflicts with War Department officials over the future status of the decimated brigade and Meagher finally requested a transfer to William T. Sherman's Western army. Meagher was given a number of mid-level assignments in the Western theater and was ultimately rewarded with the position of acting governor of Montana territory at the end of the war. During his tenure as territorial governor, Meagher was engaged in a wild drinking spree on a riverboat steaming near Fort Benton, Montana, and he fell overboard into the Missouri River under mysterious circumstances. His body was never recovered and Meagher quickly became an almost mythical figure in the lore of the Irish experience in the American Civil War.

CHAPTER IX

Twilight of Battle

By 1400 in the afternoon of December 13, 1862, Ambrose
Burnside's plan to sweep the Army of Northern Virginia from
the high ground beyond Fredericksburg had ground to a blood-
drenched halt. Only one portion of the seven-mile-long
Confederate line had been breached and that penetration had
been brief. Five divisions of Union soldiers had been badly
mauled with no tactical gains to show for their losses.
However, well over 70,000 Federal infantrymen had been barely
utilized as yet and there was still enough daylight left on this
short winter day to turn the tide of battle in favor of the North.

As Darius Couch's last available assault brigade melted
away before the hail of lead coming from the sunken road,
Burnside turned his attention once again to William Franklin's
downstream operations against Prospect Hill. Once again, the
commander of the *Army of the Potomac* became convinced that
if the men of the *Left Grand Division* could only puncture Stonewall Jackson's lines they might very well push all the way to
Marye's Heights and force the Rebels to abandon the deadly
stone wall position. Ironically, this very possibility was now
emerging as a major concern at Lee's command post on Telegraph Hill. As long columns of bluecoats continued to mass
on the edge of Fredericksburg in preparation for a new series
of assaults against Marye's Heights, the Confederate commander turned to James Longstreet and said gravely, "Gen-

eral, they are massing very heavily and will break your line I am afraid." However, the burly Georgian calmly observed the Yankee formations with his field glasses and responded, "General, if you put every man now on the other side of the river in that field to approach me over the same line and give me plenty of ammunition, I will kill them all before they reach my line." Then Longstreet warned Lee, "Look to your right, you are in some danger there, but not on my line."

The danger that the commander of the First Corps perceived was that the Federal troops deployed along the railroad embankment in front of Prospect Hill were still in possession of a springboard for a renewed all-out assault against Stonewall Jackson's less securely defended part of the Confederate line. Union reinforcements were now finally trotting across the fields between the Richmond Stage Road and the railroad tracks, while regiments from Jackson's command were desperately attempting to shove the bluecoats back from the rail embankment before they became impossible to dislodge.

One of the bloodiest encounters occurred when Colonel Edward Atkinson led a brigade of graycoats from Jubal Early's command charging out of the woods to capture several Union artillery batteries just as Union reinforcements sprinted from the Stage Road to rescue the endangered gunners. Lieutenant Edward Williams of the *114th Pennsylvania Infantry* watched in horror as Atkinson's screaming Rebels surged toward an exposed Yankee battery only seconds before the Union officer's own men were able to arrive.

> When we reached Randolph's Battery, the rebels had got to within 20 paces of it and were just on the point of taking it when we got up. We poured in a volley and gave one yell and rushed at them. They turned tail and ran and we poured it into them until they reached the woods and then we laid down in the mud and mire. Men who have been all through this war say we came in under the hottest fire they had ever seen. If we had been 3 minutes later, Randolph's Battery would have been gone.

While this regiment of colorfully dressed Zouaves had been able to check one Confederate surge, Jackson's men were now hammering away all along the railroad line, and a few minutes later a key segment of the Union position buckled. General Evander M. Law ordered two regiments of North Carolinians to smash into a portion of the railroad embankment held by two New Jersey regiments and this time it was the Yankees who ran. Colonel Hamilton Jones, of the 57th North Carolina, noted:

> We were compelled to go across the corduroy road out into the open and as the first company cleared the woods, a battery opened on it from the Bowling Green Road; yet under this fire, company after company as it cleared the woods went steadily into line without a falter or a sign of confusion and the line was formed as accurately as if on parade; then at quick step it started for the enemy's line on the railroad. We were in full view of almost the entire Confederate army on the surrounding hills and as we started there came a cheer from the hills.

The Tar Heels advanced on the rail embankment as if they were on parade and at about 400 yards the New Jersey men opened a brisk rifle fire. The Confederates had been ordered not to return fire until the enemy broke and the graycoats kept advancing in grim silence until they were about 100 yards away. At that point, the Rebels broke into a double quick and a moment later were engaging the Yankees at close quarters. As Colonel Hamilton proudly noted "there was the thunder and smoke of guns and the 57th Regiment was at the railroad; those of the enemy who had not fled were captured then and there." The Carolina men quickly surged past the railroad tracks and charged across the fields leading to the Stage Road where they encountered fresh Yankee troops who were attempting to come to the aid of the New Jersey regiments. The result was a vicious engagement of bayonets, clubbed rifles, and revolvers which sputtered into a bloody stalemate.

The battle that surged back and forth across the fields in

front of Prospect Hill was a far more evenly contested fight than the slaughter around the sunken road, but Burnside insisted that his *Left Grand Division* troops needed far more than a drawn engagement if there was going to be a turnaround in Union fortunes on this December afternoon. The commander of the *Army of the Potomac* began to suspect that he had ordered William Franklin to commit too few troops to the assault against Jackson's wing and he now attempted to rectify this oversight. He sent a new order to Franklin explaining that "your instructions of this morning are so far modified as to require an advance upon the heights immediately in your front." Burnside assumed that these instructions would be interpreted by Franklin as orders for an immediate, all-out assault against Prospect Hill with every regiment he could muster. However, his subordinate quickly squelched this idea by insisting that eight of the nine divisions available for an assault were "already engaged" in fighting the Rebels and couldn't be rapidly deployed for a general attack. Franklin was using a very liberal definition of "engagement" as most of these troops were actually little more than spectators watching a relatively small number of their comrades fight for their lives along the railroad embankment. If Burnside was really sure that the assault against Stonewall Jackson was the key to the battle, he probably should have personally crossed the Rappahannock and confronted Franklin with a specific order to carry Prospect Hill by using every available soldier in his command. Instead, the army commander seemed to veer his attention away from the battle downstream and over to Edwin Sumner's headquarters to initiate another series of bloody assaults against Marye's Heights.

Burnside found his *Right Grand Division* commander sitting in an ambulance parked in the yard of the Lacy mansion poring over reports of the disastrous attacks of the last few hours. Sumner insisted that only a breakthrough downstream could significantly improve prospects of a Union victory and exclaimed, "Everything depends on Franklin's coming up on the flank." The commander of the *Army of the Potomac* responded to Sumner's statement by pacing furiously around the Lacy garden trailed by clouds of cigar smoke. Finally, Burnside came to a moment of decision and ordered his main rival in the army, Joseph Hooker, to take charge of operations against Marye's Heights.

At 1500, Darius Couch was back in the courthouse steeple trying to spot a vulnerable point in the Confederate lines when a messenger clambered up the steps of the cupola with a message from Sumner that "Hooker has been ordered to put in everything. You must hold on until he comes in." Even the somewhat cynical Couch admitted that he began to feel more optimistic with the expected arrival of the *Center Grand Division* commander insisting, "I understood that he was to take command of the whole fighting line, the putting in of his fresh troops beside mine might make a success. His very coming was to me, therefore, like the breaking out of the sun in a storm." Couch's elation was short lived. When Hooker arrived, the commander of *I Corps* admitted, "I can't carry that hill by front assault, the only chance we have is to try to get in on the right." Hooker decided to ride forward to confer with Hancock near the front line to see if he had any ideas on how fresh troops could best be employed in a renewed assault. When Fighting Joe returned to Couch's command post his earlier enthusiasm had almost completely vanished. Hancock had insisted that

Joseph Hooker was quick to recognize the futility of Burnside's assault at Fredericksburg, but was unable to stop the slaughter.

171

*Andrew A. Humphreys ably led a division of new Pennsylvania recruits at Fredericksburg. Humphreys's greatest contribution to the **Army of the Potomac** was as Meade's chief of staff during the final Appomattox campaign.*

the Confederate line was simply unassailable at any point and Hooker exclaimed, "Well, Couch, things are in such a state I must go over and tell Burnside there is no use in trying to carry the line here."

Hooker promised Couch that he would ride quickly to meet with Burnside and return as soon as possible with clear orders to call off offensive operations for the day. However, moments after Hooker left for the Rappahannock bridges, one of Hancock's staff officers sent the corps commander the startling news that Rebel gunners seemed to be evacuating their position in the yard of the Marye house. For a moment, a new hope surged in Couch. Humphrey's division from Hooker's command was now deployed for battle and there was a slim possibility that Franklin's men had finally forced Lee to strip his defenses in Longstreet's part of the line. Couch made an emotional appeal to the newly arrived division commander, General Humphreys, "Hancock reports the enemy's falling back; now is the time for you to go in!"

Andrew A. Humphrey's division of Pennsylvanians from the *V Corps* was largely made up of new recruits who had enlisted for nine months as part of Lincoln's call for an additional 300,000 volunteers in the summer of 1862. While Union commanders were expecting new regiments of men who had enlisted for three years, state governors, such as Pennsylvania's Andrew Curtin, were forced to activate regiments of militia who agreed to only nine months of service with the national army in order to fill out the state's quota for this latest call-up. Andrew Humphreys, a 52-year-old West Point graduate, was assigned to supervise the training of these new units after he had served a stint as McClellan's chief topographical engineer. Humpreys was a solid officer who had to contend against some latent prejudice in the War Department due to his long-term friendship with his classmate, Confederate President Jefferson Davis. Despite this handicap, Humphreys's stock rose when it became apparent that he was doing an excellent job of turning novice soldiers into valuable fighting men. One of the chaplains accompanying a Pennsylvania regiment insisted that because of Humphreys' inspired leadership, "I felt eager for the fray, believing that we were going to certain victory." The new division commander himself remarked to his men as they marched out of Fredericksburg, "Your comrades are before the enemy, they have driven him and now hold the lines. You are the reserves of the army and we go in to win the day!"

Colonel Peter Allabach's brigade led the way over the canal ditch and towards the bristling defenses of the sunken road. As the brigade commander ordered his men to drop their knapsacks to provide maximum speed, a Union staff officer watched this latest assault develop from the unique perspective of a Union observation balloon. Lt. Colonel William Teall, General Sumner's son-in-law, had just gone airborne with Federal aeronaut Professor Thaddeus Lowe in the observation balloon *Eagle*, and he gasped in awe at the spectacle unfolding below him. "A view of the entire line of battle, from the extreme left to the extreme right of the line, say 6 to 8 miles, was spread out before me. The scene from this height and at this moment of the battle was magnificent beyond description. Language could not do it justice. It was a scene I never expect to live to see again."

Far below, on the swampy ground near a small tannery, Allabach's men were following Humpreys's plan to maneuver around the center of the stone wall and hit the Confederates in the sunken road at an angle. Allabach ordered his men to fix bayonets and not stop running until they had cleared the stone wall and were battling the Rebels in the sunken road. One of the Yankee attackers noted, "Our line broke into a double quick with a cheer. In going through the Second Corps men, some of our men lay down and one man pulled me violently and motioned me to lie down, but our colors were still going forward and I went."

Andrew Humphreys was conspicuously at the head of the charging line of bluecoats, a position he had secured by insisting to his officers, "young gentlemen, I intend to lead the assault and shall be happy to have the pleasure of your company." However, in some parts of the line some enlisted men outsprinted their officers and one captain insisted that "there was very little for any officer to do. The men did everything and officers and privates advanced and fell and rose like

Alfred Waud's sketch of the charge of Humphreys's division. The troops carry both national and Pennsylvania state flags.

billows on the sea." A corporal near the front of the charging Pennsylvanians related that "with a yell, we marched up the hill and were making our way across toward the enemy's works when 'whiz-whiz' came shot, shell and bullets creating such a noise as I never wish to hear again. The dead tumbled around me and the groans of the wounded made me heartsick."

A Virginia infantryman watching this bloody assault from the relative safety of the crest of Marye's Heights recalled that "I witnessed one line swept away by one fearful blast from Kershaw's men behind the stone wall. I forgot we were enemies and only remembered that they were men and it is hard to see in cold blood brave men die." Gray-coated soldiers standing in the yard of the Marye house noted that Humphreys's men were now attacking in a rapidly descending twilight that made their adversaries almost impossible to detect. Southern soldiers marveled at the fierce determination of these Pennsylvania rookies. "Every soldier knew the Rebel position; they had seen charge after charge repulsed; they had seen brigade after brigade rush forward with deadly determination only to recoil before the hailstorm of iron and lead." Now, hundreds of Rebel soldiers lined the ridge above Telegraph Road and watched the climax of a dramatic and bloody day. As one Confederate soldier recalled, "across the plain, with no martial music to thrill them, only a stillness that would strike terror into spirits less gallant, swept the dauntless brigades with serried lines and gleaming steel. It was superb!"

Allabach's bluecoats made one final sprint toward the stone wall and just as they began to close in on the sunken road, a perfectly timed volley tore the lead companies to pieces. One Yankee soldier noted in horror , "the corps seemed to be kept constantly in motion from the kick of the rebel bullets striking them; some of them must have been cut to tatters." The color sergeant of the *155th Pennsylvania* died "amid the deadly storm of leaded hail" and four successive men who took up the fallen flag were killed within seconds in volleys that "penetrated the flesh and splintered the bones of the men."

A Confederate gunner insisted that this wild twilight charge was about as one-sided as warfare could get.

There was no smoke or battle fume to obstruct the view; no wood to mask the movement; as in a grand review the whole advance could be seen in all its glory and in all its horror. The brigade came on a run and bent as it moved until it was in the shape of a half moon with the concave toward the town. Batteries opened upon them and then broke out murderous musketry. Men staggered, reeled and fell but the others pushed on as from the wall and road came a living sheet of fire and at every foot they dropped by scores; some almost reached the wall and then fell dead with their feet to the wall.

The North Carolinians and Georgians manning the stone wall now realized that this very well might be the last gasp of the Union offensive and if this attack failed the battle would probably be over. The Rebel troops were covered with burnt powder and reeling from tension and exhaustion, but they were on the verge of a major victory and knew it. As one defender explained, "Each one of us fired over 100 rounds that day. The muskets became so foul that they frequently had to be wiped out using parts of our clothing. The boys were black as burnt cork minstrels from biting the end of paper cartridges and though cold under foot we were sweating through excitement and exertion. Blood and brains were scattered everywhere. It was gruesome and sickening." Another defender noted "on their last charge some fell within a few feet of our line and it looked like a pity to kill such brave men."

As the sun prepared to slip below the horizon, hundreds of additional Yankee casualties were now sprawled in front of the stone wall, but Andrew Humphreys still had one fresh brigade to throw into the battle and he ordered Brigadier General Erastus Tyler's men into line with the warning "not to fire a gun until ordered by me to do so." Humphreys remounted his horse and led his last regiments of Pennsylvanians through ankle-deep mud towards the sunken road. An eerie silence fell over the rapidly chilling fields as Tyler's men tramped over the treacherous mix of snow and mud. Then, "a perfect shower of lead whistling, and whipping into and over our ranks" mowed down entire squads. Humphreys himself admitted "the fire, as furious as it was before, now became still hotter. The stone wall was a sheet of flame that enveloped the head and flanks of the column." Hundreds of bluecoats then ignored their commander's ban on firing and unleashed ragged volleys of their own, but they had no visible targets while their opponents could still see them. The result was gruesomely predictable. As one Confederate defender insisted, "human nature could stand no more, for the number of killed was fast counting up by thousands and half of them were down. The ranks broke and each man sought safety in flight."

While Humphreys's very amateur novices were hurling themselves against the Rebels in the deepening twilight, a unit of largely hard-bitten, long-term regulars was assembling in the gathering darkness of the streets of Fredericksburg and wondering whether the commander of the *Army of the Potomac* would ever concede that these bludgeoning attacks were not going to produce the victory he craved. General George Sykes's division contained a high proportion of United States regulars for whom nine months or even three years seemed ridiculously short terms of soldiering. These men had helped to save the rest of the army on several occasions during the past year and now they represented a final ace in the hole for Burnside as nightfall swept over the Rappahannock. The regulars were professional enough to realize that they truly were the forlorn hope of the army in this final throw of the dice, but they still grimly advanced toward the now notorious canal ditch and the even more infamous stone wall beyond. Then Sykes's men became one of the few Federal units that actually experienced a pleasant surprise on this day of slaughter. As the Yankees prepared to charge, Joe Hooker galloped onto the field and shouted for Sykes to halt the advance. Fighting Joe had spent much of the afternoon in a belligerent confrontation with Burnside attempting to convince the army commander to call off the attack on Marye's Heights and organize a wide sweep around Lee's left flank well upstream from Fredericksburg. When Burnside refused to consider his advice, the commander of the *Center Grand Division* recrossed the Rappahannock and assumed command of operations around the town. Now, as Sykes's men were preparing for their sprint into the gauntlet of fire, Hooker insisted to an aide, "I have lost as many men as my orders require me to lose," and at least one division received an almost miraculous reprieve. The assaults on Marye's Heights were not necessarily cancelled, but at the very least the ghastly procession across the fields was postponed until another day.

At about the same time that Joe Hooker was attempting to stop a Union twilight assault on one flank of the Fredericksburg line, Stonewall Jackson was organizing a Confederate attack on the other end of the bloody stretch of real estate. The aggressive Virginian viewed the defense of Prospect Hill largely in terms of a possible springboard for an offensive against the Yankees after they had battered themselves against his lines. By late afternoon, as it became increasingly apparent that William Franklin was incapable of deploying his divisions in such a way as to form a significant threat to the Confederate right flank, Jackson's energies quickly shifted over to an attack mode.

While a relatively small number of Union soldiers were fighting desperately to contest the ground between the railroad embankment and the Stage Road, most of Franklin's men appeared to be mainly spectators to the action as they deployed in a series of lines extending inland from the Rappahannock. As the sun sank lower on the horizon on this December afternoon, Stonewall Jackson was becoming convinced that if he threw every man in his four divisions against what seemed to be a milling mass of poorly deployed Yankees, he would be able to drive much of the *Army of the Potomac* right into the frigid waters of the river. As Jackson sat on his horse and weighed his options during the waning moments of daylight, one of Stonewall's aides noticed the sense of rising emotions among the men: "Those who saw him at that hour will never forget the expression of intense but suppressed excitement which his face displayed. The genius of battle seemed to have gained possession and his countenance glowed as from the glare of a great conflagration."

A few moments later J. E. B. Stuart rode up to Jackson and insisted that the Union army was so shaken from the futile assaults of the day that the Yankees were ripe for destruction in a massive counterattack. Jackson required little convincing, and the former VMI instructor called together his staff officers and began dictating orders for a bold offensive. His own light artillery batteries and Stuart's horse artillery would move forward with the infantry and provide a mobile covering fire while Rebel riflemen surged out of the woods of Prospect Hill, rolled over the Federals along the railroad and stage road, and then smashed into Franklin's other highly vulnerable divisions strung out along the Rappahannock. In a best case scenario, the bluecoats would be pinned against the river and annihilated or forced into mass surrender. While Jackson's plan was audacious and risky, it did include one major safety feature. Stonewall intended to use his mobile artillery units not only as a covering force for the infantry but also as a kind of lightning rod for the whole operation. The general's main concern was the line of powerful Union cannons deployed on the north bank of the river. Jackson had some hope that the fading daylight would make those potent weapons ineffective. But if he had underestimated their capabilities, they would initially threaten his fast moving artillery which could be quickly pulled back to the cover of the woods if the Yankee fire became really threatening.

Stonewall Jackson still had plenty of enthusiasm for the idea of a twilight offensive, but the cold reality of late day events was that it would be almost impossible to organize his entire corps for an attack during the short period of daylight that still remained. For example, Jubal Early's brigades had become scattered all over the battlefield after their successful counterthrust at Meade's assault. However, when the cantankerous division commander rode up to Jackson and explained his problem, Stonewall simply told his acting division commander to attack with every man he could round up in the next few minutes. Jackson had no reservation about beginning the offensive with a pickup force of men; he was confident that as the gray tide surged across the muddy fields, thousands of other Rebel soldiers would catch up and join the attack as it steadily gained momentum.

As the sun slipped below the horizon, Stonewall Jackson opened his pocket watch for perhaps the tenth time in the last few minutes and then gave the orders for the Confederate counterattack to begin. John Pelham's horse artillery and the Second Corps mobile batteries rumbled out of the woods, and advanced to positions where the gunners could provide covering fire for the infantry pouring forward from Prospect Hill. About 100 yards from the woods the first Confederate batteries unlimbered and unleashed volleys at the Yankees. Then, as the gunners prepared to advance to a new firing line, battery after battery of Union guns on the north side of the Rappahannock thundered in a massive response. Even Stonewall Jackson admitted that he was stunned by the intensity of the Yankee fire as "they so completely swept our front as to satisfy me that the proposed movement should be abandoned." The Union infantry on the south bank of the Rappahannock might have been poorly deployed and milling around to no real purpose, but as long as they were cov-

Union battery on the high ground north of the Rappahannock, of the type that halted Stonewall Jackson's counterattack.

ered by the Federal batteries on Stafford Heights, a Rebel counterattack would be as suicidal as the Federals' thrusts at the stone wall. Shell-shocked Confederate gunners were quickly ordered to retire and gray-coated infantrymen counted their blessings that "Old Jack" at least had enough sense to pass up this questionable opportunity for a glorious twilight offensive.

As Rebel artillerymen gratefully steered their caissons back under the cover of the woods of Prospect Hill, the early nightfall of winter descended over the seven-mile front that marked the Confederate lines at Fredericksburg and the bloody fighting of December 13, 1862, largely came to an end. Ambrose Burnside had gambled that the two-pronged assault by Franklin and Sumner would force Lee to stretch his defenses to the breaking point somewhere along the line and allow the Federal army to pour through the rupture and roll up the Rebels from either east or west. However, the Rhode Islander's gamble had turned into one of the worst Federal fiascoes of the war and had left 12,000 Union soldiers dead or wounded on the field. Now the main question circulating in the camps of both Yankee and Rebel soldiers was whether the battle of Fredericksburg was a one-day engagement that was now largely over, or whether the carnage would simply begin again as soon as the long, frigid night turned once again to day.

Maxcy Gregg (1814-1862)

Maxcy Gregg was born in Columbia, South Carolina, and attended South Carolina College. After studying law he was admitted to the bar in 1834 and became a prosperous attorney. When war with Mexico erupted in 1846, Gregg volunteered for duty with the national army, rather than joining a state volunteer regiment, and served as a major in the *12th United States Infantry Regiment*. Despite his service with the national force, he remained an ardent proponent of states' rights and soon after his state seceded he was made commanding officer of the 1st South Carolina Regiment.

Gregg played a significant role in the Confederate siege and bombardment of Fort Sumter and was soon promoted to brigade command and a general's wreath. However, while the South Carolinian seemed to perform as a very competent brigade leader in the Peninsula, Second Bull Run, and Antietam campaigns, he was never in serious contention for higher responsibility and remained a brigadier general while other men moved up to division and corps command. At the time of his death at Fredericksburg, he was viewed as one of Stonewall Jackson's most competent brigade commanders.

Thomas Cobb (1823-1862)

Thomas Cobb was a member of one of the most prominent families in Georgia and after graduation from the University of Georgia he became a highly successful lawyer and edited a 20-volume summary of Georgia legal precedents. However, Thomas was somewhat in the shadow of his older brother Howell, who served as speaker of the house from 1849 to 1851, governor of Georgia, and secretary of the navy under James Buchanan. After Lincoln's election, Howell Cobb became presiding officer at the Montgomery Convention which created the Southern Confederacy while Thomas served as a delegate from Georgia.

Thomas was elected to the Confederate Provincial Congress in Richmond but strongly preferred a field command and resigned to recruit Cobb's Legion in Georgia. After a prominent role in the Seven Days, Second Bull Run, and Antietam campaigns Cobb was promoted to brigadier general just before the battle of Fredericksburg. Cobb's defense of the sunken road became one of the legendary aspects of the battle of Fredericksburg. While the general was still alive when he was evacuated from the Fredericksburg battlefield with a leg wound, his thigh was so badly shattered that he bled to death in a nearby house.

Cavalry During the Fredericksburg Campaign

The Fredericksburg campaign was fought at a point of the Civil War in which the Confederacy still maintained a huge advantage over the Union in terms of mounted warfare. This advantage had been in place since the earliest days of the war when both background and tradition gave the Rebels an enormous lead in using soldiers on horseback. The South had proportionally a much larger pool of recruits who were used to riding a horse on a regular basis. Well-bred Southerners often saw themselves as descendants of medieval knights and many wealthy Rebels were actually more interested in serving as enlisted men in the cavalry than being commissioned in the infantry. Since Southern soldiers were expected to provide their own mounts, many men brought their best horses with them and were willing to spend considerable time caring for these animals.

On the other hand, the Union army tended to recruit its cavalry from urban areas where men were not used to riding horses, and then provided them with generally inferior mounts that could not match their Southern counterparts. The most intelligent, well-educated Union volunteers usually saw nothing particularly glamorous about serving as a private in a cavalry regiment when they could easily secure a commission in an infantry regiment. Ambitious officers viewed the infantry, not the cavalry as the route to much higher ranks.

While the Confederate cavalry continued to outmatch the Union mounted troops during the Fredericksburg campaign, the horse soldiers had relatively little impact on the outcome of the battle. J.E.B. Stuart's spectacular cavalry raid between Antietam and Fredericksburg helped Lincoln to decide to relieve McClellan, but once Burnside began his march to the Rappahannock, Rebel cavalry found it difficult to break through the Yankee screen of horsemen. Major Pelham's tiny unit of horse artillery significantly slowed the advance of the Union left wing on the day of the battle, but in most other instances gray-coated horsemen played only a peripheral role in the engagement. After the campaign ended, when Joseph Hooker replaced Burnside, the Union cavalry began a gradual improvement that would allow Yankee troops to match their Southern adversaries for the rest of the war.

CHAPTER X

Aftermath of Battle

As the early darkness of winter descended over the fields and ridges around Fredericksburg on December 13, the surviving officers and men of the opposing armies began to take stock of the dramatic events that had occurred in the last several hours. General Robert E. Lee immediately realized that he had achieved a significant defensive victory on all fronts. Messengers galloping up to his command post on Telegraph Hill informed him that not one point of the seven-mile Confederate line had been fully penetrated and only one area had been even moderately threatened. While Confederate casualty lists might have appeared long when compared to the early engagements of the war, by the standards of 1862 or later they had been very modest. The death toll in the Army of Northern Virginia was 608 men, including two brigade commanders and several regimental leaders; 4,116 soldiers had been wounded and 653 men had been captured by the enemy. Even these relatively modest figures probably overstated the damage to Lee's army as the enormous advantage of position owned by the Rebel army resulted in a much higher percentage than in most other battles of very slightly wounded soldiers. A large number of the over 4,000 wounded Rebels had only been nicked or grazed by enemy bullets and were back with their units almost immediately after the battle. By the standards of major Civil War battles, James Longstreet's corps had suffered remarkably light casualties; his five divisions had each lost an average of only 40 men killed and not many more soldiers seriously wounded, which meant that virtually every regiment in First Corps was almost fully intact for future operations. The men of Stonewall Jackson's command had been involved in much more deadly combat with the Yankees and ended the day with just over 3,600 casualties and a few regiments only marginally fit for immediate operations.

Lee was pleased with the overall direction of the battle, but he was reasonably certain the engagement would continue soon after sunrise on Sunday. This was a prospect that the Southern commander welcomed as he felt that Burnside would suffer even bloodier repulses in a second round of fighting, and the Union army might become vulnerable to a massive counterstrike that could eliminate large elements of the *Army of the Potomac* from the chessboard of the war. However, Lee was convinced that his opponent was not stupid enough to simply continue battering at the stone wall for a second day, and he expected Burnside to attempt some form of end run

Wounded men after the battle of Fredericksburg. Primitive medical capabilities and the large number of casualties after Civil War battles resulted in numerous amputations.

around the Confederate left or right flank. In order to check either of these moves, orders went out to every division commander to send fatigue parties out on nighttime digging activities. Once Confederate engineers had supervised the construction of a massive new series of fortifications, Lee breathed a sigh of relief and insisted "my army is as much strengthened by these new entrenchments as if I had received reinforcements of 20,000 men." Now, the Virginian's only real concern was a shortage of ammunition that had developed repulsing the seemingly endless flurry of Yankee attacks on Saturday. However during the night, trains rolling north from Richmond brought up the entire reserve supply of musket balls and artillery shells of the Army of Northern Virginia and by dawn on Sunday, Lee was fully prepared for the expected second round of the battle of Fredericksburg.

On the opposite side of the Rappahannock River, the commander of the *Army of the Potomac* veered between despondency and euphoria as he reviewed the accounts of Saturday's battle. The army, under Ambrose Burnside's command, had just suffered one of the most one-sided defeats of the entire Civil War. A total of 1,284 men killed, 9,600 wounded, and 1,769 captured produced a casualty list of 12,653 Union soldiers from an army in which perhaps half of the men had not fired a shot during the entire battle. The disparities in the casualty rates among different units was astounding. Three division commanders, Winfield Hancock, Andrew Humphreys, and George Meade, had seen their units almost eliminated as effective fighting forces in a single afternoon. These three Pennsylvanians had entered the battle with a combined force of about 12,000 men and had suffered 4,998 casualties, nearly 40 percent of their commands. On the other hand, one brigade of General William T. H. Brooks's division lost only four men in the entire battle, a brigade in General Albion Howe's division ended the day with exactly one fatality, and a brigade in General Amiel Whipple's division suffered no fatalities and only three men wounded. Ambrose Burnside had been placed in command of the largest body of armed men in American history to that point, but he had thrown away his single signifi-

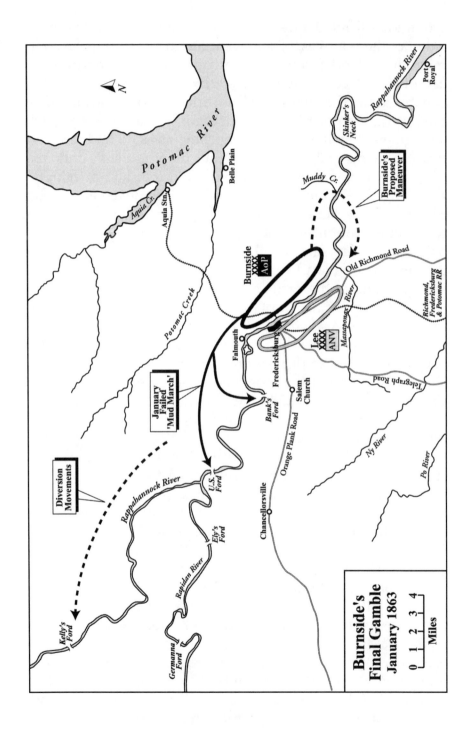

cant advantage by keeping over 50,000 men largely out of action and then failed to properly coordinate the attacks of the remaining troops that he did throw into battle. Now many of his best units were decimated and he had absolutely nothing to show for their loss.

The Union commander, unlike some other Civil War generals, freely admitted that he alone was responsible for the disaster of Saturday, but insisted that defeat had been a near thing and that just one more spirited charge might have swept the bluecoats over the stone wall and onto the crest of Marye's Heights. Burnside was now convinced that the only missing ingredient in the assaults had been his personal presence at the head of the attack force, an error he intended to rectify when he renewed the offensive on Sunday. Thus the Federal general spent the evening hours of December 13 formulating plans to personally lead his old *IX Corps* in a new, and presumably successful, attack operation.

While Burnside was planning his new offensive, a group of senior officers of the *Army of the Potomac* were sitting in the parlor of a house near the center of Fredericksburg discussing the prospects for their just defeated army. The group included George Meade, Andrew Humphreys, *V Corps* commander Daniel Butterfield, *IX Corps* commander Orlando Willcox, and a relatively junior brigade commander, Colonel Rush Hawkins. As the generals sat around the fireplace and discussed the merits and drawbacks of continuing the battle, Hawkins quietly drew a comprehensive sketch of the Confederate defenses based on his own experience and the reports of other regimental and brigade commanders. Finally, when the senior officers asked to see his sketch and passed it around the room, the seeming impossibility of carrying these works began to dawn on the generals. As Hawkins recalled, "it did not take long to convince these officers that a second attack would probably end more disastrously than the first and they united in a request that I should go at once to try to persuade Burnside that the attack ought not to be renewed."

Hawkins arrived at army headquarters in the Phillips mansion at about 2300 and was informed that Burnside was out on horseback reconnoitering the battlefield. However all three *Grand Division* commanders were present, and after Hawkins explained the reason for his visit, the generals agreed to back him in his request. When Burnside arrived around 0100 he enthusiastically embraced the young colonel and ex-claimed, "Hawkins, your brigade shall lead with the 9th New York on the right of the line and we'll make up for the bad work of today!" Burnside's enthusiasm produced an uncom-fortable silence from Sumner and Franklin, while Hooker lounged half-asleep on a cot in the corner of the parlor. Sumner approached Burnside and, as tactfully as possible, urged his superior to listen to Hawkins's objections to the planned as-sault. Then, as the army commander deliberated with Franklin, Joe Hooker suddenly sat up and "in the most frank and de-cided manner" insisted that the attack ought not to be reopened that morning.

Burnside agreed to consider canceling the attack but then rode back into Fredericksburg and suddenly appeared at Darius Couch's headquarters. It was now about 0200 and the *II Corps* commander was asleep in his makeshift headquar-ters. He was somewhat startled to see the army commander in his room but he spent the next hour reviewing every aspect of Saturday's assaults. Burnside assured his corps commander "I am perfectly satisfied that you did your best," and put on a cheerful front for most of the conversation. However, Couch later recalled, "it was plain that he felt he had led us to a great disaster. I never felt so badly for a man in my life," as he sensed Burnside wished his body was also lying in front of Marye's Heights. Finally, the commanding general returned to his own headquarters and began to compose the orders that would prevent Fredericksburg from becoming a two- or three-day bloodbath.

As Ambrose Burnside rode back and forth across the Rappahannock during this bitter cold night following the battle, the soldiers who had survived the disastrous assaults now often found themselves trapped on a frozen battlefield with their less fortunate comrades who had been killed or wounded. As hundreds of corpses lying on the bloody slopes

George G. Meade led the most successful Union assault at Fredericksburg. Shortly after assuming command of the Army of the Potomac he won the decisive victory at Gettysburg.

and fields began to freeze, their living comrades stacked them up like logs to form shields against both enemy snipers and the biting wind. Meanwhile, thousands of wounded men began crying out for help as stretcher bearers began evacuating injured men using shutters from houses as improvised stretchers. A Confederate sergeant recalled the agonized cries of his injured adversaries as "there were wounded Yankees lying between our lines sending up the most pitiful cries for help I ever heard. Some were calling for water, some calling the names of friends but none answered or went to their relief. Neither side could help. The night was cold and there is no telling how some of them suffered."

Dawn on Sunday revealed a gruesome panorama of the impact of the battle on the Union attackers. Looking over the ground from about 50 yards in front of the stone wall to the outskirts of Fredericksburg, one Confederate soldier saw "acres of dead Federal soldiers" while another Southerner insisted that a person could walk in front of the wall from one end to the other across blue-coated corpses without touching the ground. The reaction of the Confederate defenders to the thousands of wounded Yankees sprawled among the corpses was very mixed. Some Rebel soldiers coldly threatened to shoot any wounded bluecoats who groaned too loudly, while other Southerners looked for ways to help the suffering ad-versaries. The most famous "Samaritan" on the battlefield was Sergeant Richard Kirkland of the 2nd South Carolina Regi-ment. After watching the agony of the wounded Yankees dur-ing the early morning hours of Sunday, Kirkland went to his brigade commander, General Joseph B. Kershaw, and asked permission to go out on the battlefield with as many canteens as he could carry. The general insisted that Kirkland would be shot the second he stepped over the stone wall but the ser-geant insisted on trying and Kershaw responded, "Kirkland, I ought not to allow you to run a risk, but the sentiment which actuates you is so noble that I will not refuse your request, trusting that God may protect you. You may go." Kershaw would not allow Kirkland to wave a white handkerchief as he climbed over the wall and he expected the sergeant to be shot almost immediately. However as the South Carolinian knelt beside the first wounded bluecoat he faced and give him a drink of water, a cheer began breaking out from the Union lines and for over an hour the "angel of Marye's Heights" min-istered to hundreds of wounded Yankees and returned to his post totally unhurt.

Kirkland's activities were a welcome relief for a number of wounded bluecoats, but for many still uninjured Yankees, Sunday, December 14, was a day of sheer terror. Large num-bers of Union troops had been ordered to hold the ground between the swale and the canal ditch as a springboard for future assault, and when the sun rose, these men realized they had almost no protection from the Rebels perched above them on the ridge. Hundreds of Federals were hunched down be-hind the crest of the swale which offered only about six inches of cover from enemy sniper fire. The simple act of turning on one's side to retrieve a piece of hardtack from a haversack could be a fatal exercise as musket balls and canister shells whizzed overhead almost constantly.

One Union officer trapped behind the lip of the swale in-sisted that "the picture is one of my most distinct memories of the war. Eighty yards away on the ridge above us Confeder-ates were laughing and talking, cleaning muskets and clicking locks while more energetic rebels took pot shots at the cramped and half famished men lying in frozen mud, blood and sludge." Captain John Ames, who eventually became a Union general, insisted that he and his men now felt themselves effectively prisoners of war rather than functioning members of the *Army of the Potomac*. "We were so absurdly near the host of yesterday's victors that we seemed wholly in their hands and a part of their great mass; cut off and remote from the Federal army and almost within the lines of the enemy, prisoners, of course." As thirst became a major problem, bluecoats would sprint toward unused canteens on the bodies of their comrades and often pay for the water with their lives. As Captain Ames noted, "It was curious to see how strong the tobacco hunger was; men would jump to their feet and run the length of a regiment to borrow tobacco and in so doing, run the gauntlet of a hundred shots. This was so rarely accomplished in entire safety that it won the applause of our line and hearty congratulations to any one fortunate enough to save his life and sweeten it with this savory morsel."

The men trapped near Marye's Heights on Sunday initially assumed that they would soon be joined by thousands of their comrades engaged in a second round of assaults. However, as the sun began sinking into an early twilight, it became more apparent that Burnside had called off the attack. General Lee had spent most of the day on Telegraph Hill waiting for a resumption of the battle, and, of his senior commanders, only John Bell Hood had insisted that Burnside would never order another offensive. As it became obvious that Hood was correct, Lee jovially turned to Longstreet, a longtime friend of Burnside's and remarked, "General, I am losing confidence in your General Burnside." However, all day on Monday Union regiments could be seen fortifying Fredericksburg and there still seemed to be a good chance that the Federals would launch another attack. Monday night brought sheets of frigid rain sweeping across the Rappahannock, and as Southern soldiers huddled against the icy blasts, Union regiments tramped back across the river until, just before dawn, Yankee engineers dismantled all of the pontoon bridges and left the south bank of the stream to the Army of Northern Virginia. The Union army was now safely back in Falmouth but the political fall-out from the Fredericksburg campaign was just gathering momentum.

Soon after the battle of Fredericksburg ended, Burnside threw a cordon of provost guards around the Union camp and forbade reporters from leaving the area. However, at least one journalist, Henry Villard, slipped through the guards and rushed to Washington to set up a meeting with President Lincoln. Villard presented the president with the grim details of the failed assaults on Marye's Heights and insisted that every general he had encountered thought that success in this campaign was impossible, and that the army might suffer an even worse disaster unless it was withdrawn to the north side of the Rappahannock. Lincoln still held some hope that the journalist was exaggerating the seriousness of the repulse and replied with a melancholy smile, "I hope it is not so bad as all that." However, as official dispatches were transmitted from Falmouth, Lincoln and his advisers began to realize that the battle of Fredericksburg had been one of the most one-sided defeats of the war.

As details of the defeat began to become common knowledge in the North, frustrated legislators, editors, and citizens reacted with shock and horror. The *Chicago Tribune* called the period after the battle the darkest of the war, and insisted "fail-

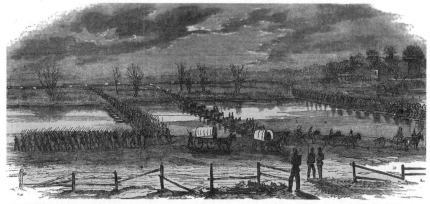

William Franklin's division recrosses the Rappahannock as part of the Union withdrawal from Fredericksburg.

ure of the army, weighty taxes, depreciation of money, want of cotton, increasing national debt, deaths in the army, no prospect of success, the continued closure of the Mississippi, all combine to produce the existing state of despondency and desperation." A Republican congressman insisted, "it really seems as though the ship of state is going to pieces in the storm," while another member of the legislature believed "the war is drawing toward a disastrous and disgraceful determination."

Since the Lincoln administration was ultimately responsible for the conduct of the war, almost every senior official connected with the White House was subjected to intense criticism. Secretary of State William Seward was denounced by one editor as "Lincoln's evil genius who has kept a sponge saturated with chloroform to Uncle Abe's nose." Edwin Stanton, the secretary of war, was pictured as "a middling murderous quack, who has uselessly sacrificed the nation's sons and brothers." Henry Halleck, commanding general of the Union army, was characterized by one newspaper as "chief of imbeciles, fit only to lead a group of generals who are the most brainless, inert set that ever the world saw." Even Secretary of the Navy Gideon Welles, who had little responsibility for the Fredericksburg campaign, was pictured as a senile old fogey with no original ideas. As one senator insisted sarcastically, "he is now examining a model of Noah's Ark with a view to its introduction into the United States Navy." A significant number of Northerners concluded that if Abraham Lincoln was responsible for the appointment of these incompetents, the president himself was incapable of prosecuting the war. A Republican senator from Michigan insisted "the president is a weak man, too weak for the occasion, and these fool or traitor generals are wasting time and yet more precious blood." Another Republican politician noted "a year ago we laughed at Honest Old Abe's grotesque genial Western jocosities, but they nauseate us now." As criticism of his war policies and the upcoming Emancipation Proclamation emerged from Republicans and Democrats alike, Lincoln admitted that it was possible that the war was lost. He explained to one longtime friend "we are now on the brink of destruction. It appears to me the Almighty is against us and I can hardly see a ray of hope." As he reviewed the long list of casualties suffered for absolutely no gain, he remarked to one adviser "if there is a worse place than hell, I am in it."

At the same time that the Lincoln administration was being lambasted for its part in the Fredericksburg disaster, the senior generals of the *Army of the Potomac* were hardly immune from the wrath of Congress and the public. The daughter of a United States senator insisted that it was almost ludicrous that a man of Burnside's limited talents could be placed in command of the largest army in the history of the republic. "His attacks were purest folly, an action that none but mad men would have attempted. Anybody would see that the enemy could make themselves impregnable except by an army able to surround them." A New Yorker echoed these sentiments by explaining that "any man with plain farmer's common sense would have seen when the first assault was made, and indeed, before the assault was made, that any attempt to break the enemy's line at that point and gain the fortified crest beyond was utterly hopeless."

While a substantial number of Northern civilians viewed the commander of the *Army of the Potomac* as the main culprit for the disaster at Fredericksburg, opinion in the officer corps of the army was more mixed. General Abner Doubleday targeted *Grand Division* commander William Franklin for his harshest criticism, charging that the general, with 55,000 men at his disposal did nothing but look on and witness the failure of Meade's desperate charge up Prospect Hill. Colonel Charles Wainright, an artillery officer in *I Corps*, charged that Franklin had basically wasted half of the *Army of the Potomac* "to make a mere demonstration," instead of seriously challenging Stonewall Jackson. Some officers insisted that Joe Hooker had done little to retrieve the situation in front of Marye's Heights because of his hatred of Burnside. Others felt that Sumner had been too far removed from the battle to exert any real influence on the outcome. However, while there was a wide spectrum of opinion regarding the person most responsible for the outcome, almost every Northerner could agree on one thing—the battle of Fredericksburg had been an embarrassing one-sided disaster that just might have been the catalyst in permanently separating the two halves of the divided nation.

This impression that the war was about to reach a climax with a settlement that recognized Confederate independence was shared by many Southerners. The *Richmond Examiner* proclaimed Fredericksburg as "a stunning defeat to the invader, a splendid victory in the defense of the sacred soil." The *Charleston Mercury* noted that "General Lee knows his business and the army has yet known such a word as fail." The *Richmond Dispatch* went even further when it called the battle of Fredericksburg "the greatest battle every fought on this continent" in which Lee's defeat of "an imposing host of Yankees demonstrated that no superiority of numbers or of preparation can avail them in a pitched battle with the forces of the Confederacy, a truth so potent that we believe they are the only people on earth who venture to deny it." Southern newspapers began to compete with one another to predict the length of time it would take for an armistice to be requested by the Yankees. The *Daily Examiner* insisted that "the battle of Fredericksburg has paralyzed and shattered Lincoln's Grand Army and it will be the work of months to put it in a condition to resume offensive operations; even if it be capable of being renovated and reorganized which is exceedingly questionable. As the *Richmond Whig* insisted, the victory at Fredericksburg "makes the whole of Lincolndom reel like a drunken man" and it would be only a matter of time until the more realistic Northerners came to their senses and recognized Southern independence.

While Lincoln was comparing the situation after Fredericksburg to a term in hell, his Confederate counterpart was enjoying the adulation of many fellow Southerners. Jefferson Davis had been out of Richmond for much of the Fredericksburg campaign as he traveled to Tennessee to consult with the senior officers of Braxton Bragg's western army. The exasperating interaction with Bragg and the other prickly generals of the Army of Tennessee was soon more than compensated for by the thrilling news of the victory in Virginia. As the president gradually made his way back to the Confederate capital, he was saluted, serenaded, and badgered to give speech after speech concerning the seemingly bright future of the Confederacy. In one address that was typical of his thoughts at this time, he told cheering Southerners that the Yankees were the "scourings of the earth" and an adversary that was both cowardly and barbaric. He joked that the earlier cry of many Northerners of "On to Richmond" had been answered for many of them; they were now in Richmond as prisoners of war! He emphasized that the combinations of the defeat at Fredericksburg and the impending Emancipation Proclamation was turning many midwesterners against the Yankee cause. The result would be the disintegration of the existing Union and the end of the war, and then "for us, future peace and prosperity."

As the bloody year of 1862 came to an end, it appeared that Lincoln's pessimism and Davis's optimism were entirely justified. The *Army of the Potomac* had still failed to win a clear-cut victory over its adversary and many Northerners were sick of a war that seemed to have no end in sight. However, the disaster that was the Fredericksburg campaign was not quite over, and Ambrose Burnside would still receive one more final humiliation before the reins of power in the huge Union army changed hands yet again.

Ambrose Burnside After Fredericksburg

While Burnside's removal as commanding general of the *Army of the Potomac* ended the most dramatic episode in his army career, the Rhode Islander continued to serve in fairly important capacities for over a year longer. In March of 1863, Burnside was appointed commander of the Department of the Ohio where he attracted huge publicity for his arrest of Confederate sympathizer Clement Vallandigham and the pursuit and capture of Rebel cavalry leader John Hunt Morgan during his spectacular raid into Ohio. Late in 1863 Burnside directed a successful defense of Knoxville, Tennessee, against his old antagonist James Longstreet, and organized a one-sided Union victory over the Rebels at the battle of Fort Sanders.

When Ulysses Grant assumed command of all Union armies in the spring of 1864, Burnside was brought east to resume command of *IX Corps* which operated independent of, but in concert with, the *Army of the Potomac*, during the Overland campaign from Wilderness to Petersburg. While Burnside performed competently during this period, his career was almost destroyed by the debacle that was called the Battle of the Crater. The corps commander was at least partially responsible for bungling the attempt to demolish the Confederate defenses at Petersburg with an underground explosion. When over 4,000 bluecoats were lost in the botched follow-up assault, Grant sacked Burnside and exiled him to almost meaningless desk assignments.

Despite Burnside's mixed war record, he became a major celebrity in his adopted state of Rhode Island, and after the war he became a director of several railroads and was elected to the govenorship three times. In 1874 he was elected to the United States Senate and died in office in September of 1881.

George Gordon Meade (1815-1872)

One of the few successful Union generals during the battle of Fredericksburg was General George Meade who led the deepest penetration of the Confederate line. Meade was born in Cadiz, Spain, the son of an American diplomat and merchant. He received a secondary education at Mount Hope Academy in Baltimore and entered West Point in 1831. Four years later Meade graduated 18th in a class of 56 members but resigned shortly afterward to pursue a career in civil engineering. Meade rejoined the army prior to the outbreak of the war with Mexico and served under Zachary Taylor at Palo Alto, Resaca de la Palma, and Monterrey, but apparently was not engaged in enough high profile responsibilities to substantially aid his career after the war. He spent most of the decade before the Civil War engaged in mundane engineering duties, and at the time of Fort Sumter was still only a captain in the regular army.

The Meade family's influence in the state of Pennsylvania prompted Governor Andrew Curtin to appoint the middle-aged captain as a brigadier general in command of one of the Keystone State's first volunteer units. The new general led his unit with distinction during the Virginia

Peninsula campaign and was severely wounded at the battle of Glendale. He recovered in time to play a major role in the battle of Second Bull Run which won him command of a division. During the subsequent battle of Antietam, Meade took temporary command of *I Corps* when Joseph Hooker was wounded and soon after received a promotion to major general.

While Meade reverted to division command for the Fredericksburg campaign, the relative success of his unit during the battle opened up new opportunities for promotion and the Pennsylvanian's career rise was dramatic. After Burnside's removal, Hooker named Meade commander of *V Corps* for the Chancellorsville campaign and then when "Fighting Joe" himself resigned in late June of 1863 the new corps commander suddenly found himself leading the entire *Army of the Potomac*. This was the most dramatic moment of Meade's career as the Confederate army had penetrated well into Pennsylvania, and only hours after assuming command the first act of the battle of Gettysburg was developing. The new commanding general was intelligent enough to accept Winfield Hancock's suggestion to fight the battle in the hills of the Pennsylvania town rather than pulling the Union army back to the Pipe Creek position that Meade initially favored. The Federal general thus orchestrated one of the most decisive victories in American history and became a national hero. However, Abraham Lincoln insisted that Meade had squandered an opportunity to annihilate Lee's army and when the first lieutenant general commission since George Washington's was handed out in 1864, it was Ulysses S. Grant who received the rank.

When Grant established his new headquarters with the *Army of the Potomac* in the spring of 1864, Meade assumed that the new senior general would appoint a fellow Westerner to command the Union's largest army. However, Grant kept the Pennsylvanian in the post, and despite their very different personalities, the two men worked fairly well together. Meade essentially spent the rest of the war as Grant's executive officer but he still influenced the senior general's strategic planning at a number of points in the final campaign of the war and was in command of the *Army of the Potomac* at Lee's final surrender.

After the Civil War, Meade commanded the Third Military District of Alabama, Georgia, and Florida, and won the respect of the many Southerners due to his fairness in Reconstruction activities. In 1869, Meade was named commander of the Military Division of the East but he had never fully recovered from his old Glendale wound and his health deteriorated until his death in November of 1872. At his death George Meade was considered one of the most highly respected, intelligent generals in either army and his name would forever be linked with the victory at Gettysburg.

CHAPTER XI

Burnside's Final Gamble

On January 1, 1863, the men of the *Army of the Potomac* and the Army of Northern Virginia welcomed the new year in very different frames of mind. This particular Thursday was a clear, crisp, frosty day on both sides of the Rappahannock River, but the sunny weather far more reflected the moods of the Rebel soldiers than their Yankee counterparts. On the south side of the river, Robert E. Lee spent much of the morning completing the paperwork that would emancipate the slaves that had come into his possession as part of his father-in-law's estate. Then the Virginian composed a congratulatory message to the men of his army which lauded their conduct during the battle of Fredericksburg but reminded them that Confederate victory was not yet a certainty.

> The war is not yet ended, the enemy is numerous and strong and the country demands of the army a renewal of the heroic efforts in her behalf. The signal manufacturers of Divine Mercy that had distinguished the eventful and glorious campaigns of the year just closing give assurances of hope that under the guidance of the same almighty hand, the coming year will be no less fruitful of events that will insure the safety, peace and happiness of our beloved country and add new luster to the already imperishable name of the Army of Northern Virginia.

The morale of the Confederacy's largest army was now at one of its highest points of the war and General Lee himself was quietly enthusiastic about the future direction of the conflict. The new corps and divisional organizations that he had put into place during the autumn seemed to be working out well as most of the divisional commanders appeared to perform their duties with enthusiasm and competence while James Longstreet and Stonewall Jackson were rapidly emerging as a seemingly unbeatable tandem of corps commanders. J.E.B. Stuart's cavalry had dramatically outclassed their Yankee counterparts and even the often outgunned Confederate artillery arm had enjoyed perhaps its best day of the war on the heights above Fredericksburg. A captain in a Georgia regiment perhaps best summarized the feelings of the men of the Rebel army as the new year began: "This army can never be whipped by all the power of Yankeedom combined and I now predict that the treaty of peace, when made, be it soon or later, will find it victorious." General James Archer, who had played a major role in repulsing the Union assault on Prospect Hill, insisted that "the prospects I think, look bright for peace since the battle of Fredericksburg and since the Democrats at the North have found their tongues." General Elisha Paxton of the legendary Stonewall Brigade was even more enthusiastic in his outlook as he noted "our independence was secured in the last campaign when we proved our capacity to beat the finest army they could bring in the field." Perhaps the most cautious person in the Army of Northern Virginia on this first day of 1863 was Robert E. Lee himself. While the commanding general exuded confidence that he could continue to outduel almost any Federal host that was thrown against him, he was also aware of the fact that the Yankees, as fellow Americans, would be just as full of courage, self-sacrifice, and enthusiasm as his own men, and that many of the people in the North were as determined to bring the seceded states back into the Union as the residents of Dixie were determined to set up their own independent nation.

Lee's insistence that the war was far from over may have been energetically disputed by thousands of his blue-coated adversaries on this New Year's Day. Throughout the Federal camps on the north bank of the Rappahannock, large numbers of Union soldiers were convinced that the war was as good as lost and that Ambrose Burnside's days as the army's commander were now limited in number. An officer in a New Jersey regiment explained to a friend at home that the disaster at Fredericksburg would almost certainly ensure Southern independence before the coming year was over. "The memory of our defeat throws a gloom over the camp. We look to a retreat to the Potomac line." A New Hampshire private suggested that "the battle has depressed the spirit, crushed the hopes and destroyed the effective power of the regiment." Union General Alpheus Williams reluctantly admitted that "the disaster at Fredericksburg affects us all deeply. I am as discouraged and blue as one well can be and I see in these operations much that astounds and confounds me and much that must discourage our troops and the people."

The men in the *Army of the Potomac* who marked the beginning of the new year were hard pressed to find anything to celebrate at the onset of 1863. The previous year had produced little enough to lift their spirits: a confused campaign around the Virginia Peninsula; an embarrassing rout at Second Bull Run; a wasted opportunity at Antietam; and finally, the disaster at Fredericksburg. Now, as their increasingly unpopular commander seemed to be groping to find some way to defeat a seemingly unbeatable Confederate army, the physical and psychological condition of the Union army was rapidly sinking to its lowest point of the war. Ambrose Burnside had become so preoccupied with developing new strategies that the men of the *Army of the Potomac* found themselves short of food, short of warm clothing, and, perhaps most frustrating, without money.

As conditions in the Union camps degenerated, more and more Federal soldiers directed their hostility toward Burnside and a number of his subordinates. Major Rufus Dawes explained to his wife that the huge Yankee army was unraveling because "this army seems to be overburdened with second rate men in high positions, common place and whiskey are too much in power for the most hopeful future." A private in a Pennsylvania regiment insisted that "it is about time something was done to relieve us if not of duty, then at least of our commanders." A journalist interviewing enlisted men and junior officers around the start of the new year was shocked at the speed in which morale was plummeting in the Federal army and the blatant lack of confidence in Burnside's leadership. He noted that "neither officers nor men have the slightest confidence in him" while insisting that if McClellan was ever restored to command "the soldiers would go crazy with joy."

During much of January of 1863 Ambrose Burnside seemed largely oblivious to the low esteem in which he was held by his men as he focused most of his energies on the twin challenges of generating plans for a renewed offensive and uncovering plots among senior officers to erode his authority with the army. These two activities soon became very interrelated when a series of end runs by his subordinates significantly affected the operations of the *Army of the Potomac*. The first attempt to circumvent Burnside's authority occurred when Generals William Franklin and William "Baldy" Smith sent Lincoln a long dispatch proposing a return to George McClellan's old strategy of attacking Richmond from the direction of the Virginia Peninsula. Both of these generals insisted that any attempt to attack the Rebels from the Rappahannock River was a strategic dead end as Lee could rapidly shift units to counter any Federal threat. Therefore, Franklin and Smith proposed concentrating virtually every Union unit in the region, including most of the Washington garrison, and moving a huge army of 250,000 men along both sides of the James River where the Federals could overwhelm any Confederate force that dared to challenge the advance. While Lincoln refused to authorize the plan because it would open the Federal capital to capture, he set a significant precedent by welcoming any other strategic ideas the generals might propose. This response was hardly a vote of confidence for Burnside's continued leadership.

While two of his senior subordinates were sending their proposals to the White House, the commander of the *Army of the Potomac* prepared to initiate a new winter offensive. Burnside had decided to push an assault force across the Rappahannock near the Seddon mansion, about seven miles downstream from Fredericksburg, and then strike the extreme right flank of the Confederate army in a massive east to west attack. Meanwhile, in order to confuse Lee as to his real intentions, the Union general planned a large scale cavalry raid across Kelly's Ford, 25 miles upstream from Falmouth. Burnside hoped that his adversary would focus on this developing threat to his left flank long enough to allow the Federals to overrun Prospect Hill from the east and then smash into Marye's Heights from its more vulnerable flank. However, just as the Rhode Islander was about to issue the orders for the new offensive, he received a cryptic directive from Lincoln stating, "I have good reason for saying you must not make a general movement of the army without letting me know," a message that essentially cancelled the operation before it actually began. Burnside did not realize it at the time, but two more of his generals had been in contact with the president and had convinced Lincoln that this latest offensive would lead to a worse disaster than Fredericksburg.

Lincoln's preemptive cancellation of the new thrust across the Rappahannock was the result of a personal interview with Generals John Newton and John Cochrane. Soon after the battle of Fredericksburg this division commander and brigade leader had begun meeting with William Franklin and "Baldy" Smith to discuss the apparent unraveling of the *Army of the Potomac*. General Newton finally proposed to his two superiors to take a leave of absence from the army and present the generals's concerns directly to members of Congress. Cochrane quickly agreed to accompany Newton to Washington and suggested using his own connections through his career in New York politics to secure access to key government officials. Soon after the two generals arrived in the capital, they secured an appointment with the president and they insisted to Lincoln that "if a crossing of the Rappahannock is attempted, and it should be unsuccessful for any reason, the influence of the disaster upon the cause of the whole country would be ruin-

Better as a military theorist and organizer than a battlefield commander, Henry Halleck exercised command of the Union armies from Washington. After being replaced by Grant, who valued his administrative ability, he agreed to stay on in the capital in a lesser post.

ous." Cochrane emphasized to the commander in chief that "to have withheld from you these facts I should not have ranked it any criminal grade below treason." Rather than insisting that these officers had circumvented the normal chain of command in their army, Lincoln responded warmly, "Generals, much good will come from this," and a short time later a telegram was on its way to Burnside ordering a postponement of the new offensive.

Ambrose Burnside had no idea that someone was interfering with his relationship with the president, but he quickly boarded a northbound train and was soon closeted in the White House with Lincoln, Halleck, and Stanton, determined to force the issue of the strategic prerogatives of the commander of the *Army of the Potomac*. The general arrived in the Oval Office carrying two documents, a revised plan for a general offensive and a letter of resignation from command of the army. Burnside was determined to make the president choose to either support his new operation or entrust responsibility for the army to someone else. By this point in the war, Lincoln had a drawer filled with resignation letters from generals and cabinet members and, for the moment, he simply tabled

Burnside's letter without comment and proceeded to the discussion of the general's plans for a new offensive. Stanton and Halleck took turns waffling on the Rhode Islander's new plan for a massive crossing of the Rappahannock upstream from Fredericksburg and neither man would either approve or disapprove of the operation. After an afternoon of unproductive haggling, the meeting broke up, and Lincoln asked Burnside to return to his hotel and wait for further orders.

The next morning the rough-whiskered general received a rejection of his resignation and a very tepid note of confidence from the president. Lincoln informed his commander that "I do not yet see how I could profit by changing command of the Army of the Potomac and if I did, I should not wish to do it by accepting the resignation of your commission." This less than ringing endorsement was concluded with a promise that a decision would be made shortly concerning Burnside's new plan. At almost the same time that the president rejected Burnside's offer to quit, he added another letter of resignation to his growing collection. Soon after the White House meeting with Burnside, Stanton, and Halleck, Lincoln sent his senior general a specific request. He asked Halleck to travel to Falmouth and evaluate Burnside's proposed plan on the spot. After he had gone over the ground and interviewed senior commanders, "Old Brains" was expected to "tell General Burnside that you do approve or that you do not approve his plan." Lincoln finished his letter with a rather harsh comment to Halleck that "your military skill is useless to me if you will not do this," and the highly sensitive senior general responded with an almost predictable letter of resignation. The president had no desire to lose the services of a general who was considered the most intelligent man in the army and Lincoln quickly backpedaled and cancelled the "request" for a personal inspection. Almost by default, Burnside's latest gamble was given tacit approval by the leadership in Washington.

The operation that neither Abraham Lincoln, Edwin Stanton, or Henry Halleck could enthusiastically support was a general movement of the *Army of the Potomac* upstream from

Falmouth toward Banks' Ford and United States Ford, respectively four miles and ten miles above Fredericksburg. A strong diversionary force would simulate preparations for a crossing downstream at Muddy Creek near the Seddon house. However, even as Burnside was finishing the last details of the operational plan, Union scouts reported to him that Lee had suspected an imminent attack in that general direction and had deployed significant forces at United States Ford; although Banks' Ford still seemed to be relatively unguarded. Burnside countered with a revised plan in which one diversionary force would feint at United States Ford while another diversion would be created across from the Seddon house. While Lee focused on the apparent threats to his line at United States Ford and Muddy Creek, Hooker's *Center Grand Division* would cross the Rappahannock just above Banks' Ford and William Franklin's men would cross just below the ford. If all went well, Union troops would be able to seize the high ground on the south bank of the river and use that position as a springboard for an advance on the vital Orange Plank Road. Once the Federals straddled that avenue, Lee would be forced to either fight the Union army on unfavorable ground or retreat in the direction of Richmond. Either move would provide the possibility of a significant Union victory, as Burnside was now determined to concentrate every available blue-coated soldier for the operation. Not only would every unit of the three main *Grand Divisions* be put into action, but Burnside now had brought up Franz Sigel's *Reserve Grand Division* to push his effective fighting force to over 150,000 men. If this huge army could engage the enemy on even moderately favorable terrain, it seemed likely to win an impressive victory.

Ambrose Burnside's operational plan was not without some merit, if it had been put into force in May instead of January. A general offensive in Virginia in winter invited two monumental drawbacks. First, the road and weather conditions in the Old Dominion in January were simply dreadful. Virginia might be part of the "sunny South" much of the year, but for two or three months in winter alternating freezes and torrential rains made for appalling campaigning conditions.

As with other unsuccessful Northern commanders, Franz Sigel was surprisingly popular during the Civil War, primarily due to his ability to rally large numbers of German immigrants to the Union cause.

Second, most of the men of the *Army of the Potomac* absolutely despised winter campaigns, and whenever they were attempted, morale plummeted. These soldiers were conditioned to operate in a campaigning season that ran from April through October, with the expectation that if decisive results were not obtained during that time period, the issue would simply be delayed until next spring. Yankee troops, in an opinion largely shared by their Rebel counterparts, generally expected their generals to have enough good sense to avoid campaigning in winter, thus permitting the men to establish reasonably comfortable winter camps for the duration of poor weather periods. Ambrose Burnside had already provoked harsh feelings from his men in the December debacle in Fredericksburg; now the prospect of campaigning in the even worse weather of January seemed almost unthinkable. The Rhode Islander had not only reduced the *Army of the Potomac* to its poorest physical state of the war, now he was about to send that army into one of the most humiliating operations in its history.

On Monday afternoon, January 19, the men of the *Army of the Potomac* began receiving orders to break camp for a march upstream toward Banks' Ford. The response in most of the units ranged from stunned silence to open derision at the operation. A captain in a Massachusetts regiment recalled that "the utmost dissatisfaction and almost insubordination was shown at the prospect of an attack." Large numbers of men in several regiments openly insisted that they would refuse to cross the Rappahannock again, while the ranks of the *42nd New York* openly hooted at Burnside's name and the troops of the *15th Massachusetts* cheered for Jefferson Davis. In one of the most dramatic mass desertions of the *Army of the Potomac*, the entire 315-man picket detachment of the *III Corps* deserted Monday night, leaving only their abandoned rifles sticking in the muddy ground. One regimental commander admitted that "every one seems to feel it is a hopeless task to try to dislodge the enemy from their works," and when the Unionists broke camp late on Tuesday morning "under threatening weather with a chilly wind blowing from the east," the mood of the army was as sullen as the skies above them.

Even as the Union army lurched upstream under leaden skies, Burnside's adversary was busy taking steps to ensure that the Yankee operation could be checkmated. Lee's spies and scouts quickly informed him of the new Federal offensive and the Virginian quickly rushed reinforcements to Kelly's Ford, Banks' Ford, and Rappahannock Station. George Pickett's division was shifted to the high ground around Salem Church, a position that Burnside expected Hooker to occupy in order to sweep against the Rebel flank. Confederate engineers plowed the ground near possible Union crossing points to facilitate the formation of muddy bogs, a commodity that would soon be in abundance naturally. By Tuesday morning Lee was feeling increasingly confident that he could inflict a stupendous defeat on Burnside's army as it attempted to unite on the south bank of the Rappahannock, and there was considerable hope among senior Confederate officers that this latest triumph would effectively end the war.

By sundown on Tuesday, most of Burnside's army was anywhere from four to eight miles north of the Falmouth camps, and as the march was halted, chilled bluecoats began seeking shelter in the woods as a light mix of rain and sleet began falling through the trees. As the temperature wavered between the freezing point and a degree or two above, the frigid drizzle gradually gained in intensity and the winds accelerated. The scene by Wednesday morning, January 21, was becoming grimmer by the moment as the Rappahannock region was subjected to a classic, "nor'easter" which produced blizzards in New England and pummeled the Old Dominion with a mix of icy rain and sleet. Most men considered these conditions about the most uncomfortable that a soldier could endure. The Unionists had no tents, no fires and, in many cases, little or no food. As one private lamented "our blankets were wet through and we found ourselves lying in a pool of ice cold water. No one got a wink of sleep and all in that cheerless wilderness of trees and mud agreed that it was the most tedious night we have ever passed." A New York officer agreed that "It was a dismal night in which enthusiasm was extinguished, in which courage was worn out, the will enfeebled and the mind stupefied."

As a wretched night gave way to a dreary day, thousands of men and hundreds of animals lurched forward toward the Rappahannock crossing points. The unbroken sea of oozing, icy mud quickly ensnared wagons, artillery caissons, and even

*The **Army of the Potomac** embarks on Burnside's infamous "Mud March." The standard-bearer at left carries colors cased against the elements. The boat-like object at right is a pontoon.*

horses. Mules drowned by the score in mud holes while hundreds of soaked, freezing soldiers were pressed into service to drag by hand the pontoon boats that would be used to span the river. As one Union general commented sarcastically, "I don't know how the world's surface looked after the flood in Noah's time, but I am certain it could not have appeared more saturated than does the present surface of the Old Dominion."

While Ambrose Burnside, himself covered with mud, rode up and down the lines exhorting his men to move forward, the Unionists were subjected to ridicule and humiliation from their adversaries on the south bank of the river. Rebel soldiers perched in trees along the Rappahannock and taunted the Yankees to come across after them. Crude signs began to appear along the river bank with arrows pointing in the direction of the Confederate capital and notations of "This way to Richmond!" Other signs taunted "Burnside stuck in the mud of the sacred soil," while Confederate soldiers sarcastically offered to help the Union engineers complete the pontoon bridges so that the "invincible" Federal army could cross to the south side to offer battle. Just as the hoots and jeers reached a crescendo, the spectacle of what was rapidly being called the "Mud March" reached a new low point.

As he watched the mood of his men become increasingly sullen, Ambrose Burnside made an ill-timed gesture to perk up the morale of the troops. A generous ration of whiskey was issued to each regiment and soon large numbers of both enlisted men and officers were staggering around in the mud, oblivious of the conditions around them. As the dole of spirits kept increasing, more and more fights began breaking out in the line of march, and by late afternoon the brawls were so widespread that Rebel soldiers on the south bank were cheering the unexpected entertainment of watching enemy soldiers pummeling one another.

By Thursday morning, even Ambrose Burnside was compelled to admit that the planned operation had turned into a fiasco, and regiment after regiment of humiliated, frozen soldiers staggered back toward their camps. Hundreds of soldiers decided that this was an excellent time to leave the war behind, and individuals and groups of men simply bolted out of the line of march and headed home, considering the war against secession largely over. As the men lurched back toward Falmouth, additional rations of whiskey were issued and large segments of the army threatened to become armed mobs. A provost marshal responsible for security arrangements on the route back to Falmouth was shocked at the unraveling of discipline in the Union army.

> There were thousands of stragglers, without any organization and completely demoralized. Where I was on a picket, there was a small station and depot of supplies for the army; there was lots of whiskey in barrels and the heads were knocked in and the men helped themselves and drank it by the pint. Many of the men were drunk, staggering toward the camps and cursing Burnside and everybody else. It looked as though the enemy could have crossed the river at that time and captured the whole army.

The nightmare of the Mud March was largely over by the evening of January 25, 1863, but the harm done to Burnside's authority was far more permanent. The army commander was now being jeered openly and was the butt of numerous jokes. As one army surgeon admitted, "when we failed at Fredericksburg, the men were as willing as ever to try again under the same commander, but an army *must* have success." A regimental commander noted that in the wake of the Mud March, "the army will be a source of great trouble to the government if things go on this way very much longer; discipline in the old regiments is merely a name, and the new regiments are easily infected with the spirit of the old." General Alpheus Williams summarized the general mood toward the continued tenure of Ambrose Burnside as commander of the army when he wrote to a friend, "I think the commander has very little confidence in himself and the army generally reciprocates the feeling."

Burnside never seemed to fully appreciate the depth to

Joseph Hooker, shown here with his staff and several foreign observers, was selected to replace Ambrose Burnside after Fredericksburg. His battlefield performance at Chancellorsville was scarcely less disastrous than Burnside's, but his reorganization of the **Army of the Potomac** *helped pave the way for later victories.*

which his popularity had sunk among enlisted men after the Mud March, but he was quite aware that a number of his generals were openly plotting to secure his removal. Thus the Rhode Islander retaliated in the third week of January by writing out a series of orders that would effectively remove eight generals from command on the charge of "having been guilty of unjust and unnecessary criticism of the actions of superior officers and having by omission or otherwise made reports and statements speaking in disparaging terms of other officers." Because of these offenses two *Grand Division* commanders, Joe Hooker and William Franklin, corps commander William "Baldy" Smith, the two generals who had visited Lincoln, John Newton and John Cochrane, and three other brigade commanders were considered "unfit to hold an important commission during a crisis like the present" and were recommended for dismissal or transfer. The commanding general had copies of the order made by his staff and boarded a train to Washington to confront the president with a choice, implement the dismissals or accept Burnside's resignation.

Abraham Lincoln received his general politely and cordially when he arrived at the White House and carefully listened to Burnside's insistence that he could no longer tolerate the level of insubordination among his deputies that was unraveling the whole army. The president told the *Army of the Potomac* commander to return to Willard's Hotel while Lincoln and his advisers carefully considered his request. The chief executive admired Burnside's honesty, humility, and selfless devotion to duty, and he began to appreciate the fact that he had added to his general's problems by allowing subordinates to initiate end runs directly to the White House. However, several of the eight generals designated for removal had important political connections in the capital and their removal to placate a commander who had just suffered two humiliating setbacks would create havoc in Congress. At the moment, the most untouchable of the eight generals on the list was Joe Hooker, who had become very friendly with several members of Lincoln's cabinet and appeared to enthusiastically support the Emancipation Proclamation, a major asset for the Radical Republican wing of the party. The handsome, dynamic *Center Grand Division* commander had made it clear that he was confident that he could devise a plan that would break the stalemate on the Rappahannock and destroy Lee's army in a single campaign, a tantalizing offer in this season of gloom in Washington.

On the morning of January 25, Ambrose Burnside returned to the executive mansion and the general waited patiently in an antechamber while Lincoln, Stanton, and Halleck held a final meeting concerning command of the *Army of the Potomac.* Apparently both Stanton and Halleck agreed with Lincoln that Burnside should be removed, but some accounts insist that both men urged the president to appoint the victor of the recent bloody battle of Stones River, William S. Rosecrans, as the new head of the largest army in the North. However, the president believed that for reasons of politics and morale among the men, the choice of successor should be limited to someone already in a position of responsibility in the *Army of the Potomac.* William Franklin was immediately eliminated from contention since Lincoln planned to fire him for his role in the Fredericksburg fiasco; Edwin Sumner was regarded as reasonably competent but too old for the highest post. Ultimately, the choice seems to have come down to two men, John Reynolds and Joe Hooker. Reynolds was generally viewed as a solid, reliable potential commanding general, but apparently the Pennsylvanian had insisted that he would only take the job if he received a higher degree of independence of action than either McClellan or Burnside had experienced. This demand for a large degree of autonomy seemed to push Lincoln in the direction of Hooker, who was the darling of Secretary of the Treasury Salmon Chase and a number of powerful Congressional leaders. The president winced at Fighting Joe's call for the appointment of a "military dictator" to exert supreme authority until the war was won but admitted "he is stronger with the country today than any other man." Finally, Burnside was summoned into Lincoln's office and told that Sumner and Franklin were to be relieved of command and that Joe Hooker would replace him as commanding general of the *Army of the Potomac*. When the Rhode Islander offered to resign entirely from the Union army, the president emphasized that he needed Burnside's services in another theater and promptly offered him command of Federal forces in the Carolinas. The outgoing general finally agreed to accept a 30-day leave and then return to service in one of a variety of capacities that would be offered. Ambrose Burnside would go on to a decidedly mixed record of command during the next two years, but by nightfall of this cold winter day, the fate of the largest army in North America was in the hands of General Joseph Hooker and one of the most disastrous campaigns of the *Army of the Potomac* was officially over.

Conclusion

The battle of Fredericksburg was probably the largest scale battle in the entire Civil War and yet has been chronicled in less detail than battles involving substantially fewer men. One of the possible reasons for this relative neglect is the fact that the battle on the Rappahannock tends to be overshadowed by the preceding clash at Antietam and the following engagements at Chancellorsville and Gettysburg. In some respects each of these three battles was more dramatic and more in doubt, than the clash over the snowy fields of Fredericksburg. A large part of the struggle for Marye's Heights parallels the dreary bloodbaths at the Somme and Verdun a half century later and invites few tantalizing discussions of "what might have happened" if one element of the battle had developed differently. However, the Fredericksburg campaign still remains one of the most significant clashes of arms in the Civil War and there are at least two fascinating questions that can be profitably considered. First, was Ambrose Burnside really as incompetent as he is often portrayed? Second, was the Union defeat as disastrous as it seems?

The first major question, the level of incompetence exhibited by Ambrose Burnside, is more complex than it initially appears. In defense of Burnside, the Rhode Islander clearly warned his superiors in Washington that he did not believe that he was qualified to command the *Army of the Potomac*, as the general seemed to have a fairly clear concept of his own abilities and limitations. During those periods before and after the Fredericksburg campaign, in which Burnside commanded a division or corps, he proved to be an adequate, if far from brilliant, general who usually earned the respect of his officers and enlisted men. He exhibited a number of excellent qualities including honesty, humility, and certainly, a lack of self-delusion about his talents. Unfortunately, Lincoln chose Burnside to command the *Army of the Potomac* more for political than military reasons and the Union cause paid the price for this decision. Burnside responded to his new position with a campaign plan that had a tolerable chance of producing a modest success if the logistics of the operation fell into place properly. However, once the plan began to unravel, Burnside demonstrated very little willingness or ability to improvise and this failing led to disaster. Yet if Burnside was a completely incompetent general he might very well have lost the whole army, a situation that was not a strong possibility at any point in the campaign. Instead, the author believes that Burnside should occupy a particular niche in the pantheon of Union generals along with at least three of his colleagues, Benjamin Butler, Nathaniel Banks, and Joe Hooker. Each of these generals suffered at least one humiliating defeat at the hands of the Rebels and each has been branded as "incompetent" by several military analysts. However, none of these men actually lost an army under their command and at certain points contributed fairly significantly to Union success. Burnside's North Carolina expedition of 1862 and his defense of Knoxville in 1863 were modest but nonetheless heartening Federal successes on a par with Butler's securing the railroad lines between Washington and the North in the opening days of the war, Banks's capture of Port Hudson in 1863, and Hooker's successful assault on Lookout Mountain during the Chattanooga campaign of the same year. Ambrose Burnside was clearly enormously outgeneralled by Robert E. Lee during the Fredericksburg campaign but he seems to have been a general who still exhibited tangible, if modest, leadership skills.

The second relevant question in a consideration of the Fredericksburg campaign revolves around the issue of the actual level of defeat inflicted upon the Union cause during this 11-week period. At first glance Fredericksburg emerges as one of the most one-sided Confederate victories of the Civil War. The Union lost nearly three times as many men as the Rebels; the Confederate battle line was never on the verge of collapsing; the Federal army was forced into a humiliating retreat from its lines. The images of blue-coated soldiers flailing hopelessly against Marye's Heights and the stone wall would become symbols of Northern frustration and ineptitude both during and after the war. This was the last battle in which Robert E. Lee, James Longstreet, and Stonewall Jackson operated as a team for the entire engagement and they were clearly at the peak of their game. The people of the Confederacy would never again be able to celebrate a victory of the Army of Northern Virginia that was as clear-cut as the battle of Fredericksburg.

There is little doubt that in a tactical and psychological sense, Fredericksburg was a huge Confederate victory and a humiliating Federal defeat. However, in the enormously important arenas of foreign diplomacy and long-term strategy the battle was very much less than decisive. The Union defeat at Fredericksburg significantly helped the Confederate cause in two ways. The Yankee retreat ensured that there would be no serious attempt to renew operations in Virginia until the next spring, and the battle and the subsequent Mud March fiasco pushed the morale of the Federal army to one of its lowest points of the war. However, in most other areas, the Confederacy gained little in this victory. The attack at Fredericksburg cost the *Army of the Potomac* perhaps 5,000 men permanently lost to the army through either death or serious wounds. This was a fairly significant loss, but would hardly cripple an army that carried almost 200,000 men on its rolls and could continue to tap into a very large Northern population. Not only were these losses made good by the beginning of the Chancellorsville campaign, but the drooping morale of the army skyrocketed with the reforms put into place by Joe Hooker during the spring of 1863. Because of the need to detach much of Longstreet's command to attend to Federal threats to the south, Lee would actually face worse, not better, numerical odds when he confronted Hooker in May.

The victory at Fredericksburg did as little to aid in securing European recognition of the Confederacy as it accomplished in evening the numerical odds between the two armies. From the perspective of foreign diplomatic implications, the key

Confederate victory of 1862 was clearly Second Bull Run. The trouncing of John Pope's Union army on the old Manassas battlefield followed by Lee's invasion of Maryland pushed pro-Southern officials in Paris and London to demand recognition of the Confederacy as it marched toward obvious military victory. However when Lee pulled his decimated army back across the Potomac after Antietam the cry for Confederate recognition became more muffled. Fredericksburg renewed the hopes of Europeans who supported the Southern cause, but this military victory was trumped by the political ace of Lincoln's Emancipation Proclamation. The disaster at Fredericksburg was an embarrassment for the Union cause, but that cause itself had now become a crusade to free the slaves, and throughout the English countryside, the celebrations of this event made it clear to the leaders of Her Majesty's government that it would take much more than Confederate repulses of the attack on Marye's Heights to make it politically feasible to recognize the secessionists as a nation. Thus the battle that had been fought along the Rappahannock on December 13, 1862, would go into the history books as the largest clash of arms on the North American continent and would always be remembered for the sheer spectacle of the panorama of blue and gray soldiers engaged in grim combat on that short winter day. However, the main impact of the battle was to set the stage for the decisive campaign season of 1863, a duel of the titans that would doom the Confederacy to eventual defeat.

Guide for the Interested Reader

While the battle of Fredericksburg was one of the largest-scale confrontations on American soil, the campaign seems to be somewhat neglected in comparison to the battle of Antietam that preceded it and the battles of Chancellorsville and Gettysburg that followed. Readers can select from a number of narratives of these other engagements but this is not the case with Fredericksburg. The only readily available narrative focusing exclusively on this duel along the Rappahannock is Edward Stackpole's *The Fredericksburg Campaign* (Mechanicsburg, 1957). General Stackpole's work is highly readable and draws upon the author's military background in World War I and World War II, but tends to be a bit simplistic in its treatment of Union and Confederate strategy. Burnside is presented as far more dull minded and unimaginative than he actually appears to have been, and there is very little treatment of what advantages might have been gained for the Union if the new commander's strategy had actually succeeded.

Stackpole's book is the only major work that focuses exclusively on a chronicle of the battle of Fredericksburg, but two volumes written more than a century apart consider the engagement in tandem with another action. Union army colonel Francis Palfrey wrote *Antietam and Fredericksburg* in 1882 while Daniel Sutherland completed *Fredericksburg and Chancellorsville: The Dare Mark Campaign* in 1998. Each of these works provides valuable insights into the Fredericksburg campaign but that battle is less prominently discussed than the other engagement that is included. A more multifaceted view of the battle is provided by Gary Gallagher's anthology *The*

Fredericksburg Campaign: Decision on the Rappahannock (Chapel Hill, 1995). Seven scholars treat such varied topics as Confederate leadership, the impact of the battle on civilians, and the aftermath of the engagement.

The relatively slim collection of books focusing extensively on Fredericksburg can be supplemented by reference to the many biographies and personal memoirs concerning major figures who participated in the battle. Ambrose Burnside's life is chronicled in two very different biographies, Benjamin Perley Poore's *Life of Burnside* (New York, 1882) and William Marvel's *Burnside* (Chapel Hill: 1991). Both of these works provide valuable insight into the Union commander's background and mindset but do not provide as comprehensive a view of Burnside's activities on the day of the battle as might be hoped. Douglas Southall Freeman's *R. E. Lee* (New York: 1934) provides excellent information on the Virginian's strategic concerns but is also somewhat spotty in chronicling the general's activities on the day of the battle.

The impact of senior lieutenants on the conduct of the battle is far better developed from a Southern perspective than a Northern one. Freeman's *Lee's Lieutenant's* (New York: 1943), Lenoir Chambers's *Stonewall Jackson* (New York: 1997), William Piston's *Lee's Tarnished Lieutenant* (Athens, GA: 1987), and Jeffrey West's *General James Longstreet: The Confederacy's Most Controversial Soldier* (New York: 1993) all provide excellent accounts of command of the left and right wings of the Confederate line at the battle. On the other hand, little has been written concerning the lives of either Edwin Sumner or William Franklin and even Walter Hebert's *Fighting Joe Hooker* (New York: 1944) is more concerned with Hooker's previous and subsequent battles than his role at Fredericksburg. Readers must make do with relatively brief accounts of mid-level commanders such as in Glenn Tucker's *Hancock the Superb* (New York, 1960) and Freeman Cleeves's *Meade of Gettysburg* (Norman, OK, 1960).

The advantage of personal memoirs is also on the side of the Confederacy. Longstreet's *From Manassas to Appomattox* (Philadelphia, 1896) provides excellent coverage of the battle for Marye's Heights, while Jubal Early's *Memoirs* give an excellent insight into action on Stonewall Jackson's flank. E. Porter Alexander's *Military Memoirs of a Confederate* (Chapel Hill, 1989) and *Fighting for the Confederacy* (Chapel Hill, 1990) present two of the most balanced accounts of the battle. Since neither of the two best Union memoir writers, Ulysses S. Grant and William T. Sherman participated in the battle, the best first person accounts by Federals are in Robert Underwood Johnson and Clarence Clough Buell's *Battles and Leaders of the Civil War* (New York, 1885) which includes General Darius Couch's "Sumner's Right Grand Division" and General William F. Smith's "Franklin's Left Grand Division."

A number of books that include discussions of particular aspects of the battle of Fredericksburg merit consideration. Benjamin W. Bacon's *Sinews of War* (Novato, CA, 1997), provides an excellent account of the fiasco surrounding the delivery of the Union pontoons. Joseph G. Bilby's *The Irish Brigade in the Civil War* (Conshohocken, PA, 1997) focuses on the gallant but futile exploits of the Irish regiments against Marye's Heights. Herman Hattaway and Archer Jones's *How the North Won* (Champagne, IL 1991) discusses the Fredericksburg campaign in connection with the other Union winter offensives of 1862-63.

Just as Fredericksburg has attracted far fewer nonfiction accounts than Antietam, Chancellorsville, and Gettysburg, the battle tends to be under-represented in other media formats. Jeff Shaara provides one of the best chronicles of the battle in his historical novel *Gods and Generals* the best-selling prequel to his father's *Killer Angels*. Military novelist Harold Coyle provides a very readable account of the battle from the perspective of two brothers serving on opposing sides in *Look Away*. The Arts and Entertainment network's award winning *Civil War Journal* includes an excellent visual chronicle of the battle in one of the best episodes of the series.

Orders of Battle

UNION ARMY

ARMY OF THE POTOMAC (Present for duty, 116,683 men)
Major General Ambrose E. Burnside

RIGHT GRAND DIVISION
Major General Edwin V. Sumner
II CORPS
Major General Darius N. Couch
  FIRST DIVISION
  Brigadier General Winfield S. Hancock
    FIRST BRIGADE
      (Killed – 108, Wounded – 729, Missing – 115 = 952 Casualties)
    Brigadier General John C. Caldwell (w)
    Colonel George W. Von Schack
      55th New Hampshire
      7th New York
      61st New York
      81st Pennsylvania
      145th Pennsylvania
    SECOND BRIGADE
      (Killed – 59, Wounded – 421, Missing – 74 = 554 Casualties)
    Brigadier General Thomas F. Meagher
      28th Massachusetts
      63rd New York
      69th New York
      88th New York
      116th Pennsylvania
    THIRD BRIGADE
      (Killed – 60, Wounded – 427, Missing – 90 = 577 Casualties)
    Colonel Samuel K. Zook
      27th Connecticut
      2nd Delaware
      52nd New York
      66th New York
      53rd Pennsylvania
    ARTILLERY
      (Killed – 1, Wounded – 4 = 5 Casualties)
      1st New York, Light Artillery Battery
      4th United States, Light Artillery Battery
  SECOND DIVISION
  Brigadier General Oliver O. Howard
    FIRST BRIGADE
      (Killed – 14, Wounded – 77, Missing – 31 = 122 Casualties)
    Brigadier General Alfred Sully

      19th Maine
      15th Massachusetts
      1st Minnesota
      34th New York
      82nd New York
      1st Company, Massachusetts Sharpshooters
      2nd Company, Minnesota Sharpshooters
SECOND BRIGADE
  (Killed – 27, Wounded – 203, Missing – 28 = 258 Casualties)
Colonel Joshua Owen
      69th Pennsylvania
      71st Pennsylvania
      72nd Pennsylvania
      106th Pennsylvania
THIRD BRIGADE
  (Killed – 63, Wounded – 419, Missing – 33 = 515 Casualties)
Colonel Norman Hall
      19th Massachusetts
      20th Massachusetts
      7th Michigan
      42nd New York
      59th New York
      127th Pennsylvania
ARTILLERY
  (Wounded – 18)
      Battery A, 1st Rhode Island Artillery
      Battery B, 1st Rhode Island Artillery

THIRD DIVISION
Brigadier General William H. French
  FIRST BRIGADE
    (Killed – 36, Wounded – 420, Missing – 64 = 520 Casualties)
  Brigadier General Nathan Kimball (w)
  Colonel John S. Mason
      14th Indiana
      24th New Jersey
      28th New Jersey
      4th Ohio
      8th Ohio
      7th West Virginia
  SECOND BRIGADE
    (Killed – 20, Wounded – 207, Missing – 64 = 291 Casualties)
  Colonel Oliver Palmer
      14th Connecticut
      108th New York
      130th Pennsylvania
  THIRD BRIGADE
    (Killed – 32, Wounded – 271, Missing – 39 = 342 Casualties)
  Colonel John Andrews

1st Delaware
4th New York
10th New York
132nd Pennsylvania
ARTILLERY
  (Killed – 1, Wounded – 7 = 8 casualties)
  1st New York, Battery G
  1st Rhode Island, Battery G
II CORPS ARTILLERY RESERVE
  (Wounded – 7)
  1st United States, Battery I
  4th United States, Battery A

IX CORPS
Brigadier General Orlando Willcox
FIRST DIVISION
Brigadier General William Burns
  FIRST BRIGADE
    (Killed – 1, Wounded – 12 = 13 Casualties)
  Colonel Orlando M. Poe
    2nd Michigan
    17th Michigan
    20th Michigan
    79th New York
  SECOND BRIGADE
    (Wounded – 7, Missing – 1 = 8 Casualties)
  Colonel Benjamin C. Christ
    29th Massachusetts
    8th Michigan
    27th New Jersey
    46th New York
    50th Pennsylvania
  THIRD BRIGADE
    (Wounded – 3)
  Colonel Daniel Leasure
    36th Massachusetts
    45th Pennsylvania
    100th Pennsylvania
  ARTILLERY
    (Wounded – 2, Missing – 1 = 3 Casualties)
    1st New York, Battery D
    3rd United States Battery L, M
SECOND DIVISION
Brigadier General Samuel D. Sturgis
  FIRST BRIGADE
    (Killed – 31, Wounded – 421, Missing – 48 = 500 Casualties)
  Brigadier General James Nagle
    2nd Maryland
    6th New Hampshire
    9th New Hampshire

48th Pennsylvania
7th Rhode Island
12th Rhode Island
SECOND BRIGADE
(Killed – 60, Wounded – 383, Missing – 38 = 481 Casualties)
Brigadier General Edward Ferrero
21st Massachusetts
35th Massachusetts
11th New Hampshire
51st New York
51st Pennsylvania
ARTILLERY
(Killed – 3, Wounded – 12 = 15 Casualties)
2nd New York, Battery L
1st Pennsylvania, Battery D
1st Rhode Island, Battery D
4th United States, Battery E
THIRD DIVISION
Brigadier General George W. Getty
FIRST BRIGADE
(Killed – 14, Wounded – 187, Missing – 54 = 255 Casualties)
Colonel Rush C. Hawkins
10th New Hampshire
13th New Hampshire
25th New Jersey
9th New York
89th New York
103rd New York
SECOND BRIGADE
(Killed – 2, Wounded – 29, Missing – 10 = 41 Casualties)
Colonel Edward Harland
8th Connecticut
11th Connecticut
15th Connecticut
16th Connecticut
21st Connecticut
4th Rhode Island
CAVALRY DIVISION OF RIGHT GRAND DIVISION
Brigadier General Alfred Pleasonton
FIRST BRIGADE
(No Reported Casualties)
Brigadier General John Farnsworth
8th Illinois
3rd Indiana
8th New York
SECOND BRIGADE
(No Reported Casualties)
Colonel David Gregg
6th New York

8th Pennsylvania
6th United States
ARTILLERY
2nd United States, Battery M

CENTER GRAND DIVISION
Major General Joseph Hooker
III CORPS
Brigadier General George Stoneman
FIRST DIVISION
Brigadier General David B. Birney
  FIRST BRIGADE
    (Killed – 14, Wounded – 106, Missing – 26 = 146 Casualties)
  Brigadier General John C. Robinson
    20th Indiana
    63rd Pennsylvania
    68th Pennsylvania
    105th Pennsylvania
    114th Pennsylvania
    141st Pennsylvania
  SECOND BRIGADE
    (Killed – 79, Wounded – 397, Missing – 153 = 629 Casualties)
  Brigadier General J. Hobart Ward
    3rd Maine
    4th Maine
    38th New York
    40th New York
    55th New York
    57th Pennsylvania
    99th Pennsylvania
  THIRD BRIGADE
    (Killed – 19, Wounded – 144, Missing – 2 = 165 Casualties)
  Colonel Hiram G. Berry
    17th Maine
    3rd Michigan
    5th Michigan
    1st New York
    37th New York
    101st New York
  ARTILLERY
    (Killed – 2, Wounded – 8 = 10 Casualties)
    1st Rhode Island, Battery E
    3rd United States, Battery F, K
SECOND DIVISION
Brigadier General Daniel E. Sickles
  FIRST BRIGADE
    (Killed – 11, Wounded – 68, Missing – 2 = 81 Casualties)
  Brigadier General Joseph B. Carr
    1st Massachusetts

    11th Massachusetts
    16th Massachusetts
    2nd New Hampshire
    11th New Jersey
    26th Pennsylvania
SECOND BRIGADE
(Wounded – 16)
Colonel George B. Hall
    70th New York
    71st New York
    72nd New York
    73rd New York
    74th New York
    120th New York
THIRD BRIGADE
(Killed – 1, Wounded – 1 = 2 Casualties)
Brigadier General Joseph Revere
    5th New Jersey
    6th New Jersey
    7th New Jersey
    8th New Jersey
    2nd New York
    115th Pennsylvania
ARTILLERY
(Missing – 1)
    1st United States, Battery H
    4th United States, Battery K
THIRD DIVISION
Brigadier General Amiel W. Whipple
  FIRST BRIGADE
  (Wounded – 3, Missing – 6 = 9 Casualties)
  Brigadier General Sanders Platt
    86th New York
    124th New York
    122nd Pennsylvania
  SECOND BRIGADE
  (Killed – 19, Wounded – 88, Missing – 11 = 118 Casualties)
  Colonel Samuel S. Carroll
    12th New Hampshire
    163rd New York
    84th Pennsylvania
    110th Pennsylvania
  ARTILLERY
  (Wounded – 1)
    1st Ohio, Battery H

V CORPS
Brigadier General Daniel Butterfield
  FIRST DIVISION
  Brigadier General Charles Griffin

FIRST BRIGADE
(Killed – 30, Wounded – 381, Missing – 89 = 500 Casualties)
Colonel James Barnes
    2nd Maine
    18th Massachusetts
    22nd Massachusetts
    1st Michigan
    13th New York
    25th New York
    118th Pennsylvania
    2nd Company, Massachusetts Sharpshooters
SECOND BRIGADE
(Killed – 23, Wounded – 193, Missing – 6 = 222 Casualties)
Colonel Jacob Sweitzer
    9th Massachusetts
    32nd Massachusetts
    4th Michigan
    14th New York
    62nd Pennsylvania
THIRD BRIGADE
(Killed – 18, Wounded – 158, Missing – 25 = 201 Casualties)
Colonel T. B. Stockton
    20th Maine
    16th Michigan
    12th New York
    17th New York
    44th New York
    83rd Pennsylvania
    Brady's Company, Michigan Sharpshooters
ARTILLERY
(Killed – 2, Wounded – 1 = 3 Casualties)
    1st Rhode Island, Battery C
    5th United States, Battery D
SHARPSHOOTERS
    1st United States Sharpshooters
SECOND DIVISION
Brigadier General George Sykes
    FIRST BRIGADE
    (Killed – 5, Wounded – 42, Missing – 4 = 51 Casualties)
    Lieutenant Colonel Robert C. Buchanan
        3rd United States
        4th United States
        12th United States
        14th United States
    SECOND BRIGADE
    (Killed – 12, Wounded – 114, Missing – 14 = 140 Casualties)
    Major George Andrews
        1st United States
        6th United States

      7th United States
      11th United States
      17th United States
      19th United States
   THIRD BRIGADE
   (Wounded – 6, Missing – 30 = 36 Casualties)
   Brigadier General Gouverneur K. Warren
      5th New York
      140th New York
      146th New York
   ARTILLERY
   (Wounded – 1)
      5th United States, Battery I
THIRD DIVISION
Brigadier General Andrew A. Humphreys
   FIRST BRIGADE
   (Killed – 52, Wounded – 321, Missing – 81 = 454 Casualties)
   Brigadier General Erastus B. Tyler
      91st Pennsylvania
      126th Pennsylvania
      129th Pennsylvania
      134th Pennsylvania
   SECOND BRIGADE
   (Killed – 63, Wounded – 448, Missing – 51 = 562 Casualties)
   Colonel Peter Allabach
      123rd Pennsylvania
      131st Pennsylvania
      133rd Pennsylvania
      155th Pennsylvania
   ARTILLERY
      1st New York, C Battery
      1st United States, E, G Batteries
   CAVALRY BRIGADE OF CENTER GRAND DIVISION
   Brigadier General William W. Averell
   (Brigade Loss, Killed – 1)
      1st Massachusetts
      3rd Pennsylvania
      4th Pennsylvania
      5th United States
   ARTILLERY
      2nd United States, Batteries B, L

LEFT GRAND DIVISION
Major General William Franklin
I CORPS
Major General John Reynolds
   FIRST DIVISION
   Brigadier General Abner Doubleday

FIRST BRIGADE
(Killed – 3, Wounded – 24, Missing – 3 = 30 Casualties)
Colonel Walter Phelps
22nd New York
24th New York
30th New York
84th New York
2nd United States Sharpshooters
SECOND BRIGADE
(Killed – 5, Wounded – 21 = 26 Casualties)
Colonel James Gavin
7th Indiana
76th New York
56th Pennsylvania
THIRD BRIGADE
(Killed – 10, Wounded – 54, Missing – 3 = 67 Casualties)
Colonel William F. Rogers
21st New York
23rd New York
35th New York
80th New York
FOURTH BRIGADE
(Killed – 9, Wounded – 40, Missing – 16 = 65 Casualties)
Brigadier General Solomon Meredith
19th Indiana
24th Michigan
2nd Wisconsin
7th Wisconsin
ARTILLERY
(Killed – 4, Wounded – 22 = 26 Casualties)
1st New York, Battery L
4th United States, Battery B
SECOND DIVISION
Brigadier General John Gibbon
FIRST BRIGADE
(Killed – 47, Wounded – 373, Missing – 55 = 475 Casualties)
Colonel Adrian Root
16th Maine
94th New York
104th New York
105th New York
107th Pennsylvania
SECOND BRIGADE
(Killed – 51, Wounded – 377, Missing – 32 = 460 Casualties)
Colonel Peter Lyle
12th Massachusetts
26th New York
90th Pennsylvania
136th Pennsylvania

THIRD BRIGADE
(Killed – 41, Wounded – 258, Missing – 15 = 314 Casualties)
Brigadier General Nelson Taylor
13th Massachusetts
83rd New York
97th New York
11th Pennsylvania
88th Pennsylvania
ARTILLERY
(Killed – 2, Wounded – 15 = 17 Casualties)
1st Pennsylvania, Batteries C, F
THIRD DIVISION
Major General George G. Meade
FIRST BRIGADE
(Killed – 47, Wounded – 386, Missing – 77 = 510 Casualties)
Colonel William Sinclair (w)
Colonel William McCandless
1st Pennsylvania Reserves
2nd Pennsylvania Reserves
6th Pennsylvania Reserves
13th Pennsylvania Reserves
121st Pennsylvania
SECOND BRIGADE
(Killed – 65, Wounded – 426, Missing – 141 = 632 Casualties)
Colonel Albert Magilton
3rd Pennsylvania Reserves
4th Pennsylvania Reserves
7th Pennsylvania Reserves
8th Pennsylvania Reserves
142nd Pennsylvania
THIRD BRIGADE
(Killed – 56, Wounded – 410, Missing – 215 = 681 Casualties)
Brigadier General C. Feger Jackson (k)
Colonel Joseph Fisher
5th Pennsylvania Reserves
9th Pennsylvania Reserves
10th Pennsylvania Reserves
11th Pennsylvania Reserves
12th Pennsylvania Reserves
ARTILLERY
(Killed – 7, Wounded – 19, Missing – 4 = 30 Casualties)
1st Pennsylvania, Batteries, A, B, G
5th United States, Battery C

VI CORPS
Major General William F. Smith
FIRST DIVISION
Brigadier General William T. Brooks
FIRST BRIGADE
(Killed – 18, Wounded – 94, Missing – 50 = 162 Casualties)

Colonel Alfred Torbert
 1st New Jersey
 2nd New Jersey
 3rd New Jersey
 4th New Jersey
 15th New Jersey
 23rd New Jersey
SECOND BRIGADE
(Killed – 4, Wounded – 13 = 17 Casualties)
Colonel Henry L. Cake
 5th Maine
 16th New York
 27th New York
 121st New York
 96th Pennsylvania
THIRD BRIGADE
(Wounded – 10)
Brigadier General David A. Russell
 18th New York
 31st New York
 95th Pennsylvania
SECOND DIVISION
Brigadier General Albion P. Howe
 FIRST BRIGADE
 (Wounded – 26, Missing – 3 = 29 Casualties)
 Brigadier General Calvin Pratt
  6th Maine
  43rd New York
  49th Pennsylvania
  119th Pennsylvania
  5th Wisconsin
 SECOND BRIGADE
 (Killed – 21, Wounded – 121, Missing – 2 = 144 Casualties)
 Colonel Henry Whiting
  26th New Jersey
  2nd Vermont
  4th Vermont
  5th Vermont
  6th Vermont
 THIRD BRIGADE
 (Killed – 1, Wounded – 14 = 15 Casualties)
 Brigadier General Francis L. Vinton (w)
 Colonel Robert F. Taylor
  21st New Jersey
  20th New York
  33rd New York
  59th New York
  77th New York

ARTILLERY
(Wounded – 1)
1st Maryland, Battery B
5th United States, Battery F
THIRD DIVISION
Brigadier General John Newton
FIRST BRIGADE
(Killed – 2, Wounded – 19, Missing – 3 = 24 Casualties)
Brigadier General John Cochrane
65th New York
67th New York
122nd New York
23rd Pennsylvania
82nd Pennsylvania
SECOND BRIGADE
(Killed – 3, Wounded – 14 = 17 Casualties)
Brigadier General Charles Devens
7th Massachusetts
10th Massachusetts
37th Massachusetts
36th New York
2nd Rhode Island
THIRD BRIGADE
(Wounded – 6, Missing – 6 = 12 Casualties)
Colonel Thomas Rowley
62nd New York
93rd Pennsylvania
98th Pennsylvania
102nd Pennsylvania
139th Pennsylvania
ARTILLERY
(Killed – 2, Wounded – 8 = 10 Casualties)
1st Pennsylvania, Batteries C, D
2nd United States, Battery G
CAVALRY BRIGADE OF LEFT GRAND DIVISION
(Killed – 1, Wounded – 3 = 4 Casualties)
Colonel David McM. Gregg
1st Maine
1st New Jersey
2nd New York
10th New York
1st Pennsylvania
TOTAL UNION CASUALTIES = 1,282 Killed, 9,517 Wounded,
1,816 Captured or Missing = 12, 615

CONFEDERATE ARMY

ARMY OF NORTHERN VIRGINIA (Present for duty, 78,513 men)
General Robert E. Lee

FIRST ARMY CORPS
Lieutenant General James Longstreet
MC LAW'S DIVISION
Major General Lafayette McLaws
    KERSHAW'S BRIGADE
    (Killed – 38, Wounded – 341 = 379 Casualties)
    Brigadier General Joseph Kershaw
        2nd South Carolina
        3rd South Carolina
        7th South Carolina
        8th South Carolina
        15th South Carolina
    BARKSDALE'S BRIGADE
    (Killed – 29, Wounded – 151, Missing – 62 = 242 Casualties)
    Brigadier General William Barksdale
        13th Mississippi
        17th Mississippi
        18th Mississippi
        21st Mississippi
    COBB'S BRIGADE
    (Killed – 33, Wounded – 198, Missing – 4 = 235 Casualties)
    Brigadier General Thomas Cobb (k)
    Colonel Robert McMillan
        16th Georgia
        18th Georgia
        24th Georgia
        Cobb's Legion (Georgia)
        Phillips's Legion (Georgia)
    SEMMES'S BRIGADE
    (Wounded – 2)
    Brigadier General Paul Semmes
        10th Georgia
        50th Georgia
        51st Georgia
        53rd Georgia
    ARTILLERY
    (Wounded – 2)
        1st Richmond Howitzers (Virginia)
        Troup Artillery (Georgia)
ANDERSON'S DIVISION
Major General Richard Anderson
    WILCOX'S BRIGADE
    (Killed – 3, Wounded – 15 = 18 Casualties)

Brigadier General Cadmus Wilcox
    8th Alabama
    9th Alabama
    10th Alabama
    11th Alabama
    14th Alabama
MAHONE'S BRIGADE
    (Killed – 2, Wounded – 6 = 8 Casualties)
Brigadier General William Mahone
    6th Virginia
    12th Virginia
    16th Virginia
    41st Virginia
    61st Virginia
FEATHERSTON'S BRIGADE
    (Killed – 5, Wounded – 38 = 43 Casualties)
Brigadier General W.S. Featherston
    12th Mississippi
    16th Mississippi
    19th Mississippi
    48th Mississippi (5 Companies)
WRIGHT'S BRIGADE
    (Killed – 2, Wounded – 1 = 3 Casualties)
Brigadier General A. R. Wright
    3rd Georgia
    22nd Georgia
    48th Gerogia
    2nd Georgia Battalion
PERRY'S BRIGADE
    (Killed – 7, Wounded – 38, Missing – 44 = 89 Casualties)
Brigadier General E. A Perry
    2nd Florida
    5th Florida
    8th Florida
ARTILLERY
    (Killed – 1, Wounded – 8 = 9 Casualties)
    Donaldsonville Artillery (Louisiana)
    Norfolk Light Artillery Blues (Virginia)
PICKETT'S DIVISION
    (Division losses, Killed – 3, Wounded – 50, Missing – 1 = 54 Casualties)
Major General George E. Pickett
    GARNETT'S BRIGADE
Brigadier General Richard B. Garnett
    8th Virginia
    18th Virginia
    19th Virginia
    28th Virginia
    56th Virginia

ARMISTEAD'S BRIGADE
Brigadier General Lewis A. Armistead
    9th Virginia
    14th Virginia
    38th Virginia
    53rd Virginia
    57th Virginia
KEMPER'S BRIGADE
Brigadier General James L. Kemper
    1st Virginia
    3rd Virginia
    7th Virginia
    11th Virginia
    24th Virginia
JENKINS'S BRIGADE
Brigadier General Micah Jenkins
    1st South Carolina
    2nd South Carolina
    5th South Carolina
    6th South Carolina
    Hampton's Legion (South Carolina)
    Palmettos Sharpshooters (South Carolina)
CORSE'S BRIGADE
Brigadier General Montgomery D. Corse
    15th Virginia
    17th Virginia
    30th Virginia
    32nd Virginia
ARTILLERY
    Fauquier Artillery (Virginia)
    Richmond Fayette Artillery (Virginia)
HOOD'S DIVISION
Major General John B. Hood
  LAW'S BRIGADE
    (Killed – 50, Wounded – 164, Missing – 5 = 219 Casualties)
  Brigadier General E. McIvor Law
    4th Alabama
    44th Alabama
    6th North Carolina
    54th North Carolina
    57th North Carolina
  ROBERTSON'S BRIGADE
    (Killed – 1, Wounded – 4 = 5 Casualties)
  Brigadier General J. B. Robertson
    3rd Arkansas
    1st Texas
    4th Texas
    5th Texas

ANDERSON'S BRIGADE
(Killed – 2, Wounded – 8, Missing – 4 = 14 Casualties)
Brigadier General George T. Anderson
1st Georgia Regulars
7th Georgia
8th Georgia
9th Georgia
11th Georgia
TOOMBS'S BRIGADE
(Killed – 1, Wounded – 12, Missing – 2 = 15 Casualties)
Col. H. L. Benning
2nd Georgia
15th Georgia
17th Georgia
20th Georgia
ARTILLERY
German Artillery Battery (South Carolina)
Palmetto Light Artillery Battery (South Carolina)
Rowan Artillery Battery (North Carolina)
RANSOM'S DIVISION
Brigadier General Robert Ransom
RANSOM'S BRIGADE
(Killed – 27, Wounded – 127 = 154 Casualties)
Brigadier General Robert Ransom
24th North Carolina
25th North Carolina
35th North Carolina
49th North Carolina
COOKE'S BRIGADE
(Killed – 52, Wounded – 328 = 380 Casualties)
Brigadier General J. R. Cooke (w)
Colonel E. D. Hall
15th North Carolina
27th North Carolina
46th North Carolina
48th North Carolina
ARTILLERY
COOPER'S BATTERY (Virginia)
CORPS ARTILLERY
(Killed – 4, Wounded – 35 = 39 Casualties)
Washington Artillery (Louisiana)
Alexander's Battalion (Virginia)
Madison Light Artillery (Louisiana)
Bedford Artillery (Virginia)
Rhetts' Battery (South Carolina)
SECOND ARMY CORPS
Lieutenant General Thomas J. Jackson
HILL'S DIVISION
Major General Daniel H. Hill

FIRST BRIGADE
(Killed – 2, Wounded – 14 = 16 Casualties)
Brigadier General Robert E. Rodes
    3rd Alabama
    5th Alabama
    6th Alabama
    12th Alabama
    26th Alabama
SECOND BRIGADE
(Killed – 2, Wounded – 25 = 27 Casualties)
Brigadier General George Doles
    4th Georgia
    44th Georgia
    1st North Carolina
    3rd North Carolina
THIRD BRIGADE
(Wounded – 15)
Brigadier General A. H. Colquitt
    13th Alabama
    6th Georgia
    23rd Georgia
    27th Georgia
    28th Georgia
FOURTH BRIGADE
(Killed – 1, Wounded – 12 = 13 Casualties)
Brigadier General Alfred Iverson
    5th North Carolina
    12th North Carolina
    20th North Carolina
    23rd North Carolina
FIFTH BRIGADE
(Killed – 8, Wounded – 51 = 59 Casualties)
Colonel Bryan Grimes
    2nd North Carolina
    4th North Carolina
    14th North Carolina
    30th North Carolina
ARTILLERY
(Killed – 4, Wounded – 8 = 12 Casualties)
    Jefferson Davis Artillery (Alabama)
    King William Artillery (Virginia)
    Morris Artillery (Virginia)
    Orange Artillery (Virginia)
LIGHT DIVISION
Major General Ambrose P. Hill
  FIRST BRIGADE
  (Killed – 10, Wounded – 73 = 83 Casualties)
  Colonel J. M Brockenbrough
    40th Virginia

47th Virginia
55th Virginia
22nd Virginia Battalion
SECOND BRIGADE
(Killed and Wounded = 363)
Brigadier General Maxcy Gregg (k)
Colonel D. H. Hamilton
    1st South Carolina Rifles
    12th South Carolina
    13th South Carolina
    14th South Carolina
THIRD BRIGADE
(Killed – 42, Wounded – 288 = 330 Casualties)
Brigadier General Edward Thomas
    14th Georgia
    35th Georgia
    45th Georgia
    49th Georgia
FOURTH BRIGADE
(Killed – 62, Wounded – 257, Missing – 216 = 535 Casualties)
Brigadier General James Lane
    7th North Carolina
    18th North Carolina
    28th North Carolina
    33rd North Carolina
    37th North Carolina
FIFTH BRIGADE
(Killed – 40, Wounded – 211, Missing – 166 = 417 Casualties)
Brigadier General James J. Archer
    5th Alabama Battalion
    19th Georgia
    1st Tennessee
    7th Tennessee
    14th Tennessee
SIXTH BRIGADE
(Killed – 16, Wounded – 153 = 169 Casualties)
Brigadier General William D. Pender (w)
Colonel Alfred Scales
    13th North Carolina
    16th North Carolina
    22nd North Carolina
    34th North Carolina
    38th North Carolina
ARTILLERY
(Killed – 11, Wounded – 88 = 99 Casualties)
    Branch Artillery Battery (North Carolina) (section)
    Crenshaw's Artillery Battery (Virginia) (section)
    Fredericksburg Artillery Battery (Virginia)
    Johnson's Artillery Battery (Virginia) (section)

Letcher Artillery Battery (Virginia)
Pee Dee Artillery Battery (South Carolina)
Purcell Artillery Battery (Virginia)

EWELL'S DIVISION
Brigadier General Jubal A. Early

LAWTON'S BRIGADE
(Killed – 86, Wounded – 633 = 719 Casualties)
Colonel E. N. Atkinson (w,c)
Colonel Clement Evans
13th Georgia
26th Georgia
31st Georgia
38th Georgia
60th Georgia
61st Georgia

TRIMBLE'S BRIGADE
(Killed – 8, Wounded – 98 = 106 Casualties)
Colonel Robert F. Hoke
15th Alabama
12th Georgia
21st Georgia
21st North Carolina
1st North Carolina Battalion

EARLY'S BRIGADE
(Killed – 17, Wounded – 140 = 157 Casualties)
Colonel James A. Walker
13th Virginia
25th Virginia
31st Virginia
44th Virginia
49th Virginia
52nd Virginia
58th Virginia

HAYS'S BRIGADE
(Killed – 9, Wounded – 44, Missing – 1 = 54 Casualties)
Brigadier General Harry T. Hays
5th Louisiana
6th Louisiana
7th Louisiana
8th Louisiana
9th Louisiana

ARTILLERY
(Killed – 4, Wounded – 21 = 25 Casualties)
Charlottesville Artillery Battery (Virginia)
Chesapeake Artillery Battery (Maryland)
Courtney Artillery Battery (Virginia)
Guard Artillery Battery (Louisiana)
Staunton Artillery Battery (Virginia)

JACKSON'S DIVISION
Brigadier General William B. Taliaferro
    FIRST BRIGADE
        (Killed – 3, Wounded – 44, Missing – 1 = 48 Casualties)
    Brigadier General E. F. Paxton
        2nd Virginia
        4th Virginia
        5th Virginia
        27th Virginia
        33rd Virginia
    SECOND BRIGADE
        (Killed – 3, Wounded – 34 = 37 Casualties)
    Brigadier General John R. Jones
        21st Virginia
        42nd Virginia
        48th Virginia
        1st Virginia Battalion
    THIRD BRIGADE
        (Wounded – 9)
    Colonel E. T. H. Warren
        47th Alabama
        48th Alabama
        10th Virginia
        23rd Virginia
        37th Virginia
    FOURTH BRIGADE
        (Killed – 2, Wounded – 35 = 37 Casualties)
    Colonel Edmund Pendleton
        1st Louisiana
        2nd Louisiana
        10th Louisiana
        14th Louisiana
        15th Louisiana
    ARTILLERY
        (Killed – 2, Wounded – 48, Missing – 1 = 51 Casualties)
        Carpenter's Battery (Virginia)
        Danville Artillery Battery (Virginia)
        Hampden Artillery Battery (Virginia)
        Lee Artillery Battery (Virginia)
        Lusk's Battery (Virginia)
    RESERVE ARTILLERY
        (Killed – 10, Wounded – 26 = 36 Casualties)
    Brigadier General William N. Pendleton
        Brown's Battalion (Virginia)
        Sumter Battalion (Georgia)
        Nelson's Battalion (Virginia)
        Ells' Battery (Georgia)
        Hanover Artillery Battery (Virginia)

CAVALRY
Major General J. E. B. Stuart
    FIRST BRIGADE
        Brigadier General Wade Hampton
            1st North Carolina
            1st South Carolina
            2nd South Carolina
            Cobb's Legion (Georgia)
            Phillips's Legion (Georgia)
    SECOND BRIGADE
    Brigadier General Fitzhugh Lee
            1st Virginia
            2nd Virginia
            4th Virginia
            5th Virginia
    THIRD BRIGADE
        (Wounded – 7)
    Brigadier General W. H. F. Lee
            2nd North Carolina
            9th Virginia
            10th Virginia
            13th Virginia
            15th Virginia
    ARTILLERY
        (Killed – 3, Wounded – 22 = 25 Casualties)
    Major John Pelham
            Breathed's Battery (Virginia)
            Chew's Battery (Virginia)
            Hart's Battery (South Carolina)
            Henry's Battery (Virginia)
            Moorman's Battery (Virginia)
TOTAL CONFEDERATE CASUALTIES
605 KILLED, 4,240 WOUNDED, 507 CAPTURED OR MISSING = 5,352

Index